THE DAUGHTER TRAP

THE DAUGHTER TRAP

Taking Care of Mom and Dad...and You

LAUREL KENNEDY

Thomas Dunne Books
St. Martin's Press
New York

THOMAS DUNNE BOOKS.
An imprint of St. Martin's Press.

THE DAUGHTER TRAP. Copyright © 2010 by Laurel Kennedy. All rights reserved. Printed in the United States of America. For information, address St. Martin's Press, 175 Fifth Avenue, New York, N.Y. 10010.

www.thomasdunnebooks.com
www.stmartins.com

Library of Congress Cataloging-in-Publication Data

Kennedy, Laurel.
    The daughter trap : taking care of mom and dad . . . and you / Laurel Kennedy.—1st ed.
        p.   cm.
    Includes bibliographical references and index.
    ISBN 978-0-312-38510-1 (alk. paper)
    1. Aging parents—Care—United States.   2. Aging parents—Family relationships—United States.   3. Adult children of aging parents—United States—Psychology.   I. Title.
    HQ1063.6.K46 2010
    649.8084'60973—dc22

                                                        2009040286

First Edition: April 2010

10 9 8 7 6 5 4 3 2 1

To Mom and Dad. For everything.

CONTENTS

The third category of quotes are from male caregivers. Men proved much more reticent about offering up personal information, so for the most part, quotes from men just include their names sans descriptive data. We hope you'll find the stories from these male caregivers compelling enough without the additional information.

It has been a privilege to meet these caregivers and hear their stories. With the rise of the Internet, the dissolution of extended families, geographic dispersion of clans, and rise in employed parents, the oral tradition has faded in America. This was my first exposure to that oral tradition, the telling of tales, the sharing of stories and life lessons, and it was wonderful. Perhaps next time, we'll be able to post live recordings of interviews on our Web site, so people can experience the stories viscerally, hearing the pain and the joy expressed by intonation as well as in words.

AUTHOR'S NOTE

The Daughter Trap was conceptualized as a way to give caregivers a voice. Literally. The book features quotes from three different categories of caregivers, and I wanted to explain why they are sourced differently. The vast majority of quotes are pulled from transcripts of more than 200 hours of phone interviews with female caregivers. Because we had the luxury of time during these one-hour interviews, we were able to gather extensive demographic information, such as marital status, presence of children, and adult siblings. You'll find that type of descriptive information following each woman's name at the end of these interview-based quotes.

The second category of quotes are from women participating in Internet chat rooms. Because we pulled these live off the Web, no descriptive demographic information is available. The language of the Internet chat room is informal and quick, so quotes have been filled in or grammatically corrected as needed, and the accompanying attribution is the individual's self-designated user name. Some of the names are quite creative and definitely revealing. All of their stories are riveting, and so honest they hurt.

ACKNOWLEDGMENTS

I couldn't have done it without you. All of you. As everyone knows, any attempt to generate an all-inclusive list undoubtedly forgets someone, so I won't even try. But there are key figures who kept me motivated and mobilized along the path to publication.

Unending gratitude to the generous women—and men—who willingly shared their caregiving stories. This book is yours. Your honesty, courage, and charitable spirit demonstrate the true meaning of love. To the dedicated experts, authorities, and academics who contributed their experiences, their research, and their time, you have performed a mitzvah for families everywhere.

To Janis Hines, who served as litmus test for concepts, early reader for drafts, and empathetic mentor throughout. To Marti Barletta, who steered me through the ins and outs of this crazy world called publishing. To Mollie Glick, agent nonpareil, who believed in the book and the author from the outset. To Marcia Markland, who championed both the book and the cause, bringing it to life and to market. To Melissa McDill, who gave *The Daughter Trap* a visual look. Many thanks.

To Kevin McGirr, who, like so many, has lived the caregiver role and included me in his circle of care. You inspire us.

To my siblings, for helping us to avoid "the daughter trap" and other caregiving snares outlined in this book.

To Kristin James and Linda Eatherton, my constant friends, reliable cheerleaders, and life coaches, for always being there.

To Cristina and Nicholas, may you never have to experience the caregiver's dilemma, unless it's by choice.

Caregiving is a journey. Whether you have just begun to travel this road or are nearing its end, I hope *The Daughter Trap* provides you with guidance and support, and the knowledge that you are not alone. We are here for you. If you wish to reach out to fellow caregivers and share your insights, please visit www.daughtertrap .com and join the online conversation. The Web site chat room is open around the clock for people around the world, because caring never ends.

PREFACE

Writing this book was an act of love, and an act of desperation. An act of love because I wanted to do the best possible job of caring for my parents. An act of desperation because there was nowhere to turn when I had a question.

I'm sure the following questions will sound frighteningly familiar to many of you:

How do we find a caregiver for Dad?

How can we convince Mom to take her medication?

How do we pick the best rehab facility—with just twenty-four hours to find one?

How do we find a board-certified geriatrician?

How can we get someone to relieve Dad for a few hours?

How do we track medical expenses from multiple sources with multiple payers?

Where do we dispute double billing on medical charges?

How do we convince Dad to continue with physical therapy on his own dime?

How do we get a doctor to pay attention to a drug's side effects?

Who sorts out the pills for next week?
Have the prescriptions been filled recently?
How do we calm a dementia patient to avoid a meltdown?
How do we make sure Mom eats the meals we've prepared?
Who can be in the ER when I'm out of town and Dad has an attack
    at 3 A.M.?
How do we address issues of personal hygiene?
How can we get Mom to socialize in her new living situation?

These represent just a few of the questions most of us will face when caring for our parents. Get ready, because the questions come up fast and need answers almost immediately, despite the dearth of helpful resources to resolve them.

I quickly discovered that I was not alone in my situation, or in my confusion. I undertook a little impromptu research and posed an elder care question at parties, just asking people: "Hey, do you find that your parents need extra help these days and that it's hard to find?" The flood gates would open. People literally poured their hearts out, expressing their universal frustration with the lack of a single-source solution at best, or starting point at worst.

Hopefully, *The Daughter Trap* will be a starting point on a few levels. A starting point for you and your family as you begin to explore elder care alternatives. A starting point for private-sector providers, who can bring their creativity and expertise to bear on the growing elder care problem. Note that I say private-sector solutions, not public-sector solutions. First, because our government has enough on its plate trying to figure out health care. Second, because the private sector always gets there faster, better, and usually, cheaper. Third, because there are any number of private-sector innovations already being tested and close to commercial launch. Go for it!

Frankly, I don't care who gets there first. But I do care, passionately, about making affordable elder care solutions accessible to all. If you care about that too, please share your thoughts and ideas with other like-minded caregivers and concerned citizens at www.daughtertrap.com. Together, we can reshape the world, making it a healthier and happier place for elders, and their friends and families.

THE PROBLEM

1. FROM DAUGHTER TRACK TO DAUGHTER TRAP

It was so subtle in the beginning. My sister and I would talk about how odd Mom was acting . . . kind of like a giggly teenager. Then we noticed that she was wearing the same two outfits every time we saw her, despite having closets full of clothes. The biggest "tell" for us was that their condo wasn't as clean as it once was. My mom always prided herself on keeping a clean house. It took much, much longer to realize that Mom had dementia than it should have, because our dad was compensating for her decline, covering up so we wouldn't notice anything and confront them.   *—Janet, daughter of a dementia patient*

You know your parents are going to die, but it's not something you think about. Now that my mother is gone, I think about my dad dying. I never did when they were both alive.

—Sarah, daughter of a widowed father

The Daughter Trap Defined

Daddy's little princess. Mommy's little helper. Since earliest childhood, our selves have been defined in relation to our parents.

Whom do we favor physically? Whose eyes do we have? Whose hands? Whose capabilities did we inherit? Do we ride a bike like Mom? Have an artistic bent like Dad? Do we share personality traits with our parents—a sense of humor, a piercing intelligence, an easygoing nature, an empathetic soul? Whether you argue on the side of nature or nurture, there is no argument that parents shape our lives.

So what happens when our parents can no longer parent? When time robs them of physical strength and beauty? When their basic nature begins to erode? Whom do they turn to for help? A daughter.

> When I think of people I'm responsible for, who I take care of, my dad's right up there. Sometimes I get pissed off because I already have kids and a husband and a job to worry about. Some days, worrying about my dad is just one thing too many.
>
> —Sheila, mother of two, wife

It's rarely even an overtly stated question. No one asks a daughter if she can be responsible for her parents. As if it was the natural order of things, the extended family assumes that a daughter will step up to the plate to handle matters. For no other reason than because she's a woman. Married or not. Working or not. Children or not. Nearby or not. Willing or not. Male siblings or not. Elder care is perceived to be a daughter's obligation.

Somewhere along the line, aging parents came to view the existence of a daughter as something of an economic and social security blanket, a guarantee against the insulation, isolation, and insults of old age. The daughter-dependent aging paradigm may have worked in an agrarian society, where large extended families farmed the homestead together, or in the idyllic 1950s, when

Dad went to work and Mom stayed home to "keep house," but not today.

The model for a model daughter got broken when baby boomer women established lifetime careers outside the home while continuing to undertake full-time responsibility for the household. Add the demands of caring for an often-critical and frail parent to the already-delicate work-life balance of the nuclear family, and you've pushed a woman toward her personal tipping point.

Who Pays the Toll?

The Daughter Trap is here to lift the veil from this socially proscribed topic and give voice to what overstressed daughters are thinking about the elder care burden: Enough! We explore the cultural legacy that creates the daughter trap, examine it in the unflinching light of day, and remove the guilt associated with simply being out of the resources—whether time, space, patience, or money—needed to add on the load of full-time care for a senior parent.

While it may take a village to raise a child, it takes a whole lot more to sustain an aging senior. At first glance, elder care appears to be the near-perfect analog of child care. Both involve first-order needs encompassing the basic activities of daily living such as eating, bathing, dressing, toileting, mobility, grooming, and sleeping. But it is a far different matter to change the dirty diaper of an eight-month-old than an eighty-year-old.

Senior care is serious business. It takes a huge emotional toll on the senior and extended family, a physical toll on the caregivers, a financial toll on retirement savings, and an economic toll on businesses and local communities. Never before have so few drained down a system so quickly, and we are sitting at the very beginning of a senior-care sine curve that will accelerate at a pace and achieve a height of unprecedented proportions.

Yet regardless of the demographic writing on the wall, virtually nothing has been done to prepare for the senior onslaught. Despite the fact that almost 80 percent of all women work outside the home, elder care is still viewed as the exclusive province of daughters. Unlike the child care corollary, few community-based or private-sector support services exist to lighten the load of adult daughters, and employers appear oblivious to the problem.

The solution is simple: Boomer women need to unite and effect the same type of revolutionary changes on the elder care front that they so successfully achieved in the child care domain.

The Daughter Trap Manifesto

Like everything else about the baby boom generation, the elder care problem looms large, a function of the sheer numbers constituting the largest age cohort in history. Firmly entrenched in middle age, with their own senior years creeping over the horizon, boomers are grappling with the many aspects of the elder care quandary.

The Daughter Trap explores the elder care issue from a variety of angles. It examines the societal norms—many, like women's liberation, brought about by ardent boomer lobbying—that conspire to place the mantle of elder care firmly on a daughter's shoulders. The discussion moves toward more hidebound and traditional expectations of female roles, which have proved impervious to an onslaught of feminist and egalitarian assaults.

Fearless when it comes to addressing taboo issues head-on, *The Daughter Trap* takes an unblinking look at the elder care dynamic and questions why society shuns it, employers ignore it, parents expect it, and women accept it and then let their brothers off the hook. Few issues rival that of sibling rivalry when it comes to the psychological fallout from caring for aging parents.

Perhaps it's stating the obvious, but there is a very simple reason that people avoid the topic of aging on both the personal and professional levels. It's scary. While child care discussions are replete with positive language and a future focus, elder care discussions are laden with negative language and a terminal focus. Even considering the prospect of elder care summons up the specter of one's own mortality, so it understandably becomes a verboten topic to be avoided at all costs.

The problem for our society is that avoidance costs. By not anticipating the support needs of an age band more than seventy-eight-million persons strong, we are about to be hit by a tsunami-force depletion of medical and health-support services—community assets ranging from transportation to housing to Medicare and Medicaid funding accounts to business resources.

The Emotional Maelstrom

The Daughter Trap grants women the permission to vent the visceral emotions evoked by elder care and to demand help from whatever sources can help, be they structured social institutions, religious organizations, legislative representatives, medical professionals, concerned employers, or an informal support circle. Through the voices of women in the throes of the daughter trap, we also acknowledge the unique benefits that accrue to the caregiver. Women repeatedly talked about developing a deeper connection with a parent through care delivery and described a soulful, spiritual bond that they had never experienced before with anyone.

In an unprecedented move, *The Daughter Trap* speaks frankly to aging parents, encouraging them to discuss their lifestyle options with adult children and figure out solutions that work for all parties instead of dictating the terms of engagement and demanding compliance. Elders are asked to examine their needs and expectations against the objective reality of their children's lives, not just the isolated benchmark of personal preference or a long-held vision.

Do an elder's adult children have the time between the demands of career and child care to run yet another household? Do they have the skills to deliver medical care or physical therapy? Do they have the funds to pay for clothing, food, medication, housekeeping, and transportation services if needed? And elders are reminded of the power resident in that magic phrase "thank you." Sometimes that's all it takes to smooth over a touchy situation and to renew the ability of an exhausted caregiver to soldier on.

Giving credit where credit is due, *The Daughter Trap* throws a nod in the direction of the "good guys," those men who defy convention and rate among the very best of elder caregivers. By dint of their mere presence, these models of manhood serve a vital function in the senior community, simply by providing male companionship for aging men as their ranks thin.

After thoroughly exploring the personal side of the caregiving equation, *The Daughter Trap* turns to third-party concerns. These include policy prescriptions at the legislative level; necessary changes in the medical and health community's approach to geriatric care; the enabling role of private-sector corporations as employers and alternative service providers; and the daughter-directed, convention-shattering, grassroots movement that will ignite the afterburners behind entrenched traditions.

Laying the Trap

When we thought Dad would be unable to live alone after surgery, there wasn't even a thought that he might live with my brother.

—*Ruth, sister, wife, mother, daughter*

My brother never would have noticed the grimy kitchen cabinets or understood what it meant. Until my mom called him up on an incoherent rant, he didn't believe anything was wrong.

—*Jill, geographically distant daughter*

Ask any daughter of aging parents how she ended up in the daughter trap, and more often than not, you'll discover that she doesn't really know. There is no line of demarcation, rarely a single critical incident that marks the official beginning of the daughter trap. Often it starts with subtle changes in her parents' mental or physical status, then a series of small but cumulative health events, followed by a long, slow decline. The initial clues are easy to miss, because to robust individuals, they're mere blips on the radar screen of life. To a senior, they're early indicators of failing faculties.

It may begin with more frequent bouts of forgetfulness. Or a favorite recipe that gets botched in the making. Or a string of excuses for why a parent has stopped going to visit friends. Or visible discomfort walking or getting out of a chair. Or overflowing wastebaskets throughout the house. Nothing that shouts "decline in progress," just a series of slightly odd incidents that tweak the status quo.

My first clue came when I went home for the holidays. Mom kept touching me, as if to make sure that I was real, and was really there.

> She was completely scatty. Couldn't stay focused on anything. Couldn't
> follow a recipe. Couldn't make a bed. Couldn't do the laundry. I
> thought she was just worried about my dad's health and distracted.
> Turns out, I was wrong. She was the one in trouble.
>
> —*Pam, single, consultant*

When the daughter trap gets sprung, women often find them-selves grappling with an issue they thought was laid to rest years ago. Where once these women chose between work and children, a dilemma known as the mommy track, now the choice is be-tween work and parents, a dilemma known as the daughter track. What makes this track a trap is its inevitability—it is not really a choice at all. There are no solutions that are easy or that fully satisfy everyone's needs.

Also missing from the equation is a representative political ac-tion group to lobby businesses and Congress on behalf of the col-lective interests of caretaking boomers. This may strike you as odd, given the proliferation of organizations that claim women and boomers as a primary constituency, but it is indicative of a cul-tural phenomenon (elder care) that is hidden in plain sight.

In a *New York Times* article, the journalist Jane Gross presented the case of several successful executives who got on board with full-time caregiving and off the career track.[1] Fortunately, each of the women interviewed—a radio news anchor, a lawyer, and a non-profit group executive director—was in a financial position to quit working or, as in some cases, to relocate halfway across the country. For most cash-strapped Americans, that is simply not a viable option.

A Corporate Imperative

One potential effect of the daughter trap is a brain drain in cor-porate America. Increasingly, companies are seeing accomplished women walk away when parental-care responsibilities impinge on the job, because there are few alternative paths available to them. In a study of more than 5,100 Americans conducted by the sociologist Phyllis Moen, the reason proffered by most women for early retirement was the need to care for aging parents; for men, an attractive buyout offer.[2]

No workplace solutions available adequately address the long-term realities of elder care. At the moment, a caregiving daughter has three options: Leave. Retire. Quit. Formal leaves of absence are limited to twelve weeks and, with rare exception, are given without pay. Alternatives like telecommuting or a compressed schedule might work, assuming the nature of the job will accommodate the erratic schedule of caretaking—like lengthy daytime doctor's appointments, unexpected health emergencies, chauffeuring duties, food shopping, physical therapy, and home maintenance.

Predictable schedules are tough to maintain because, as one woman pointed out, when parents are involved, "Everything takes longer. Everything. Something as simple as getting into the car becomes a huge ordeal when you're unsteady on your feet, moving slowly from arthritis, and need to use a walker. If stairs are involved—forget it! You're in for a thirty-minute ordeal."

It doesn't matter if the boomer daughter is the CEO of a major corporation requiring global travel and eighteen-hour workdays. Even if her brothers live in town and hold down 9-to-5 jobs, the primary responsibility will still fall on a daughter's shoulders. Unless, of course, there is an amenable daughter-in-law living within striking distance willing to take up the charge.

> The minute my mother-in-law moved in, she just abdicated responsibility. It was as if she was waiting for someone to take over for her. Which made things even tougher on me. I had to wait on her hand

and foot. When my husband and I went out with friends, I'd make her meal and put it in the refrigerator with instructions. We'd come home and it would still be there untouched. It made me wonder, was she even eating when she lived alone? Thinking back, I'd have to say that she was in decline, losing track of life and getting very forgetful about things like eating and bathing.

—Adelaide, married, operations executive, mother of three

The Need for Redress

When it comes to adult caregiving, it's *go time* for American society. How can a nation that so ardently champions the rights of every minority extant treat the plight of some forty-four million family caregivers and their extended families as if each was a one-off event? The fact is that elder care affects virtually every family in the United States either directly or indirectly.

In a *New York Times* interview, Judy Feder, dean of the Georgetown University Public Policy Institute, summarized the situation in two pointed questions: "Should this burden fall solely on the individual and the family? And can we really expect this arrangement to keep doing the job as a larger and larger population comes to grip with it?"[3] In a word, the answer is a resounding "No!"

The situation is grim. According to recent studies, more than fifteen million baby boomers[4] now care for an ailing parent, with more than half providing some type of help weekly and one-quarter now living with a parent.[5] Medicare alleviates some of the financial pain in acute-care situations, but the majority of elder-care needs constitute the sort of mundane support services that whittle away at the modest savings of seniors and drain the retirement accounts of middle-aged children. The cost of care is astounding—$38,896 per year on average for assisted living and more than double that amount ($74,208 per year) for a nursing home or home health aides.[6]

Squeeze Play

As America continues to go gray in a major way, the demands on baby boomer women will escalate. Leading-edge boomers (born between 1946 and 1955) will find themselves challenged as never before: negotiating with more factions, responsible for more people, more susceptible to market fluctuations, juggling more financial obligations, grappling with new technologies, postponing retirement plans, forgoing expensive indulgences—all at a time when their predecessors were marking time until they got the gold watch.

When prior generations turned sixty, their mental radar locked in on a new heading, south or west to retirement havens in Florida, Arizona, or California. Reaping the benefits from a lifetime of work, often for a single employer; confident in the security of a defined benefit program with cost-of-living adjustments; and buffered by the availability of inexpensive health insurance, retirees lived out their lives in the supportive cocoon of corporate subsidies.

Today's preretirees face a much more uncertain future. Few, if any, employers offer retiree health benefits, forcing the elderly to rely on Medicare and purchased supplemental insurance. It is the rare throwback company that provides costly defined benefits, and most prefer to shift the burden of risk to the employee through defined-contribution plans like 401(k)s. If a boomer loses a job, it will take them 50 percent longer to find a new one than in the seventies, and that job will earn a lower real wage that likely will stay flat irrespective of productivity gains.[7]

Inching toward retirement and just beginning to experience the debilitating physical effects of aging themselves, older boomers will be required to navigate the arbitrary health care system on behalf of their elderly parents while holding down a full-time job to pump up their pension (the lucky few) or aggressively saving for retirement to replace funds lost in the dot-com market implosion or never set aside.

For boomers, parenting never seems to stop. On the homefront, boomers will be welcoming unemployed boomerang-generation college graduates who return to the nest until they save enough for a nest egg of their own or complete the graduate degree necessary for many positions. Boomer parents reported being either the primary (33 percent) or secondary (35 percent) means of financial support for a child over eighteen.[8]

While boomerangs reclaim their old rooms, younger children will jockey for position, elbowing siblings aside for their share of already-limited parental time and attention. Riddled with angst, boomers worry about balancing caregiving with other duties (37 percent) and having enough time for their nuclear family (25 percent).[9] Caring for aging parents takes a toll at work as well. One-third of boomer women and one-fourth of boomer men said they missed work because of an elder care obligation.[10] A telling statistic, one that puts the time requirements of nurturing into perspective and bodes ill for caregiving daughters, is this: most women will spend seventeen years raising children and eighteen years caring for aged parents![11]

> You've got to circle the wagons . . . cling to certain things that are yours and yours alone. Don't give up your own life. Draw a line in the sand and stop there, or people will suck you dry.
>
> —Peggy, daughter, single, communications executive

The Hidden Costs

A study sponsored by the National Alliance for Caregiving and AARP placed the number of family caregivers in the United States at approximately 44.4 million. The services they provided to elderly and disabled adults had an estimated market value of $257 billion, far exceeding the combined costs of home-health and skilled nursing care.[12]

We should be grateful that families willingly embrace the caregiving burden, because if health care costs progress apace, only the privileged few will be able to afford the medical help they need. In 2006, one investment firm forecasted the amount a couple retiring that year without employer health benefits would need to cover out-of-pocket health expenses during retirement. The amount: a staggering $200,000.[13] The Employee Benefit Research Institute concurred. Its 2006 Retirement Confidence Survey pegged the number at $210,000, assuming the fifty-five-year-old couple would live to age ninety.[14]

Any way you look at it, elder care costs. It takes an emotional toll on the adult children. It imposes a financial drain on the seniors and family members who cover the often not-so-incidental costs. It places a physical strain on those providing hands-on care. The open question remains: How will boomers, architects of radical social movements, reshape the face of aging? And more important, how will they pay for it?

A Woman's Role / A Daughter's Choice

Buffered financially by healthy savings. On the cusp of paying off mortgages and college tuitions. Settled into a satisfying career track. Contributing to their church and community. When boomers finally reach the point where they can visualize their retired future, they may discover that parents will figure prominently in that vision.

Finding the parent-child tables turned can be a demoralizing experience for all involved. Powerful father figures resent having to forfeit control over their future, their finances, even their own bodies to children or appointed professionals. Adult children re-awaken the ghosts of old slights and youthful failings long laid to rest as they spend more time with parents and siblings, often in the home where they grew up.

> I find that my patience runs out. I never used to get impatient with her. At times she can be a little demanding.
>
> —Terry, mother of teenagers, divorced, consultant

> Having my mom around is like being the parent of a rebellious teenager. I do all the work so she can find something wrong with everything. No matter what I say or do, she will take the opposite point of view . . . just to be contrary.   —Julie, divorced, entrepreneur, no children

Why is caring for elderly parents viewed as the almost-exclusive purview of women? Call it tradition. Call it gender typing. Call it sexism. But whatever acts as the primary driver, seven out of ten times it is a woman who has primary responsibility for the aging parent, who becomes either the hands-on caregiver or the care coordinator.

Admittedly, there are some terrific male caregivers—sons and sons-in-law who dote on their elderly relatives and deliver superb care. But they are the exception to the rule, and their efforts are noted and singled out for lofty praise, praise that is sadly missing from a daughter's world because it's expected that she'll deliver care on demand.

Welcome to the real world—my world. Equality between men and women was a lofty feminist goal but turned out to be an empty promise. I feel like I have the brunt of the responsibility at home, for my children, my parents and his!

—Martie, marketing executive, married, mother of two young children

Caretaking may sound like a kinder, gentler occupation, but it is not for the faint of heart or physically fragile. Family members providing care report a 51 percent incidence of sleep disorders and a 41 percent incidence of back pain.[15] The more care given, the higher the physical and emotional toll. Family caregivers providing more than thirty-six hours of care a week experience twice the rate of anxiety and depression as noncaregivers.[16]

It's like virginity versus sex. There are people who have been there, who have had to care for a sick or dying parent, and then there are those with no personal experience. People either get it, or they don't.

—Lydia, divorced, executive, no children

Although recent data suggests that more men are becoming involved in caregiving, it really comes down to what your definition of *involved* is. At the end of the day, women lose an average of 11.5 working years because of caregiving responsibilities, men just 1.3 years. The numbers speak for themselves. By 2010, more than ten million working women will provide some form of caregiving assistance.[17]

Men and women simply view caretaking differently. To women, it's all about making people feel better. To men, it's getting things done. In interviews, women repeated a familiar refrain, "He'll do all the hands-off stuff, like running errands or shopping for groceries. But give his dad a bath or put on lotion? No way!"

They have it easier all around. Women are the emotional caretakers. Men either don't have to, because a woman's already taking care of it, or they choose not to go there. Sometimes I wish I could be that emotionally removed.   —*Clara, married, homemaker, mother of two*

Putting aside the fact that individually it's different, women are more intuitive. They have the ability to anticipate what's going to happen next, to interpret what goes unsaid. Men see that as being alarmist. Women see it as being aware.   —*Pam, single, consultant*

Men just throw money at problems. My brother will do anything to avoid getting personally involved. On the other hand, he's very reliable. If I give him a specific assignment, he'll do it.

—*Julie, divorced, entrepreneur, no children*

Despite the inequities and the lack of recognition and gratitude for providing elder care, women persevere. It appears that an emotional radar comes as standard equipment in the female psyche, and it simply cannot be turned off. Where there is physical need, women address it. Where there is emotional hunger, women feed it. Where there is paralyzing fear, women calm it. Because they care. Because they can. Because it's a daughter's prerogative. Because it's the definition of *family*.

Narcissism and Aging

Research for this book showed that seniors spent far too little time discussing elder care alternatives like continuing-care communities and far too much time discussing "those places," aka nursing homes. The unwillingness to consider lifestyle options that would minimize demands on the extended family leaves many seniors without a backup plan.

I've never heard of an elderly person who wants to go to a nursing home. Even though they may need to go, they fight it tooth and nail to the very end and then some.   —*Kathy, elder advocate*

When push comes to shove, seniors will find they have two options: being proactive and choosing their final residential environment or not being proactive and defaulting into the least-desirable living arrangement, a nursing home. Many seniors obstinately attempt to bully children into doing what they, the parent, want. When this tactic doesn't work and the senior is ready to consider alternatives, they frequently find those options foreclosed on by deteriorating health or mental status. It's now too late and the choices have disappeared, because the elder has become too frail or too poor to meet entrance criteria for a desirable residence.

The eventual outcome from the ostrich approach is the need for very expensive, frequently unreliable private home care until available funds are exhausted. Finally, when the money runs out, the senior ends up in the very place they wanted to avoid—a nursing home. Only this time they'll enter as a Medicaid patient, going wherever a qualified bed is available, regardless of care quality or geographic location. Choice exits the equation.

Redefining Families in the Age of the Aged

When the patriarch or matriarch yields control, the family dynamic undergoes a sea change. All members of the extended family redefine their duties, reassess their obligations, and reexamine long-standing rituals and roles. Adult children realize that they are about to become orphans, abandoned (however unwillingly) by the people who have anchored their existence since conception.

Grandchildren may be called on to serve as chauffeurs or

companions for grandparents they may not know that well or like that much. Adult siblings may try to renegotiate relationships, competing on the basis of who does the best job caring for Mom and Dad.

Spouses may demonstrate a profound degree of empathy or attempt to avoid the situation, knowing it foreshadows the death of their own parents. Friends and neighbors often act as proxy family members when geography or schedules make it impossible for the caregiver to take care of business. It's an emotional minefield for all involved, and nobody hands out flak jackets.

Recently, I got my own taste of the role of friend as stand-in-caregiver. It came in the form of a frantic call from a friend in California whose mom, over eighty, returned from wintering in Florida to discover that her Chicago apartment building was going condo. Windows were being replaced in subzero weather and she had to move all the furniture (including a heavy china cabinet, dressers, and buffet) six feet from the walls and vacate the apartment for three days, starting the next day!

You can imagine the degree of anxiety on everyone's part. There wasn't even time for my friend to catch a plane and rush to her mother's aid. In less than twenty-four hours, from almost one thousand miles away, she was supposed to figure out where her mom could stay during the renovation and who would move and cover the furniture, filter all the particulate matter from the air so her mom's asthma wouldn't activate, clean up the residue on the furniture and carpet, and move the furniture back in place. Interestingly, her mom never even mentioned the problem to my friend's brother.

Anyone with a senior parent can tell you that this situation is fairly typical. The damnedest things happen to seniors at the most inopportune times, when they are at their most vulnerable emotionally and have lost both their resilience and ability to cope. In the case of an elder with senile dementia, it can be enough to throw them into a tailspin that lasts for weeks, requires medication, and that marks a downturn from which they may never rebound.

> I was so embarrassed for my dad. My daughter came into the house and tossed him the car keys, saying "Grandpa, are you okay? You left the car running with the keys in it." He just wanted to crawl in a hole and die. No one's ever brought it up since.
>
> —*Pru, divorced, business owner, three kids*

The boomerang phenomenon, college graduates returning home to live, is gaining momentum. Some view it as the by-product of a competitive graduate-school admissions process, a ridiculously expensive rental market, or a desire to delay growing up for as long as possible. To others, this is a heaven-sent partial solution to the aging-parent conundrum. The 2000 United States census, the first to measure multigenerational trends, determined that 3.9 million households accommodated three or more generations under one roof.[18]

Grads are old enough to understand the problem, savvy enough to alleviate the problem, mature enough to handle the problem, and, unfortunately, smart enough to exploit it by demanding perks in return for helping out. There are few things that can take an elder out of their self-directed musings faster than the antics of an overgrown teenager and their friends.

> One of the nice things is that my dad knows more about my family now. He's more concerned than he's ever been because my mom's not around to take care of it. He finds my children entertaining and he's genuinely lonely.   —*Sheila, mother of two, wife*

When the kids are home from school, he takes them to a steakhouse for a "boys' night out," complete with cigars and drinks. They think it's a hoot and it makes me feel wonderful to see how much Dad enjoys them.

—*Donna, mother of two boys, telecommunications worker, remarried*

Younger children can be a great distraction and provide a good cover story for having an adult check in on an aging parent living in the same home. A friend with school-age children always asks the babysitter to keep an ear open for her mother while in the house. "Mom would be absolutely mortified if I hired a sitter to stay with her. She'd never speak to me again! But she completely understands the idea of me hiring a babysitter so as not to bother her. The truth is, the kids would be perfectly fine alone."

Love, hate, sadness, joy, anxiety, relief, fear, confidence, and, finally, closure. All in all, senior care can be a volatile emotional mix rendered inert only by the death of the parent or the emergence of a new family order.

Today's family order has indeed been reordered. Two-thirds of boomer parents contribute to the financial support of their adult children, many of whom have returned to the empty nest. Fully 25 percent of boomers live with one of their elderly parents. Multigenerational households, thought to have died out with the family farm, have been resurrected and reconfigured.

The twenty-first century brings with it a singular confluence of events. An unprecedented number of the "old old," those whose lives have been extended by medical and diagnostic advances, need to be integrated into the family fold. Young adults who left for college never planning to return now can't afford to strike out on their own and are bouncing back to the welcoming arms of parents.

Boomers find themselves sandwiched in the middle of dependent generations, diverting funds from retirement savings to cover the costs of an expanding and demanding household. Three generations of adults resident under one roof represent one of the fastest-growing family configurations, emerging not a moment too soon. When Mom and Dad need emergency backup to care for their mom and dad, they can turn to an embedded solution: their adult kids.

The family circle, once thought to be circling the drain, resurfaces with renewed vigor in modern form. Yet trapped at the epicenter of it all remains the pivotal figure of the adult daughter. One of the strongest tethers ensnaring adult daughters is the misguided feminist belief in an egalitarian division of labor on the work front and the home front. Such a division never happened and it never will.

2. THE MOMENT
FOR A MOVEMENT

Welcome to the real world—my world. True equality is a lofty goal. But it's a platitude. Most people work today because they have to work. Everything's expensive. In my case, I feel like I have the brunt of responsibility. I'm the sibling responsible for keeping tabs on Mom. I'm also helping with my in-laws and their needs. Throw a pail of water on it. So much depends on people's jobs and roles and your kids', your parents' situation. If I had gotten married ten years younger, my mom wouldn't have stopped what she was doing to help take care of my kids. She was busy volunteering and wouldn't have been as accessible. It's not her responsibility and she wouldn't like it if she HAD to do it. She did the mom thing and is done with it. Feels that it's my job to raise the kids, and it is. Unfortunately, despite the fact I work full time just like he does, my husband feels the same way.

—*Mariel, mother of two, one of four siblings*

It's true that feminism opened doors in the workplace for us to achieve higher goals. But there is still a glass ceiling. It just allowed women to take on ALL of the responsibility outside the home, plus most of the responsibility inside the home. Now we do double or triple duty. Taking care of our own kids and aging parents. Our day has increased. Not sure it's gotten better, but for sure it's gotten to be a bigger responsibility. Economically, we're supposed to have more things now. Maybe we do have more material things. I know a lot of women whose husbands don't help at all . . . they end up doing everything themselves.

—Adelaide, married, mother of three, one of eight siblings

It was a more innocent time. When all things appeared possible. When social justice was a front-page issue. When issues of equality were at the forefront of the political agenda. In 1966, when the National Organization for Women (NOW) was formed, founders espoused lofty ideals in the broadest of terms. The statement of purpose includes a phrase that stands as a silent testament to the audacity of the movement and the inevitability of its failure to reach the stated goal: "The purpose of NOW is to take action to bring women into full participation in the mainstream of American society now, exercising all the privileges and responsibilities thereof in **truly equal partnership with men**" (my emphasis).[1]

We wish. Not a single person interviewed for this book, not a single man or woman of my acquaintance for that matter, believes that, more than forty years later, women are anywhere near the goal of truly equal partnership. If anything, women are feeling even more overwhelmed, swamped by some of the backwash from the women's-liberation movement. Pressured to do a yeoman's job on both the work and home fronts, with husbands and partners providing lots of moral (but a lot less physical) support, women know where that proverbial buck stops—with them.

As a radical feminist, I think part of the deal is, men are more abstract thinkers. They don't notice the details. It's just easier to do it yourself than explain what needs to be done.   —*Jo, divorced, one of three siblings*

At the VA, visiting my dad, I saw people who didn't give a rip. Their sons would show up the day they checked in and the day they checked out, mostly to see if the money was all there. That nurturing gene is just missing in men. They'll cede the caretaking job to us and it stinks!   —*Rusty, divorced, two sons, one of five siblings*

In terms of career options and choices, yes, the women's movement has helped. In reality, the thing that I see, even as open-minded to feminist ideals as my ex-husband was, there is still that expectation that you are the primary caregiver in the family. Caring for kids or parents or having dinner ready. Even though sure, you can work all you want. His idea was "get your cake and eat it too." You get to have it all and do it all. I see a few people who are not that way, but for the most part, the woman ends up with the major role of parenting.

—*Catherine, mother of two*

Less Is Less

Sadly, there are fewer bucks of any kind paid to women. According to one recent poll, 90 percent of American women believe they get paid less than their male peers for the same work.[2] As it turns out, they have good reason for that belief. Professors Philip N. Cohen (University of North Carolina at Chapel Hill) and Matt L. Huffman (University of California at Irvine) did a deep dive through the 2000 United States census data and discovered that, on average, women earn a mere 81 percent of what male colleagues bring home for the same job.

For those tempted to dismiss the news as an artifact of statistical sampling, it is worth mentioning that this extremely robust finding is based on more than 1.3 million workers reporting in from seventy-nine metropolitan locations and accounting for more than 30,000 job classifications.[3] Not a blip on the radar screen, and definitely not a statistical anomaly.

Only when women executives break through the glass ceiling to the very highest ranks of senior management does the pay gap narrow to nine percent—still a fair piece away from parity.[4] In a particularly unfortunate turn of events, it appears that the number of women achieving this lofty goal, or even the more moderate level of executive, has dropped by 13 percent in the last decade, falling from 32 percent in 1990 to 19 percent in 2000.[5]

The unequal-pay news actually gets worse, courtesy of a female double-whammy effect. You get paid less working for a woman and managing women. Professors Cohen and Huffman discovered that men who work for women managers earn less than men reporting to men.[6] A separate team of researchers (Professor Cheri Ostroff from Columbia University and Leanne E. Atwater of Arizona State University West) uncovered the fact that both men and women who supervised departments with a large female census made less money than those managing male-dominant areas.[7]

Earning less means having less money available to defray health care costs and to retain the support services that enable women to continue to work and provide care. Women are penalized in their paychecks for their gender, for their age, for having children, for being married—and may even find themselves targeted by other women based on that most fundamental choice: whether to work outside the home or not.

Something Gets Sacrificed

In a pendulum response typifying the physics of change, radical feminist forces took the idea of equality to the extreme, slinging rhetoric that demeaned more traditional career paths, unintentionally fostering a feeling of condescension between employed professionals and their at-home counterparts. In her wonderfully funny book titled *To Hell with All That,* Caitlin Flanagan summarizes the dilemma nicely:

> What few will admit—because it is painful, because it reveals the unpleasant truth that life presents a series of choices, each of which precludes a host of other attractive possibilities—is that whichever decision a woman makes, she will lose something of incalculable value. The kind of relationship formed between a child and a mother who is home all day caring for him is substantively different from that formed between a child and a woman who is gone many hours a week. The former relationship is more intimate, more private, filled with more moments of maternal frustration—and even despair—and with more moments of the transcendence that comes from mothering a small child.
>
> Yet when a woman works outside the home, she uses the best of her mind and education, exerting her authority and power on the world beyond her doorstep. We respect women who stay home with their children, but it's the ones who work—the ones who spend their days taking part in the commerce and traffic of the adult world—who seem to have retained the most of their former selves.[8]

The internal dissension between those who work inside and those who work outside the home bifurcated the women's movement, disenfranchising a significant number of supporters. It also radicalized the current NOW agenda into a direction far afield from founder designs.

> We do it to ourselves. Or let it happen. I was home with my kids, so the assumption was "she's home, she'll have the time to deal with things," and everyone thought I could do it all. I took on way too much responsibility and didn't take care of myself. I should have insisted my husband be more helpful.
>
> —*Anne, wife, mother of two, one of three siblings*

At a time when elder care touches one in five households in the United States,[9] when the over-sixty-five population is growing nearly four times faster than the under-sixty-five group,[10] when women carry a disproportionate share of the caregiving burden it is incomprehensible that NOW relegates elder care to the status of "other," a mere secondary concern. The NOW key-issues roster of six priority subjects includes a number of matters that touch the lives of most women and a few that reflect minority interests only.

Take for example priority issue number 5—lesbian rights. Although undeniably a worthy cause, fewer than 1 percent of American women self-identify as homosexual,[11] and these women are already championed by well-endowed niche interest groups like the National Gay and Lesbian Task Force, the National Center for Lesbian Rights, and the Family Pride Coalition. Elder caregivers lack equally powerful and politicized representation.

Pursuing these narrow issues has rendered NOW a pale shadow of itself, with its initial vision unrealized and its current purpose unrecognizable. Women, especially baby boomer–age women caring for multiple generations, find themselves adrift without an anchor, bereft of a philosophical coxswain to call the beat and direction for the caregiving trials. This predicament represents a pivotal moment for NOW—a chance to reestablish its relevancy, to recapture momentum, and to reignite the passion of women around a resonant cause. NOW can either seize the opportunity to advocate for elder caregivers, the overwhelming majority being women, or walk away from a worthy cause and a needful constituency.

> We're not equal at everything, but I like being a woman so I can be more emotional. It's a whole different way of approaching things. My husband does a lot of things his dad didn't do like change diapers and talk about sex with his children. But we're not equals as parents. I definitely went on more play dates and arranged them. I'm the one who worries about homework being done. I feel that thanks to feminism I have more options. —*Bridget, wife, mother of two*

Clock Watching

Under the old model of marriage and family, women stayed home to care for the children and household. Under the new model of marriage and family, women are expected to have full-time jobs—no, make that meaningful careers—while sharing responsibility for hearth and home with their partners. Only the division of labor never quite works out equally. It is most definitely a lopsided affair, with women shouldering the brunt of the housekeeping burden, no thanks to their spouses.

> I'm so tired of getting "the look" at parties. I almost hate to go anywhere anymore because of that awkward "what do you do for a living?" moment. When a guy asks, they seem to think it's kind of cool that I'm a full-time mom. When a woman asks, they either start backpedaling, muttering things like "how nice for your kids" or "that's

worthwhile work too" or there's this really uncomfortable silence followed by a glance over my shoulder to see who they can network
with. They can't get away from me fast enough.

—Seema, wife, mother of two

Have you been patronized lately? If you're a full-time mom who no
longer works outside the home, the answer is a resounding "Yes!"

—Caroline, wife, nonpracticing lawyer, mom

According to a 2008 study released by the University of Michigan's Institute for Social Research, husbands create seven hours of
housework a week for women, while having a wife saves men from
about an hour of housework a week.[12] Admittedly, the average
amount of housework performed by a woman has decreased by
nine hours since 1976 to seventeen hours on average, while men
added seven hours to their home workload for an average of thirteen hours. When kids enter the equation, the hours climb and the
gender gap widens.

You can talk women's liberation, but my husband's generation (he's
older) wasn't sensitized, taught, or trained to recognize the needs of
others. Everything was done for the boys. We still don't raise boys
with that expectation. We should teach them how to take care of a
family, how to anticipate the needs of others. Men have a sense of
entitlement. Despite all our hard work on behalf of women, it seems
you can't have it all.   *—Harriet, married, no children, one sibling*

Men and women have different roles that they've been taught in life.
I'm one of those women who feel I can be equal to a man and in turn
think men should be equal to women. Men should have more knowledge about what we are doing as caregivers.

—Lydia, wife, mother, one of six

Married moms with 3-plus kids logged twenty-eight hours of housework per week, while dads weighed in for roughly ten hours per week. Not unexpectedly, families with more than three kids increased that total weekly workload by an additional eight hours. The big surprise is who bears the brunt of that increase. Mom ends up with the lion's share, adding eleven hours to her weekly workload, while Dad actually reduces his contribution to chores by three hours, letting Mom pick up his slack—hardly what one might term an equitable division of labor.

> So many guys are emotionally detached or busy in a "manly" way—they use it as an excuse. I think of that sometimes, in terms of the example we're setting for our son. That's the lesson I'm trying to impart. Men get off too easily. It's the tradition I was raised in.
>
> —Bethany, wife, mother, sister

As with so many ambitious initiatives, execution of feminist principles fell far short of the goal of gender equality. When the women's movement told us that we could "have it all," little did we know that they meant we could have all the work to ourselves. The problem is a familiar one: faulty assumptions. It was assumed that men would fall in line because they would recognize the obvious fairness of splitting things equally. But that thinking defies fundamental logic as well as basic economic principles.

> It got misinterpreted. It sent the message to men that they're off the hook. That women can do it all for themselves. You don't have any accountability to your spouse. To women, it said you can be even stronger, do it all by yourself and you don't need anybody else. Neither message is right. We need someone who's got our back, to shoulder the burden when we can't. There's a need for partnership in this

life . . . with friends, spouses, coworkers. That's what makes life work. Some of us misinterpreted female empowerment to mean you don't need those connections. You should succeed on your own. The nuances got lost.   —*Beth, wife, mother of three, sister*

Rational Choice

Students of economics and the social sciences will be familiar with rational-choice theory, which holds that people act out of self-interest and will make the choice that maximizes their personal outcome while minimizing the cost of achieving that outcome. Another popular way of framing up rational choice is in terms of cost-benefit: if benefits outweigh costs, people will take the plunge.

Equality? Like that's going to happen! Men and women are different, period. While it's a good thing to strive for, it's never going to happen.
                                            —*Renee, single, no children*

If we apply rational-choice theory to the caregiving or home-making situations, it's clear why men haven't enthusiastically embraced the idea of true equality. They don't have to and they don't want to. Men asked themselves the primal question, What's in it for me? When the answer was simply more work and perhaps a slightly happier spouse or child, the payoff wasn't viewed as big enough to justify expanding their workload.

I see some men who try to do their part in elder care. For the most part, that's not a realistic expectation. So many men grew up in a culture with a different role model. I do see that there are men who have stepped up to the plate and taken full or equal share of the work. Men seem to feel at a loss. They don't know how to care for

parents. They're not comfortable with the physical aspects of caregiving. Part of it is social. Part of it is their brain. They just don't see
what needs to be done. Men don't listen, they hear. Men don't see,
they look.　　　　　　　　　　　　　　　　　　　*—Claudia, wife, mother*

One can argue that intrinsic rewards such as being a better
helpmate; mastering new tasks; or enjoying improved relationships with child, parent, or spouse should suffice as incentives for
men to share the load. Reality proves otherwise. This begs the
question, Should extrinsic rewards be offered as an inducement
to get these hyperrational beings to lend a hand? If so, should those
same inducements also be made available to the women who already willingly take up the task day after day? That's complicated,
because it's a potential subject big enough to merit another book.
The purpose here is simply to underscore that elder care falls into
the same category as housework and child care and is thus relegated on a gender basis to women. Men don't consider it their
problem or part of their purview.

And so women soldier on. They see what needs to be done and
they do it. Whether "it" refers to child care or elder care. Simply
put: because women care, they take care. They take care of their
children. They take care of their homes. They take care of
their relatives. They take care of their spouse. They take care
of their careers. They take care of just about everyone and everything but themselves, fulfilling the "Others first" credo of Moms
everywhere. Who will speak for them?

A Missing Voice

Elder care needs a poster child. Although we write that tongue-in-
cheek, the elder cause is missing a telegenic face and a memorable
voice that will resonate with the general public and imbue the is-

sue with a sense of urgency. People need a reason to care, which means they need a person to fixate on, a living focal point— someone who can humanize the story either as the physical embodiment of the condition or whose life has been affected by it. Media-savvy charities have seen awareness and donations skyrocket when a popular celebrity steps forward to publicly champion an issue.

The Michael J. Fox Foundation for Parkinson's Research is one of the most successful models of a celeb cause that works, having raised more than $120 million for research into treatment and a cure.[13] The Alzheimer's Association has a raft of celebrities endorsing their efforts, chief among them actor David Hyde Pierce, also known as Niles Crane from the sitcom *Frasier*. Marie Osmond spearheads the American Heart Association's *Go Red for Women* program to raise awareness of the insidious disease that killed her mother, father, and grandmother.

Elder care has simply failed to ignite the firestorm of attention that an issue of this magnitude rightfully merits. Much of the blame for that sits at the feet of mass media. There are a number of contributing factors. Unlike young children or baby animals who are the popular choice for feature segments, old people aren't sexy, riveting, or particularly attractive subjects for the camera. Electronic media wants a great visual and a quick sound-bite. The elder-care problem delivers neither.

Another reason for relegating elder care to the back pages: middle-aged and older people are not the demographic sweet spot coveted by advertisers. Lest we forget, media mergers have consolidated control of print and broadcast outlets into the hands of a few mega corporations. In the news business, it's all about business and advertising dollars. With the exception of hard news involving police action or taxes, editorial decisions are strongly determined by the demographic it will index against. If forced to choose between covering the latest celebutante or discussing elder needs, guess which topic polls higher with the age segment eighteen to thirty-five.

MIA in the Media

Yet another mitigating factor influencing media coverage: elder care is a fairly complex story and has significant financial and sweeping policy implications that take time to be researched and explained. Time is money in the news game, and thus elder care is relegated to the back burner. When it does get covered, elder care is generally given series or special-feature treatment, which allows for deeper but much less frequent exposure, when what is needed is consistent, visible, and recurrent "above the fold" coverage.

A more subtle but more potent reason for the dearth of publicity may be simple fear. At the end of the day, reporters are people too, susceptible to the same aversion to end-of-life issues and the inevitable physical and mental declines associated with old age that the rest of us suffer. Actually, this point is amplified for on-camera talent, where physical appearance can outstrip reporting ability on the hiring-attributes scale. With a very few notable exceptions (individuals like Barbara Walters, Katie Couric, or Diane Sawyer), network news is a young person's, especially a younger woman's, bailiwick.

Not only are there fewer women in front of the camera than men, there are significantly fewer older women in visible positions. In point of fact, there are 40 percent fewer women between fifty and fifty-nine holding down news analyst, reporter, or correspondent jobs than holding positions in the workforce overall according to the 2000 census.[14] This is the same age bracket most actively involved in caring for elderly relatives. Because caregiver peers are MIA by dint of being underrepresented overall in the media, elder caregivers have the least likelihood of any employed age group at finding a sympathetic ear and kindred caregiver among media decision makers.

On the upside, this may prove to be a self-correcting problem. Thanks to the Internet, electronic media, and the aging of the United States population, the problem of sympathetic points of contact may be resolved over time as more people see their own parents failing or struggling with grandparent issues. Elder care remains a cause in search of a spokesperson and a media platform.

Leveraging Assets

There is a stultifying leadership vacuum in the elder care arena. While any number of estimable groups now grapple with the issues of aging and caregiving, no one person or organization has surfaced to act as a point of coalescence in a way that has riveted the country or instigated sweeping action in Congress. Rather, there are parallel movements forward on a number of fronts in relatively minor, incremental ways. Proverbial baby steps on the legislative and policy agenda for an issue that is literally a matter of life and death for the affected constituency. Time's a-wasting!

Elder care needs a champion. Elder care needs a leader to coordinate efforts, to aggregate funds, to consolidate public-relations activities, to advocate for the cause in a compelling way that focuses media attention with laserlike precision on a well-articulated set of goals. It is easy to understand the diffusion of effort. Elder care is a massive issue.

Although far from infinite, the number of elder care touchpoints is overwhelming. Consider that on one Web site's resource roster, there are 105 individual listings for groups involved in some aspect of elder care. There are forty-seven entries under the banner of disease-specific and health-related agencies alone. Each lobbying for their cause, each vying for funding and donations, each only partially concerned with the plight of the elderly population, each working different missions and visions.

The National Alliance for Caregiving, a coalition comprising some twenty-seven complementary organizations, developed a seminal proposal at its 2001 Caregiver Empowerment Summit outlining a logical approach for advancing the elder care cause, beginning with three key tasks:

1. *Task 1—Strengthen the national coalition of natural allies to address caregiver problems*
   - Identify likely allies (among corporations, professional groups, organized labor, insurance companies, faith communities, foundations, health care organizations);
   - Be a conduit for information to these allies;
   - Help allies promote activism among their constituents;
   - Develop common ground among coalition members around caregivers' needs;
   - Create a political agenda on caregiving; and
   - Create a "Caregiver Bill of Rights"—a list of principles that constitute essential supports for caregiving.

2. *Task 2—Develop a public awareness campaign*
   - Hire a public relations firm to conduct a multi-faceted public awareness campaign that will, among other things, help family caregivers to self-identify and create greater recognition of caregiving among the general public; and
   - Use a variety of strategies to heighten the awareness of elected officials and policymakers about caregiving issues. Strategies could include having major national meetings sponsored by international and national entities, such as the White House, Congress, and the UN.

3. *Task 3—Develop a grassroots plan to promote activism*
   - Create a grassroots task force of summit participants to identify state and local organizations that include family caregivers and develop a means for communicating with them, such as through Web site links;
   - Identify "natural leaders" at state and local levels;
   - Develop a database of individual caregivers; and
   - Train local leaders on how to advocate effectively.[15]

This is a terrific work plan. But, as anyone who has ever served on a committee or board knows, voluntary cooperation is great—when it happens. Usually, voluntary activities are downgraded on the priority list to secondary concerns whenever conflicts arise. Granted, voluntary efforts are important, but they qualify as "nice tos" versus "need tos." Despite the best of intentions, when something's got to give, it's usually activities off the corporate charter, like coalition efforts.

Voluntary activities don't affect performance reviews, promotions, or payment and compensation, nor do they advance personal agendas or increase power bases—all the reasons that motivate people to take action. Effecting fundamental change requires a unique driver, a charismatic apostle, or a compelling incentive to keep benevolent contributors on task and on schedule. Given its sweeping scope and all the attendant motivational requirements, the job description for elder care advocate is beginning to sound a lot like that of a superhero.

Superhero Wanted

- Faster than a speeding bullet (bias to action)
- More powerful than a locomotive (political clout)

- Able to leap tall buildings in a single bound (physical stamina)
- It's a bird! (soars over obstacles)
- It's a plane! (on time to the destination)
- It's . . . a strange visitor . . . with powers and abilities far beyond those of mortal men! (the will to succeed and compel others to join the quest)
- Fights a never-ending battle for truth, justice, and the American way (relentlessly pursues the ultimate objective—a better quality of life for elders and caregivers)

There's a real opportunity here for an association, a foundation, a corporation, or another willing entity to champion the elder care cause and become an institutional hero. Elder care has all the elements that make for a compelling and sustainable story line: families in crisis, financial disaster, emotional blowups, health traumas, insurance fraud, physical abuse, sibling rivalries, administrative snafus, middle-of-the-night phone calls, emergency room visits—and the list goes on. If reality-TV producers really want to capture some high drama, they ought to develop a show about families dealing with elder care.

> You know that commercial "I can bring home the bacon, fry it up in a pan"? When I have a really bad workday . . . on Wednesday, I had back-to-back bad workdays. I can't bring home the bacon, because I'm too tired to go to the store or even order it in and I care less that you're a man. —*Cindy, self-employed, married, mother of two*

For corporations in search of a meaningful cause, one that reaches across generations, one that materially affects their workforce, one that would make a remarkable contribution to society as a whole, one that could be "owned" in the sense of serving as point guard, look no further than elder care. This is an opportunity for a visionary CEO to exercise true leadership that transcends commercial transactions.

Resolving the elder care crisis will require a deft touch, inspired management, and prophetic foresight, supported by a well-conceived, longitudinal action plan that achieves critical mass by drawing down on multiple funding sources and volunteer bases. Coordination is key to ensure that objectives get met in priority order, minimizing donor fatigue, volunteer exhaustion, and legislator overload. The reward: improving the quality of life for millions by solving a social problem that transects every aspect of modern life.

> In the twenty-first century, family care-givers continue to be the most neglected group of the health and long-term care system, despite their contributions worth $257 billion (2000 dollars) in unpaid services and support—more than double the annual spending on home care and nursing home care combined.[16]

The Value of Precedent

Elder care is neither a woman's issue nor a man's issue. It's a human issue. It affects everyone in the family, in the community, in the country. It's burning through resources at an alarming pace, more than $309 billion per year by some estimates.[17] Sundry groups address elder care from a variety of perspectives: tax credits, Medicare payments, leaves of absence, medical education, respite help, interfamily cash transfers, transport vouchers. There's an idea floated every minute and the competition for funding is intense.

How can elder care proponents gain traction? How can they grab headlines, focus attention, and prompt state and federal legislatures to take action? How can they ramp up a rapid response?

Fortunately, a precedent exists. Women need to do for elder care in the twenty-first century what they did for child care in the twentieth century: relentlessly pursue a common goal and help shape a multidimensional response with private-sector initiatives leading the way.

It hasn't been easy, but there are lessons to be learned from the evolution of child care services that can accelerate the adoption of elder care programs.

Lesson 1: Don't wait for the government.
Lesson 2: Build a compelling financial argument for employers.
Lesson 3: Let the free-market engine drive innovative solutions.

Like child care, the biggest issue in elder care is the availability of services. Like child care, competitive forces should conspire to solve price inflation and make elder care more affordable.

The Care and Feeding of Child Care

A brief history tracing federal child care financing illustrates that initial child care programs were conceived in response to the Depression, as a way for the government to stimulate the economy by creating caregiver jobs. Since the primary motivation behind the Works Progress Administration (WPA) emergency nursery schools was employment versus child development, as soon as the economy gathered steam, the programs were disbanded.[18]

Then the United States entered into World War II. Between the war effort and the draft, critical jobs were vacated and new jobs created in war industries that required women to work outside the home. Congress helped make it possible for mothers to work by converting WPA dollars to Lanham Act dollars, which funded child care facilities in war-production areas. In just four years of operation, the program affected approximately 600,000 children at some 3,102 centers in forty-seven states, with a disproportionate share allocated to California, whose geographic proximity made it a hotbed of wartime industry.[19]

Almost twenty years later, a succession of legislation was enacted beginning with Head Start under Lyndon Johnson's administration, designed for families with very low incomes. Next, the so-called working poor enjoyed some relief when Title XX of the Social Services Amendments of 1974, followed by the 1981 Social Services Block Grant, the 1988 Family Support Act, the Child Care and Development Block Grant and Title IV-A At-Risk Child Care.[20]

Despite the multiple, successive initiatives, middle-income women enjoyed little relief. Most programs were expressly designed to help lower-income families move toward employment by taking the child care issue off the table. When assistance did become available to the moderately well-off, it took the form of tax credits rather than rebates, direct payments, or special subsidies. Not until 1954 did the IRS recognize a tax deduction for dependent care, limiting it to widows and widowers, married women whose spouses could not work, and the divorced or legally separated.

Getting Some Credit

In 2008, the child- and dependent-care tax credit afforded relief equal to 35 percent of qualifying expenses, depending on earned household income, adjusted for any employer contributions, and after meeting a number of qualifying criteria regarding age of child, provider, residency and the like.[21] Implicitly, the current governmental-funding approach reflects a resistance to organized, institutionalized child care. This may be a reflection of the American character and its fierce dedication to the principles of self-reliance and independence. It may be a reflection of the nagging guilt women feel when they relinquish child-rearing responsibility to a third party. But it flies in the face of a reality where women compose 46 percent of the United States workforce.[22]

Employers turned out to be slightly more responsive to the child care plight and, thanks to benefits consultants, more creative in their response. Although the 1981 Block Grant's alleged purpose was to stimulate employer interest in on-site child care centers, it was a secondary concept, the dependent-care expense account, that caught the attention of business.

The former option comes bundled with all the attendant liability exposure, physical-plant changes, personnel costs, insurance expense, compliance demands, and oversight requirements. The latter option comes pretty much unencumbered, easy to explain and administer, and at an extremely low cost to employers when folded into the popular cafeteria-style benefit plans. Despite an impressive history and proven successes, child care went nowhere until benefits consultants figured out a way to exploit tax law changes that made client companies appear family friendly at little to no cost. But the price of caring for loved ones is steep for the average American.

Peace of Mind, at a Price

No doubt about it, child care is expensive; elder care, even more so. At one of the most benefits-progressive companies on the planet, Google, child care subsidies got way out of hand, reaching a high of almost $37,000 a year per child. That's more than three times the Silicon Valley average of roughly $12,000 a year at companies like Cisco Systems and Oracle.[23]

According to the National Association of Child Care Resource and Referral Agencies, the average annual fees for full-time child-center care for an infant range from $4,560–$15,895; for a four-year-old, the range is $4,055–$11,680.[24] Compare those statistics with the annual elder care costs assembled by the American Association of Homes and Services for the Aging: $68,985 for a semiprivate nursing-home room; $35,628 for an assisted-living-facility placement; $32,064 to live at a nonprofit continuing-care community. It's a big ticket, and fully 40 percent of the expense comes out of private pockets, either elder retirement savings or those of their adult children.[25]

Hidden Costs

In a phone survey conducted in 2007, the National Alliance for Caregiving/Evercare revealed that for families supporting elders aging in place at home, local caregivers estimate their out-of-pocket expenses at around $5,500 a year, while long-distance caregivers believe the number is closer to $8,728 annually.[26] The cash outlays purchased household goods and food (42%), transportation (39%), medical copayments and drugs (31%), clothing (21%), and home repair and maintenance (13%).[27]

The study also included a written diary section. This careful daily tracking of expenses revealed that diarists, most of whom resided with the elder, spent $14,832 per year for live-ins—$14,064 was spent by diarists taking care of elders at long distance and $8,496 by those caring for elders locally.[28]

These findings suggest that actual out-of-pocket expenses are significantly higher than people realize or are willing to admit, since the spending is viewed as a necessity, not an option. Most caregivers can't really establish an annual budget, because they can't anticipate the dramatic and sometimes severe changes in health status among the elderly. It's a situation that will only get worse as the aging population in the United States swells to unprecedented size.

What We've Learned

Superheroes need apply. If you've got what it takes to lead a social revolution . . . to inspire a movement, to ignite dramatic action, to intercede on behalf of elders, make yourself known!

Turn up the heat on Congress and vote in representatives willing to act on behalf of elders and their caregivers. Perhaps a dedicated PAC is the answer.

Precedents exist. Let's borrow a page from the fight for child care and look to the private sector for lower cost, readily available, innovative elder care solutions.

CGM. No, it's not a text message. It stands for consumer-generated media, just one of the ways to deploy the Internet to effect change.

3. NOT-SO-GREAT EXPECTATIONS

When the first major health crisis happens to an elder person in your family, it hits you—things will never really be okay again. Certainly, they'll never be the same again. When the elder is a parent, you'll sense the subtle vibrations as the tectonic plates of your relationship shift. In psychology, this transition is called filial maturity. The parent becomes child and the child becomes parent.

While this might indeed be the cycle of life and an inevitable part of the evolutionary process, it generates a tremendous sense of unease. There is something comforting, even as an adult, in knowing that your mom and dad are around and have your back. When that bedrock foundation erodes, it resets your internal compass without the security of a true north.

Now, your once robust, energetic, and independent parent has been leveled—perhaps by a fall, a surgery, a heart attack, a series of TIAs, or a chronic condition like diabetes that just grinds them down, bit by bit over time. Whatever the specific nature of the health crisis, your parent comes out of it a little bit "less" than before. Less confident. Less sure-footed. Less mentally facile. Less independent. And less of your parent translates into more work for you, the caregiver.

Caregiving is debilitating on a number of levels beyond the obvious physical and financial toll it takes. Genes being predictive, you see what the future may hold for you, and it's not pretty. There will be the inevitable physical decline and, often, an even more rapid mental deterioration. You begin to ponder your own mortality. You reexamine your place in the world. You question your legacy and values. On a more pragmatic level, you start to navigate the logistical logjam that has just become your life, figuring out how to maintain your job, your marriage, your home, and your social life. You try to squeeze thirty hours of commitments into a twenty-four-hour day.

> The question again is when will this end? She (grandmother) has no idea the impact this (a bad fall requiring hospitalization) has on everyone else. It will again be up to my mother and I [sic] to care for her if she needs help, impacting our lives and free time. Last May/June/July were taken up with the surgery and then having to be there every day to help her and now this. . . . When will it be a fall that breaks a hip?
>
> —Seirith

In addition to the stress of managing your parent's health and recovery plan, emotional turbulence churns and foments throughout the extended family unit. Siblings revert to childhood roles (the baby, the dependable one, the organizer, the oldest, the smartest) and hang on for dear life, hoping that embracing the known and established will mitigate the impact of the unknown and recent. Life partners lend their support to varying degrees, but there's always a slight undercurrent of obligation, a sense that such support has limits and you're edging perilously close. Children do what children do—demand attention and act out if they perceive a slight or imbalance in their apportioned share of your interest.

You're a strong independent woman, and you've always been able to cope without calling in reinforcements. Well, not this time. This is, as they say, bigger than the both of you. Or the three of you. Or the four of you. Because this signal event is only the beginning of the care stream. This marks where the true challenge of caregiving starts.

When a parent prepares for release from the hospital, the question of where they go next is pretty straightforward. That destination depends on their after-care or continuing-assistance needs; they can go home with outside help or may require more skilled care at a nursing home or rehab center. What isn't straightforward is the parental expectation. While you're busy exploring external settings, your parent will likely be planning on resuming business as usual, returning to their own home—or yours!

For many of us, the care choices are murky and ill defined. There may not be a critical event that serves as a catalyst to a dramatic lifestyle change. Rather, such change may be the result of a series of individual deficits, each small in itself, each contributing to an aggregate, noticeable decline in the ability of a parent to perform acts of daily living: the type of incremental changes that the affected person doesn't notice, but loved ones do.

I wonder if the elderly will EVER learn that they are not able to do the same things as they used to be able to do. My mom said two weeks ago, while I was there for her shower, "Let me see if I can get

out of the tub by myself." I asked, "Why?" She said, "To see if I can."
Of course I didn't let her. She broke two ribs tripping over her kitty's
litter box!   —*Kolleen, divorced, two children*

Recognize the moment for what it is—the beginning of a new
world order for your family. Now is the time to set realistic expectations, determine family roles in the care plan, and assess where
outside support will be needed. In this game, everyone gets to play.

Why We Do It

There are as many reasons for assuming the parent-care mantle as
there are people who assume it. In general, kinkeeper motivations group into five categories ranging from the practical to the
metaphysical. Social exchange theory holds that it's a matter of
reciprocity, or filial "payback," for the food, shelter, clothing,
education, and socialization provided by parents.[1] Taken to the
extreme, there are even cultures and cults where this obligation
continues after the parent is dead, requiring rituals, sacrifices, or
offerings to appease the gods and make for a smooth transition in
the afterlife.[2]

Attachment theory views elder care as a natural expression of
the filial bond and affection that exist between parent and child.
Under this theory, instead of a weighty obligation or "have to,"
elder care represents the physical expression of an emotional
bond. Put another way, it pays to be nice to your kids![3]

Socialization theory purports that, although filial norms may
vary across any number of psychodemographic variables (age, income, marital status, culture, race, religious beliefs, traditional
values, etc.), women are socialized to be kinkeepers, to nurture
and provide care, and that the very act of caring provides them
with a necessary connection to the world.[4]

Moral imperative theory says that you must care, that it is an inherited obligation bestowed by dint of birth. This imperative stands as a bedrock belief in societies defined by the Judeo-Christian ethic, where behavior is governed by the Ten Commandments, which include the directive to "Honor thy father and thy mother" (Exodus 20:12). It is also observed in Confucian philosophy and across Asian cultures. Researchers found elder respect so pervasive in the Far East that a vocabulary has arisen in Tagalog, Thai, and Chinese to define the concept of the debt and gratitude owed to parents, as well as their important social status.[5]

Filial maturity theory asserts that the role reversal from cared for to caring for represents a midlife marker, one of the developmental tasks along the path to maturity.[6] Researchers differ on whether a single crisis triggers the realization of role reversal or if role reversal represents a point along the development continuum, but all agree that it is an inevitable milestone.

Regardless of individual philosophical perspective or personal motivation, every adult with a living parent or relative will be touched by the demands of elder care in some way. Whether that's providing hands-on care, supervising care delivery from afar, being badgered to help with care by siblings, paying for care, organizing care, or actively avoiding giving care, elder care will be on the mental radar screen of most adults in America.

For additional proof of how pervasive the elder care need will be, consider the increase in the parent-support ratio. In 1950 there were three persons eighty-five and older for every one hundred persons aged fifty to sixty-four. Over the next fifty years, this number is expected to increase nearly tenfold, to twenty-nine.[7] How ready are we for the challenge? How ready are our parents to accept the help they'll need?

Boundaries and Barriers

If you're one of the fortunate few, you can skip this chapter. In the elder care context, you qualify for the designation of "fortunate" if

- your parents did an outstanding job of financial and life planning, anticipating every contingency, and have begun executing their plan
- your parents are wealthy and can readily afford 24/7 in-home assistance, a personal case worker to coordinate care, and a financial adviser to change course in turbulent financial markets
- your parents have already moved into a continuing-care community that has made a lifelong commitment to care for them
- you have a generous sibling or relative with the willingness, the nuclear family situation, and the financial and physical wherewithal to care for your parents

Now that the fortunate few of you have skipped ahead, the rest of us can try to get a handle on our parents' not-so-great expectations.

The Rolling Stones said it all in their lyric "you can't always get what you want." That line should be adopted as the anthem of aging. We all want to retain the vibrancy, the independence, the relevance of our youth. But biology and gravity work against us. There is a difference between our physical abilities at twenty-five, forty-five, sixty-five and eighty-five. Like it or not, it's a fact.

We lose roughly one-third of our hearing, mostly in the upper registers. We see muscle mass diminish at age thirty. We have a tough time getting up in the morning, thanks to musculoskeletal decline. We start developing cataracts and presbyopia as early as thirty-five. We experience diminished senses of smell and taste. We acquire wrinkles, creases, and folds as connective tissue loses strength and elasticity.[8]

We find short-term memory beginning to fail. We have difficulty finding words. We take longer to make critical mental connections as neuroplasticity falters. Long story short: Our living
situations must evolve to accommodate and compensate for the
physical and mental changes associated with aging. While that
logic is inescapable, denial is an even more powerful nostrum for
coping. Not an effective one, but an extremely popular one.

> If something needs to be fixed in the apartment, I have to keep calling
> to make sure he gets it done. After Mom died, I found a letter from
> the insurance company. Dad hadn't made a payment and there was a
> rebate on it.   —Cindy, self-employed, mother of two, one brother

It is an interesting dichotomy that the seniors most reluctant to
acknowledge aging, those who dig in their heels and refuse to
make accommodations, actually wall themselves off from the
very mechanisms and assists that would help maintain their
coveted independence. Sadly, they operate from the expectation
that the world should change to accommodate them, rather than
the reverse. This is an obviously flawed and egocentric logic at
work, itself testimony to misfiring synapses.

The expectation that the world should change for elders begs
the question—how exactly do they think that will happen? It appears that seniors with this expectation look to their adult children to make it happen, to function as intermediaries who smooth
the way and navigate the system as parental proxies. How parents
co-opt these adult children into willing (or not) advocates is simplicity itself—a generously applied dollop of guilt.

Guilt is a great control mechanism. Parents have had a lifetime
to fine tune their technique. When it comes to elder care, you will
be attending a master class in manipulation as your folks apply
pressure here, ease up there, playing siblings off one another,

ensnaring friends and extended family in the argument—all in an attempt to force you to accept, and make possible, the living situation of their choice. Which is great if what they want is workable and affordable.

> When my mom died they had been married for fifty years and he had never done any of this stuff. He doesn't want to do it because my mom did. The first time he was going to Florida to visit his cousin, he had never bought clothes. He wanted to know "Where do I go to buy pants? I know where to get my underwear and socks, but I don't know where to buy pants." I never realized how much my mother did for my father until she died. It's not just that he doesn't know how to use a microwave—he didn't know it was in the house. He wanted to know if they still made those "little things in tins" my mom made us when they went out on Saturday night.
>
> —Cindy, self-employed, mother of two, one brother

Understandably, almost all elders prefer to age in place and die at home. Unfortunately, given current support systems, that is rarely possible or affordable. With increasing age comes increasing frailty and increasing complexity of health issues. As longevity increases, the demands on caregivers increase as well. Your mother may have cared for her mother in her dotage, but that meant Grandma was probably in her late seventies. Today it's more likely that an older parent is in their late eighties or early nineties, and all the attendant ills of advanced age require skill and attention beyond the ability of one person or one family unit to provide.

You won't be alone facing this issue. Some 34.8 million Americans now care for someone older than fifty.[9] Between 15 and 25 percent of the workforce supports a loved one in need of assistance, a number expected to double by 2010, according to the MetLife Mature Market Institute.[10] According to the United States Census

Bureau, the fastest-growing population segment in the United States between 2000 and 2050 will be people over age eighty-five. Their projected growth rate of 389% is more than three times more rapid than the next-fastest-growing group: people ages sixty-five to eighty-four. This is no longer a situation that families can cope with themselves without organized, systemic, institutional support. It is a social pandemic screaming for redress.

Like the early days of child care, people are cobbling together a solution based on limited knowledge, limited resources, and even more limited time. For the good of society and sanity of employees, this approach has got to stop. All members of the community— governmental, religious, philanthropic, business—need to be engaged in providing a many-tentacled, holistic system of support that can be accessed when and where needed at an affordable price.

At What Price?

> The single most important variable to never spending any time
> in a nursing home is having a daughter.
>
> —DR. JOHN MURPHY, PRIMARY CARE PHYSICIAN[11]

At the end of the day, it's that simple. Elder care is viewed as a daughter's obligation, even by the medical community. Despite statistics that show 40 percent of caregivers are men,[12] that number reflects linguistic and definitional nit-picking versus the daily reality of caregiving. The grinding, intimate, personal care that involves gross bodily fluids and demeaning tasks falls to women.

> I only got into it with my brother once. He had a big trade show coming up in Hilton Head. I said to my brother, "We'll be at the hospital with Dad all day. Terry [her husband] will come by about 4 P.M. If Dad is

released to come home, we'll get him home, but we want you to spend the night with Dad. It makes more sense for you to do it, because your schedule is more flexible and you can work from anywhere."

The second thing I said was, "I can't help Dad if he has to go to the bathroom . . ." My dad is six feet tall. I can't physically help him. ". . . and HE'S YOUR FATHER!" Until that moment, I hadn't said to him, "I cleared out Mother's apartment. I gave it away. I inventoried it. Now I'm at Dad's apartment once a month where I go through his bills, pick the place up, throw stuff out of the refrigerator." It was an emotional thing for me when Dad said, "What's wrong with this? Your Mom bought it." That was very emotional for me. "I'm asking you to spend the night with your father. I think your answer should be 'What time should I be there?'"

—Cindy, self-employed, mother of two, one brother

It comes down to the difference between theory and practice. A 2001 study determined that, while men and women expressed similar views regarding filial obligations when speaking hypothetically, they differed on the nature of that support.[13] Findings from a British study conducted a decade earlier established the premise, underscoring the fact that adult sons ante up with monetary support while daughters perform the more intimate, personal caregiving chores such as activities of daily living.[14]

Most male caregivers do so at arm's length and in less-intense situations, preferring to manage and finance services rather than provide direct care. Yes, the same men who wallow in an unholy stew of sweat, skank, and funk on the wrestling mat or in the locker room are put off when asked to deal with simple tasks like changing a parent's sanitary brief.

Who can blame them? There is nothing glamorous or rewarding about bathing or toileting an adult who is crabby from chronic pain, the humiliation of having to be handled, or a lifetime of disappointments. Even under the best conditions, with a happy and grateful patient, it's hard physical labor. Every time I talk with a caregiver and ask how they're feeling, I automatically expect to hear the words "bad back" come up in the conversation, quickly followed by a riff on physical and mental exhaustion and a large helping of lack of acknowledgment.

> Please, Please, Please. If the thought of taking in your N [narcissistic] mother or father ever crosses your mind "STOP!" You will grow old and tired trying to make them happy in their old age and they will hate you for it anyway. You will be endangering your relationship with your spouse and other family members. I love my mother but I do not like her at all. She is mean to everyone but especially to her children, the ones she should love the most. She is bitter and always has been and now that she is eighty-four and living with my husband and I [sic], she has gotten so much worse.   —*EmmieK*

Assuming that one daughter can meet the myriad needs of a frail senior is ludicrous. By some accounts, it can take as many as seven people (a geriatrician, nurse practitioner, social worker, and four licensed practical nurses) to support a single frail elder, with a price tag in excess of $250,000 a year depending on where you live in the country, whether you contract directly, and if you comply with federal employment and taxation law.

Of course, that breathtaking price tag doesn't factor in the opportunity cost to the family caregivers. The National Alliance for Caregiving and AARP believe that the average employed caregiver finds themselves forced to reduce hours worked, which affects related pay and benefits by roughly 40 percent.[15] Additionally, unpaid caregivers who also ante up cash for their elderly relative contribute an average of $2,441 per year.[16]

The burden of care rests squarely on the shoulders of the baby boomers, those born between 1946 and 1964, who are literally mortgaging their own future to supplement Mom and Dad. If boomers didn't get thumped by the dot-com financial crash in 2000, they find themselves in the position of diverting funds once earmarked for retirement to pay for their parents' care-associated expenses.

In almost two hundred interviews conducted by the consulting firm Age Lessons on this topic, fewer than a handful of caregivers mentioned that their parents ever considered the imposition on their children of the financial double whammy—the fact that caregivers were not only meeting unanticipated expenses (the parents') but also drawing down their own savings and earning less, which impacted the caregivers' social security benefits and prospects for advancement as well as current lifestyle. The elders' total focus was on their own personal comfort without regard to the tsunami effect on their adult children and families.

More than 40 percent of boomers already provide personal assistance or contribute financially to their parents, according to a 2007 *USA Today/ABC News/Gallup* poll.[17] That means almost thirty-two million people are compromising their future to fill in the gaps in the elder care system. Net net: caregivers trying to do the right thing for their parents are doing the wrong thing for themselves and their own children in the long run.

Trading Options

Anyone who has investigated professional elder care alternatives can tell you that the cost is staggering. Beyond the monetary cost of facilities and personnel is the psychological cost of providing anything other than the best care possible. Since only the wealthy can afford the "country club" quality facilities, it leaves the average person feeling like a failure, forced to compromise on the quality of care they'd like to provide because of the financial realities of the marketplace.

A 2008 Genworth Financial study determined that the average cost for a private room in a nursing home in the United States hit $209 per day, or $76,460 per year. Families opting for an assisted-living facility felt the crunch to the tune of $36,090 per year, a whopping 25 percent increase in four years. Those who chose in-home care at the lowest end of the spectrum, a non-Medicare-certified helper, paid out $18 per hour for housekeeping tasks and $19 per hour for home-health-aide services like bathing, dressing, grooming, ambulation, and medication assistance. Even those relatively independent households that tapped into adult-day-care services ran up a tab of $59 per day on average, or $15,000 per year for five-day-a-week participation.[18]

In typically American style, kinkeepers aren't waiting for the government to devise a solution. Instead, they have jury-rigged ad hoc networks of friends, neighbors, families, and church and volunteer organizations to maintain elders at home. Unfortunately, these informal arrangements involve tenuous commitments and linkages that teeter on the brink of dissolution as goodwill waxes and wanes and schedules change unpredictably. This leaves the caregiver in a continuous state of anxiety, uncertain from day to day whether the network will hold.

Never Assume

There was nothing subtle about it. The battle of wills started with my father repeating the mantra that "Mother and I want to stay here in the condo. We don't want to live in one of those places." That was the first salvo—lay it off on Mom. It was followed by a period when every time we saw him, he made certain to tell us about yet another of his friends whose children invited them to move in. When we didn't take the bait, he switched tactics and agreed to tour the continuing care communities in their area. But it was clear from the outset that he was only there for the free meals and to placate us.

Next, he tried to convince a recently divorced daughter, months after she bought a condo, to sell and move in with them as a caregiver with nary a nod to her need for privacy, the financial hit involved, where her furniture would go, and the fact that she had to work to build up her social security because of her ex-husband's spendthrift ways.

Through multiple hospitalizations and surgical procedures, he never once acknowledged the burden it placed on us. My siblings and I all work. My mom had dementia, so with every hospitalization, someone had to take days off to stay with Mom because she would not accept or cooperate with a caregiver she didn't know. Someone else would have to take off to sit with Dad, because, as anyone who has been hospitalized knows, you need a vigilant advocate by your side. Eventually, we just had to say "We're out of time. When it happens again, and it will, who is going to take care of Mom?" Finally, at that point, he was out of options. By then, it was too late for my mom.   —Lake, divorced, self-employed

In truth, often little thought is given to where parents will live out their final years, when mental and medical problems intensify. While standard retirement planning may have landed seniors in the active-retirement community of their choice in the 1970s and 1980s, financial assumptions underpinning those plans rarely anticipated just how successful modern medicine would be in prolonging life. Adding a decade or more to someone's life span may enrich them experientially, but it also completely blows apart their financial plan. Now people get to live longer, only to end up sicker and poorer.

> In no way, shape, or form did I ever imagine I would care for my dad. My mom was nine years younger than my dad. It has profoundly affected my life. When I think of people that I'm responsible for, take care of, my dad's right up there. It's not part of my brother's life. I look for things my brother doesn't look for. Dad dresses very nice. We always thought it was my mom, but it's not, it's my dad. He's got great taste. You learn a lot about someone when their spouse is not around. —*Cindy, self-employed, mother of two, one brother*

By convention or precedent, many elderly parents assume that their children will take care of them. Because there is so little discussion of want, need, and intent, no one really knows what it is that mom and dad are counting on. Meanwhile, Mom and Dad expect to get what they want, when they want it, in the manner they want it and assume that their children will make it happen. Like a vestigial organ, the agrarian concept of children as "living life insurance" holds many in a viselike grip. Those experiencing the emotional blackmail of such an expectation describe it as more of an iron fist in a velvet glove. As incredible as it may seem, less advance planning often goes on in the elder care arena than people put into the purchase of a car or a big-screen television.

> My grandparents both died at home one day of heart attacks. The biggest disservice to us was that my parents didn't think they could go in any other manner.
> —*Peggy, mother with dementia, father suffered serial strokes*

A cautionary note to those who make assumptions about the actions of others: A wise boss of mine once pointed out, "When you assume, you make an ass out of u and me." At the time, I thought it was a stupid and trite comment. In the context of elder care assumptions, it's one of the smartest things I've heard. You can never assume anything.

To adult children we say, Don't assume your parents want to live alone. Don't assume your parents want to live with you. Don't assume your parents have saved any money. Don't assume your parents have saved enough money. Don't assume your parents will remain physically able to care for themselves. Don't assume your parents will remain mentally able to care for themselves. Don't assume your parents will continue to drive. Don't assume your parents will be able to handle financial matters. Don't assume your parents will take their medication properly. Don't assume your parents can modify their home to accommodate senior needs. Don't assume your parents will recognize their needs and be willing or able to communicate them to you. Don't assume your parents will maintain a social network. Don't assume your parents will see to their spiritual health. Don't assume your parents will continue to act like parents.

To senior parents we say, Don't assume your children will want you to move in. Don't assume your children won't want you to move in. Don't assume your children will be able to do your shopping and errands. Don't assume your children will be able to clean your home. Don't assume your children will do the laundry. Don't assume your children will do the cooking. Don't assume your children can supplement your income or pay your rent. Don't assume your children can attend doctor's appointments. Don't assume your children can handle home maintenance and upkeep. Don't assume your children's family wants to spend every free moment with you. Don't assume your children will maintain your wardrobe. Don't assume your children are on call to run interference for all the necessities of your daily life. Don't assume your children will continue to act like children.

To adult siblings we say, Don't assume a sibling will step up to care for your parents. Don't assume a sibling can step up. Don't assume a sibling can afford to step up. Don't assume a sibling can physically step up. Don't assume a sibling has the time to step up. Don't assume a sibling who does step up can do so indefinitely. Don't assume a sibling has room in their home. Don't assume that their home can be modified for senior safety. Don't assume a sibling's spouse will agree. Don't assume a sibling's children will agree. Don't assume a sibling can reduce their work hours. Don't assume a sibling's schedule affords the flexibility to go to doctor's appointments or physical therapy with your folks. Don't assume a sibling can handle parental finances. Don't assume a sibling can take the pressure of 24/7 elder care. Don't assume if a sibling steps up, you're totally off the hook.

Here's a classic example of the problem with assumptions. If parents assume a married daughter living nearby will take them into her home, bear in mind how quickly life situations can change. That daughter may return to work to bolster her own retirement savings. She may switch jobs to one requiring extensive travel or one with little flexibility in hours or officing, leaving no one home to prepare meals or provide assistance with the activities of daily living. She may get divorced and be forced to vacate that large home in the familiar neighborhood. She or her husband may become ill and physically incapable of caring for a parent. She may get caught in a foreclosure situation, losing her home and moving to a much smaller apartment. She or her kids simply may not be willing to accept an extra adult into the family's home.

Firmly rooted in the American farming tradition is the concept of aging in place, of remaining an active and contributing member of society, ensconced in the bosom of one's family, until death. Oh, that that was possible today. For most of us, it's not. We don't live in large, extended family units farming a shared homestead with everyone assigned roles commensurate with their productive capacity. We live in ever-shrinking nuclear units, dispersed because of an economic diaspora that finds families scattered from coast to coast with little contact and less interdependency.

> It's so frustrating. We talk about three times a week. I always call. He never calls. I say "Just checking to see if you're dead." He thinks that's funny.
>   —Cindy

Even if parents remain in the home and town where their families were raised, adult children have long since spread their wings and flown to pursue opportunities elsewhere. The twentieth-century ideal of a close-knit, physically proximate family is ephemeral at best. Family ties no longer bind. Instead, collectives of friends and neighbors have assumed the mantle of faux family, marking significant events like graduations, birthdays, and anniversaries, serving as twenty-first-century doppelgangers, stand-ins for aunts, uncles, cousins, and grandparents.

Me First

A peculiar thing happens as parents age. People who formerly lived exclusively to provide for their children begin to experience a gradual shift in focus, from other-directed, self-sublimating behavior to inner-directed, self-absorbed behavior. The switch gets flipped from "we" or "thee" to "me." In a sense it's a rite of passage, one that demarcates the point where parents and adult children switch roles. However, it can generate an odd sense of displacement as adult children realize that once-devoted parents no longer place their independent children first, above their own wants and needs. After all, who would willingly give up the chance to be the center of anyone's universe?

> The dawning truth (is) that I was blessed with a mother who put her overwhelming concern for appearances before anyone's feelings. Including her own daughter's.   —*Kathy, Internet chat room*

This reversal of fortunes can be a healthy development in many regards, as resources get redistributed to support the elderly parent's pursuit of long-delayed interests. The caveat here is that such behavior operates within socially acceptable limits. Problems can emerge when an overactive id overwhelms a healthy, rediscovered ego and the narcissistic parent emerges.

Mirror, Mirror

> My youngest brother is the only one [of the four of us] who stays in touch with my dad intermittently. Dad was a raging, violent alcoholic and we all cut him off as soon as we could. The brother who reestablished a relationship with him is the genetic carbon copy of my dad. He looks EXACTLY like my dad. People do double takes. So you can imagine when my self-absorbed, narcissistic dad looks at him in the hospital and said "who the hell are you?" So typical an exchange . . . it's always got to be about my dad . . . he's got to be the center of attention.   —*Hailey, single, one of four siblings*

As their ability to influence the world outside narrows, elders begin to look inward and backward, dwelling on their panoply of ills and the life that used to be. In response, many seniors lash out by trying to control their immediate environment and the people closest to them. With diminished external stimuli, their focus shifts with laser precision to issues revolving around self. Here are just a few of the ways this right-seeking behavior and need to control exhibits itself in daily life:

• When elders pick up the phone to make a call, they simply expect the recipient to be available. Because they want them to be.
• When elders misplace an article, they didn't lose it. You moved it.
• When elders decide to go shopping, they expect a ride to be available. Because they want it to be.
• When elders queue for services, they expect to be able to cut to the head of the line. Because they believe it's their right.
• When elders can't hear a television unless the volume is cranked up high, it's not because they're hard of hearing. It's that your hearing is too sensitive.
• When elders send their food back in a restaurant because it's too bland, it's not because their taste buds have lost sensitivity. It's because the chef can't cook (or you picked a bad restaurant).
• When elders trip while walking, it's not because their muscles have atrophied. It's because there was a twig on the sidewalk or the cement was uneven or you were walking too fast.

> I just thought Mom was "different." She has always been demanding, acts entitled to everything . . . like it should be handed out to her just because. [She's] self-centered and has NEVER EVER been able to utter those simple little words of "I'm sorry." Most of the time, she knows exactly what she is doing and she does things to intentionally inflict harm onto others. She can be very sly around other people, especially if she wants something from them, but if they do not do exactly what she wants . . . oh boy, look out!   —BJ

I've witnessed my mother time and time again set the stage, pounce, then pretend she is confused. I think with age she is a tad forgetful so it is much easier to catch her in her lies than it used to be . . . when caught in her lie, she resorts to other means such as bawling, anything to take the attention off her to play a victim and get the attention where it should be—Oh poor, poor X. My mother has been nasty from day one and continues to get nastier by the year.　　—*Allyson*

Whatever problem a narcissist encounters, the answer is always the same—someone else is to blame and needs to wise up and adjust to the senior's requirements. In her book *Why Is It Always About You?* Sandy Hotchkiss details the "seven deadly sins of narcissism" in excruciating and familiar detail.[19] They include:

1. *Shamelessness*
2. *Magical thinking*
3. *Arrogance*
4. *Envy*
5. *Entitlement*
6. *Exploitation*
7. *Bad boundaries*

The *Diagnostic and Statistical Manual of Mental Disorders* defines *narcissism* as a "pervasive pattern of grandiosity, need for admiration and lack of empathy."[20] There is little room for empathy in a brain determined to assign blame and deflect self-examination.

Every story that my grandmother tells revolves around her. When she talks about my mom as a child, it always is about how someone complimented my grandmother on what a talented child she had. If anyone in my family does anything successful, my grandmother takes

credit for it. She claims she taught my brother how to talk in a weekend of babysitting, that my cousin has her talent for music, etc. It all
goes back to her. She is the queen and must be praised.   —*Cleofet*

Law of the Land Versus Law of the Heart

In those dark moments, when exhausted caregivers retreat to the
ugly place in their brain, there begins an internal discussion on
the topic of, Do I really have to do this? When parents are particularly trying, abusive, or obstreperous, one can ask, Nothing
seems to please them, so why do I even try? Good question.

A cautionary note for parents: Caretaking is optional. There is
no federal law governing filial obligations to parents or relatives—
financial or otherwise. There also is no federal or state law governing the provision of physical care to an elderly relative. Although
parents may view it as a child's legal duty and obligation, in twenty
of fifty states, there is absolutely no legal imperative to care for an
older adult.

The thirty states with filial-responsibility laws generally address
issues like financial support for indigent elders and reimbursement
to the state for expenses such as home care or Medicaid.[21] Even
where filial-responsibility laws are in place, there appears to be a
tacit agreement not to enforce them. So parents, the next time
you're feeling testy and tempted to make a comment about the dinner someone prepared or how your driver is driving, remember
that old adage "play nice" is relevant even in old age. If you don't
play nice, you may be playing alone.

What We've Learned

Elder care is a personal prerogative. We do it out of love, obligation, or
guilt, but not because we have to.

"Thank you": these are the two most powerful words in our vocabulary. Seniors—use them often!

When making plans for finances and care in the long term, be aware that situations change and there may not be a family lifeline available. Assume nothing.

4. SIBLING RIVALRIES REVISITED

I do understand about siblings that won't help—got one myself. Well, truthfully, he helps when he wants to and when I've nagged enough I'm sick to death of myself.

—Sue

I have one sibling that may call [Mom], or may not, may visit, but usually not. I knew, realistically I would be the one doing the majority of caregiving, I just didn't think it would be everything. It's gotten to the point where I don't expect anything at all from him.

—Beautiful Day (online chat name)

For the past almost ten years, I have been the primary caregiver for my dad, who is now ninety-eight. This is not the problem. The problem is the anti-siblings (one anti-sister and one anti-brother) who are selfish and narcissistic beyond belief. They will do nothing for either my dad or myself that might in the least inconvenience them, or cause them to give up even the smallest thing. They become angry at me if I ask for help, suggest something they might do, or express something I need.

—SJ (online chat name)

All of my brothers and sisters would do anything for my mom except
for one brother and one sister who are geographically far away and
not as emotionally connected. My mother says, "I couldn't be more
blessed."   —Adelaide, married, mother of three, one of eight siblings

We're all grown up now and dealing with grown-up problems
like elder care, right? Well, partially. The extent to which adult
siblings actually deal with and resolve parent-care problems is
almost certainly correlated with their ability to resolve or ignore
sibling-rivalry issues. So while the problems are definitely adult
sized, the ego interaction is likely to be all about one's inner
child, the child who feels unloved and unrecognized for their life
accomplishments.

It's ironic because his parents didn't coddle my husband, but his sister
got everything she wanted, including a private college. Then she moved
away, got married and only came back once a year. It's interesting to
me that she couldn't be bothered with her own mother, but she took
care of her husband's mother and father. She's a scientist, a cytotech-
nologist. Things are cut and dried, not emotional. She just didn't
want to deal with it. She almost purposely came when she knew it
would be too late.

—Adelaide, married, mother of three, one of eight siblings

If you find yourself identifying with that description, don't
worry. You are not alone. Fully one-third of adults report that
their sibling relationships are strained, with unresolved conflict
undulating beneath the surface like a varicose vein.[1] Research
simply underscores what every child knows to be true—try
though they might, parents love unequally. The only difference is
that with age, parents are just more open about it. Age acts like a

giant magnifying glass, amplifying all that is good and bad about our personalities and our relationships. If you resented your siblings growing up, you likely still do.

Here are the facts about sibling rivalry:

- It's real—parents admit to having favorites.
- It intensifies—age exacerbates slights.
- It's mutable—labels and roles can change.
- It's predictable—gender and birth order count.
- It starts young—one-year-olds pick sides.[2]

Everything you thought you knew and experienced regarding sibling rivalry is about to get worse as your parents become more dependent on their children for emotional and physical support. Think of it as the emotional equivalent of a wrestling smackdown. For parents, the constraints of polite behavior erode with age, and brutal honesty becomes the new order of the day. For siblings, long-buried, festering antipathy rears its ugly head as internecine competition begins anew for the dwindling supply of Mom's and Dad's remaining attention.

Here's one of the theories I've got about this guy thing. My brothers were so emotionally fragile or stunted, or so unable to acknowledge Mom's condition, that they just shut down completely. They abdicated and left me holding the bag. Fear was the complete driver. They were afraid of losing her. Unfortunately, that turned into an inability to solve the problem. They were pissed they couldn't fix it, and that rendered them absolutely helpless. Deer in the headlight time. They all demonstrated a complete inability to process emotion. Who knows? Maybe it was something genetic, something about how they were socialized. Women just seem so much more able to take in emotion faster and process it.   —Hailey, single, one of four siblings

Mom Liked You Better

If you honestly think your mom liked your sister or brother better, she probably did. Despite years of denial and claims of equal and undying love, a 1997 study by Cornell University and Louisiana State University determined that 80 percent of older mothers admitted to having a favorite among their adult offspring, and an equal percentage of adult children say that they knew it. What's really interesting is that, although adult children accurately identified the existence of favoritism, close to half the time (41 percent), those same adults were dead wrong when identifying the favorite sibling.[3] So be careful who you emotionally punish or attack for being the favorite. It just may be the wrong sibling.

> Time to call the "golden sister" and tell her I did the last hospital thing, so this one [managing a hospitalization] is your turn! NOT!
>
> —Nancy

> My brother flies in and out of town to visit friends and to golf. If it works out for him, or if he needs a free place to stay, then he calls my dad. You'd think it was the second coming. Dad gets all excited and it's all he can talk about for weeks. Which is saying something because my dad barely communicates with the rest of us at all. It makes me really angry that my sister and I are the ones who have to plan our lives around Dad, but we're completely taken for granted, dismissed, and discounted.   —Lynn, one of five siblings

At the end of the day, it all may be a moot point, since it appears that aging parents are less able or interested in bestowing their attention on adult children. In a 2002 follow-up study, Cornell and Louisiana State University researchers were surprised to learn that as mothers age, feelings about their children become more ambivalent.[4] This phenomenon may simply be an extension of the tendency with age to turn inward, become more contemplative, and consider larger issues than the now-independent children.

In theory, love may be a birthright. In reality, life achievements such as getting married, completing college, and securing financial success influence aging parents' perception of their adult children. It appears that in later life, love is earned, or at least apportioned, based on accomplishments.[5] Speculation suggests that this outcomes-based assessment may have more to do with self-interest than anything else.

Elders recognize that they may one day need to lean on children for financial or other assistance, and they naturally gravitate to those more able to provide such support—a very pragmatic reason indeed to continue cultivating a favorite child. Although as the next anecdote underscores, financial solvency does not always serve as a sound indicator of a child's willingness to provide support.

> My brother has the resources and finances to help out . . . but just won't. I had to beg him to help with a few co-pay medical bills. I was hoping (silly me) that he would pick up the $300.00 tab just to have someone stop in while I'm away. Forget that. This is a brother remodeling his $3 million home . . . yes, you heard right. I just feel so angry at him, and confused as to why he won't help his family.   —Sue

Even if they are self-sufficient and not looking to lay the groundwork for a future caregiving scenario, parents guilty of overt favoritism can be expected to exacerbate the situation in their dotage, fomenting unrest and competition among their offspring as a means of exerting control and focusing attention on (or diverting it from) themselves.

Daniel does nothing, just comes to visit a couple times per year. Takes her to Dad's grave. He installed the mezuzah when Mom moved, but that was his deal, not hers. Anne doesn't do much either. Maybe she acts as a sounding board, but I think my mom talks to me more. Morrie will run errands like Home Depot and take her to eat. Fortunately for me, my mom's great fun to be with and the kids love her. Plus, she can afford to hire the help she needs, because otherwise it would all be on me.   —*Mariel, mother of two, one of four siblings*

Love 'Em Versus Leave 'Em

Whether you love them, tolerate them, or ignore them, your sibling relationships will be the longest lived in your interpersonal network. Longer than your parents. Longer than your spouse. Longer than your children. Longer than your best friend. No one on the planet knows more about the real you and the influences that shaped who you are today. Friends may fade away. Spouses may divorce. Colleagues may leave for new jobs. Children may move on with their own lives. But your siblings remain inextricably linked to you by blood and experience.

In fact, as Americans experience ever-increasing life spans, sibling relationships are extending anywhere from sixty to eighty-odd years. Given that context, it seems like it would be a good idea to resolve one's differences, doesn't it? But as we all know, logic has nothing to do with it.

What's Your Sibling Type?

Sibling rivalry is a common experience, but types of sibling relationships differ. Professor Deborah T. Gold of Duke University was the first researcher to identify five different types of sibling relationships, categorized by degree of emotional involvement with their siblings:

1. *intimate*—*thoroughly devoted and involved in each other's lives*
2. *congenial*—*siblings viewed as friends, but spouse and children come first*
3. *loyal*—*there for each other during family celebrations and crises*
4. *apathetic*—*indifferent and uninterested in each other's lives*
5. *hostile*—*actively angry, antagonistic, resentful*

Roughly two-thirds of the sibling relationships studied were classified as congenial (34 percent) or loyal (30 percent), and only 11 percent were overtly hostile.[6]

> Many of us have brothers and sisters who won't help because it will disrupt their happy lives. I ignore my brothers and sisters and pretend I am an only child! It's discouraging, disappointing, and sad that they won't help Mom, which in turn would help me.
>
> —*Daughter (online name)*

> I am in the same boat as you, drained, sick, tired and POed . . . When a dad is 88 years old, there is no changing them. And your sibs, you will find, they will come around when they want something from Dad, or when they think they are missing out on a scrap that might have gotten by them.   —*Janie*

Where do you sit on the sibling love-hate scale? Many of the influences that keep siblings close have nothing to do with emotional ties. Instead, it's all about practical matters or gender. A study of 7,700 siblings found that half had spoken or face-to-face contact at least once a month. Sisters reported the most contact, and brothers the least, with brother-sister pairs somewhere in the middle. Those who lived the closest—within two miles of each other—had the most interaction. Oldest children, wealthier children, more educated children, and those with a living parent communicated more often.[7]

A Glimmer of Hope

Since it looks like your siblings are here to stay, it's probably a good thing that you actually can influence the relationship. You're not stuck with the labels and preconceptions of the past if you don't want to be. Among the trigger events that researchers believe can redefine sibling relationships are a move away from home, the illness and death of a parent, marriage, and the vulnerable time when one's own children leave home. Each major event opens fissures in our emotional armor that can allow siblings to penetrate the social veneer and reconnect on a visceral level.

You also could just wait things out. The bromide "Time heals all wounds" may apply as readily to sibling rivalries as to other situations. Turns out that eight of ten senior siblings (age 60 plus) claim that they have a good relationship with their brothers and sisters.[8] One researcher described sibling relationships as following an hourglass pattern, with high levels of involvement in youth and old age and lower levels of involvement in middle adulthood, when nuclear family concerns dominate.[9]

Men put on blinders until you can't ignore it anymore. Until somebody's in the hospital, they ignore it. Mom is proactive with doctors, investigated shoulder replacement on her own. Did research on the Internet, decided to move forward that way. No one was involved with this except me. It was OK for me to fasten her bra for her, but not to wipe her butt. She needed a caretaker. In rehab you wear your own clothes. I went through to do laundry or pick out clothes that would work in rehab. My brother never brought dirty clothes home to

be washed. He went to see her pretty often. I suggested we coordinate and trade off so there would always be someone there instead
of two at once. He just doesn't think.

—*Mariel, mother of two, one of four siblings*

Initially, when it was time to talk about the move, everyone had differ-
ing points of view until they saw how bad Dad was, and Mom wasn't
capable. Men seem to take the "let them be, live their own lives" approach. One brother and I could see what was happening.

—*Peggy, single, three brothers*

Rivalry in Action

How do you know if you and your siblings are stuck channeling the
jealousies of youth? Pretty simple really. Do you find yourself getting emotional before you even make a phone call to discuss a care
issue with a sibling? When you talk about elder care with friends,
do you minimize sibling contributions? Do you complain to your
spouse about a brother or sister "doing nothing"? Do you make a
point of making the point with your parent that your brother hasn't
called lately, or your sister didn't send a birthday card?

Do you feel compelled to continuously make comparisons
between your contributions and those of siblings on everything
from who spends the most time with your parent to who cleans
the most, runs the most errands, attends the most doctors appointments, cooks the most, buys the most clothes, entertains them
the most, drives them the most, contributes the most money, and
simply does the most overall? Then you've got a bad case of sibling
rivalry.

All families are not good. We sent [the sister-in-law] a detailed accounting a few weeks after my mother-in-law's funeral. Then we

wrote her a check for half of all that was left. And then the questions
started. She was willing to take the time and spend the money to come
in and meet with the accountant, but not to see her mom before she
died.   —*Adelaide, married, mother of three, one of eight siblings*

Sibling rivalry: Why do we have it? This is a complicated
question at a very complicated time of our life. Biological clocks
are ticking or, in this case, winding down. There is limited time
available for us to make that last-ditch attempt to win approval
from Mom and Dad; to demonstrate definitively that we are
every bit as good, smart, competent, funny, accomplished, successful or attractive as the favored sibling. That our children are
as good. That our spouse is as worthy. That our life matters as
much. Aware that time is running out, we scramble to attain
much-vaunted "closure" in the hopes of achieving an outcome
that we want.

Generally I avoid them [siblings] . . . but we recently had a crisis with
Dad and my work schedule was crazy, so I asked for help. . . . [T]heir
blatant lack of caring, their blasé attitude, and the enormous effort it
takes to get them to do the smallest bit wears me down, and makes
the task of caregiving so much harder. . . . When I am unable to
be there for Dad they do NOT step up to the plate. They don't care
enough about Dad's well-being to do that. And they don't care
enough about me to pitch in and help out.   —*SJ (online chat name)*

Sibling rivalry: Why should we resolve it? On one level, we
still believe that we can reshape the parent-child relationship and
our feelings about it. On some level, as our parents near the end
of their lives, we are forced to confront the issue of our own mortality. On another level, we realize in our gut that we are about to
become orphans, emotionally bereft without a parent to anchor

us in the world. On yet another level, we yearn for a long-lost or never-achieved intimacy with siblings who share a blood tie, an almost tribal connection that will become more important as our parents pass.

> Now in come the family dynamics. I made the promise that we all—my siblings and I—have to be in agreement to have the feeding tube removed. If one of us doesn't want it, then we won't do it. My oldest brother says that he "won't sit and watch Dad starve to death." This brother is being selfish, I think. He wants Dad here because he's not ready to let him go. Dad would want to go and be with Mom. He wouldn't want to lay in bed and have people change his diaper.
>
> —DJMay515 (online name)

Communication Patterns

Parents are the mechanism that keeps adult siblings connected. As long as our parents draw breath, they function much like the communications hub in a computer network. They connect multiple users (children) to the network (family), concentrate the signals (messages) received, clean up (neutralize) the messages, then regenerate and redistribute those messages to other connected users (children).

Here's how it works in real life: child number 1 calls up to inform their parents about a recent promotion, waxing ecstatic about the great new title, the size of the pay raise, the huge new office, and all the executive perquisites that come with the position, like a luxury car and country-club membership. Knowing that child number 2 has always been keenly competitive with child number 1 and that child number 3 was recently bypassed for a promotion, Mom serves up the information about child number 1 differently to each sibling, with a delicate spin designed to maximize positive reception.

To child number 2, she simply conveys very factual information about the promotion, deleting any reference to the perks or money. When speaking with child number 3, Mom intentionally downplays the whole event, just mentioning the promotion as an aside. Her goal: create awareness instead of angst that will only amplify sibling rivalries. Message received, filtered, homogenized, amplified, and forwarded to multiple parties for receipt. How's that for an informal grapevine!

I walked into intensive care, and immediately knew she would never come home. Just my gut. My mom was catheterized. They had given her a pill because she tried to pull out a ventilator. It was everything she didn't want to happen to her. They just stripped her pride away because that was their drill—even though everyone knew it was a lost cause. Meanwhile my brothers were freaking clueless. Mom had a living will, but her doctors weren't aware of it, because my brothers were so divorced from the situation that they hadn't alerted the doctor to that. I talked with the doctor on Sunday about it. He was like "What!?" The doctor was shocked to learn that there was a DNR and specific health directives in writing. You could tell he knew immediately what they had done to my mom. So I asked him, "Knowing this [that a DNR was in place], what does it mean for my mom now that she's on a vent?" My middle brother would have nothing to do with it. Wouldn't even talk about removing the vent. My oldest brother said "No, she can move in with me." Yeah. Sure. Mom didn't like this sister-in-law in the best of times and sure as hell wouldn't want to die in her care. My youngest brother lives in Colorado. I called him and said, "Come immediately and pack a dark suit. This is it." —Hailey, single, one of four siblings

The Psychological Caregiver

While sibling rivalry is a fact that can't be minimized, there's another fact of life and of impending parental death that almost always exacerbates the sibling situation and can't be overlooked: Someone has to be the primary caregiver. One person gets the first call. One person gets listed as the medical contact. One person gets asked first about care preferences. One person coordinates service providers. And that one person is generally a woman, be it a daughter or a daughter-in-law who lives nearby.

> When my husband and I go over there, we invent reasons to be in my dad's house. One of us distracts my dad, and I go through the refrigerator and throw out the expired stuff. He got mad and said "I suspected you were roaming my house." Then he got mad because I was sitting at his desk. I looked at the stamps and there were 37 cent stamps. "OK, Miss Snoopy, look behind them and you'll see the make-up stamps." I check around for that kind of thing. My brother does not do that. They [brother and his wife] haven't been to my dad's house since my mom died . . . the first time was a month ago. I'm the one who takes care of that. I'm the one who takes care of birthday presents, cards. That is my inherited responsibility.
> —Cindy, self-employed, mother of two, one brother

> . . . [Y]ou are not alone in having an uncaring family. I also did not consider my material or financial needs [when agreeing to provide care] and now wish that I had. I sometimes wonder what went wrong that I so totally do not advocate for my own well-being. I step up to the plate and do what needs to be done for Dad, but what about me?
> —SJ (online chat name)

They are the first line of defense for the parent, the first to see caregiving action, the people literally elbow deep in care issues. The ones to wipe butts, to comb hair, to brush teeth, to cook meals, to supervise caregivers, to argue with doctors, to run to the pharmacy, to pick up supplies, to handle laundry, to organize closets. The ones with the most visceral experience of caregiving. Those who literally see, hear, smell, taste, and touch the parent on a daily basis. The kind of care that cannot be delivered long distance or over the phone or on the occasional weekend.

My brother lives in another state. He is single with no real attachments or career. He comes down once a year and stays a few days. He calls about once a week and that is it.

—*MaggieMay (online name)*

I went to visit Dad . . . and that particular brother was there when I got there. Dad's back was itching. I sat him up, pulled the gown together in the back, and laid him back down. Presto, he was calm. Brother just stood there. Dad tried to say something. I asked if he wanted his bottom teeth. He nodded. I got them, rinsed them, and put them in. Brother just stood there. I asked if he [Dad] wanted his glasses. He nodded. I got them and put them on him. Brother just stood there. When putting on his [Dad's] glasses, I noticed his left eye was swollen. I went and got the nurse who looked at it and decided it was a broken blood vessel probably from coughing too hard. Brother just stood there, only this time he blinked!

—*DJMay515 (online name)*

And, yes, these caregivers deserve our gratitude. And, yes, if you're the primary caregiver, you deserve recognition from your

parents and your siblings for your sacrifices. Because there is
no rest for the primary caregiver. Whether on-site or off-site,
there is no off switch from the burden of worry and care about
the elder.

> Usually he [brother] calls to tell me what I've done wrong. . . . And he
> snarls at me if I take too long to answer or I've misunderstood the
> question or I'm not giving him the exact information he wanted. Oh,
> and we have joint power of attorney—to act separately or together.
> A fact that he throws in my face whenever he doesn't like what I've
> done and is threatening to undo it. A lovely situation all the way
> around.   —Sue

Much like the term *psychological parent* that has become part of
the American social services lexicon, there has evolved an elder
care corollary of the *psychological caregiver*. Whereas the *psychological parent* is defined as a person whom the child considers to be a
parent regardless of biological or legal ties, the elder care corollary of *psychological caregiver* is a person whom the elder views as
an advocate and support system.

A recent study by Karl Pillemer and Jill Suitor identified several factors that dictated who mothers believed would most
likely serve as the primary caregiver.[10] Chief among the selection
factors: emotional closeness, similarity of gender, and comparable attitudes.

> Sib[ling] then said I know I haven't been involved, but I need to
> look at her finances and start keeping up with things. I said nothing
> had changed. Sib knows [mother's] fine and with the sale of her
> house she can go wherever she desires. I hate to say this and I
> know you're already thinking it. . . . Sib's concerned about her inheritance.   —Beautiful Day (online chat name)

It is only the one brother who doesn't think we should have the PEG [feeding tube] removed. He also told me on the phone this morning that I should limit my "dad stuff" to an hour a day. I have [Dad's] house to drop by and check on, we have Dad's dog at our house, we need to sell his car and eventually, the house. I pay his bills. I bring his laundry home from the nursing home and do it for him, AND I haven't missed a day seeing him since this began. Not to mention the fill-in time that I spend just thinking about him. I don't think it's possible to limit it to an hour a day. I'm not sure how you compartmentalize and put it away.   —DJMay515 (online name)

So let's give the primary caregiver a round of applause and a very big break, both literally and physically. Let's take Mom or Dad for a week now and then to spell our sibling. Or give them a night on the town, our compliments. Or send a gift card they can use to treat themselves. And let's promise to never, ever second-guess the decisions the primary caregiver makes about the elder they love enough to care for daily. The subject of noninterference brings us to the issue of "pigeon" siblings.

My husband's side of the family is another story. His mom was eighty-four. We just went and picked her up. We did not get much support from his sister. It was so hard, because I kept saying to his sister, "Your mom is failing." She didn't visit her mom once during the seven months she lived with us. She never saw her, and was supposed to come the day her mom died at four in morning. So she never saw her until the funeral. Then she was bitching about cheaper caskets. I said, "No, we're having this casket and putting her in a special outfit." In the end, she [sister-in-law] was still cheaping out. Since that time, my husband is no longer close to his sister and he's gravitated toward my family. He does everything for my mother.

—Adelaide, married, mother of three, one of eight siblings

Pigeon People

It is evident . . . that this is a VERY common thread among family care-givers. Often the sibling who becomes the caregiver becomes used and abused as the "family mule" . . . and the others either gladly step to the sidelines and disappear altogether . . . or become "pigeons." They occasionally fly in . . . flap their wings . . . squawk around . . . drop their pigeon poop . . . and fly off . . . not to be seen again for who knows how long.   —*Samwise (online name)*

Pigeon siblings . . . they fly in, poop all over everything, and fly out!
                                                    —*SJ (online chat name)*

So for the siblings who are calling you up to berate you, or swooping in to leave pigeon droppings and then swooping out, perhaps just threaten them a little bit with the "Okay, you know better than me, so when are you picking up Mom?" line. That might quiet them down—a lot.   —*Daughter (online chat name)*

Beware of the pigeon people! In the words of Internet chat rooms, pigeon siblings fly in from out of town, make a quick pass over the situation, shit over everything, and then fly away. It's one of the funniest and most visually apt descriptions we've run across for those geographically or emotionally distant siblings who appear on the caregiving scene occasionally to assuage their guilt. Or do they really appear in order to keep tabs on their inheritance?

You'll often find pigeon siblings spending more time bankside than bedside, consulting with financial advisers as to the status of parental bank accounts and investment portfolios instead of meeting with physicians and therapists. Another favorite feeding ground popular with pigeon siblings is Mom's jewelry box. Health care institutions warn against bringing fine jewelry onto their premises, so the good bijoux gets boxed and sent back home, where it makes fine pickings for the pigeons while the dutiful daughter is busy tending to the caretaking business.

Pigeon siblings make their presence known by unilateral, intrusive, and uninvited interventions. They stir things up with providers of financial and medical services who aren't really sure what the pigeon sibling's status is, so you end up getting deluged with calls not only from the pigeon sibling who isn't getting the obeisance they consider their due but also from the providers trying diligently to keep family members informed without treading on privacy boundaries.

> They're going to argue when we pull the money out of Bear Stearns. Marty because it's attached to my dad. They'll be distrustful of Ira. Bottom line is . . . we're the ones who are here. We're in the best position to take care of it. We're also in a better financial situation than anyone else. Mom needs to have some liquidity. When she needed the 24/7 caretaker, we were writing big checks every week.
>
> —Mariel, mother of two

> I have two sisters and I thought when the time came to care for my elderly father, I could rely on them. I came to find out when I asked for their help, both have refused to assist me. I never prepared for going this alone. I have spent the last four months doing nothing but taking care of my father's financial issues, health care, doing everything from grocery shopping to moving him and supporting him daily. He ran out of money for living, he's having health issues, and it's just more than one person should have to bear on their own. Over the past four months, I've lost my business, my savings, and my sanity.
>
> —Gina

Two things you can count on pigeon siblings doing: doling out large dollops of useless, unsolicited, and unwelcome advice and asserting rapacious, avaricious "rights" when it comes to financial matters like divvying proceeds from a house sale, liquidating a portfolio, or distributing estate jewelry.

Double Whammy

Apathetic and hostile sibling relationships can tax an elder's limited reserves, materially affecting his or her quality of life and care. Arguments, disaffection, and trash talking make it almost impossible to have an intelligent discussion about parental health and welfare issues. Adult children who revert to childhood roles need to check themselves if they plan on supporting parents in any meaningful way and keep the focus squarely where it belongs: on the parents.

> I will always resent that she [sister-in-law] didn't care for her mother, who would have loved to have lived with her or have her close by. One time she said to me, "Her [mother's] friends are around, they'll take care of her." Like it was their job, not hers.
>
> —Adelaide, married, mother of three, one of eight siblings

Rather than count coup, toting up the verbal hits on envied siblings, caregivers need to understand that setting aside personal slights is part of the caregiver package. Yes, it's time to grow up and suck it up. It might help to remember that there's a "double whammy" effect at play. Children model what they see, which means your kids are paying attention to how you care for your parents and how you relate to your adult siblings. This will shape their attitudes and expectations about caring for you and dealing with their own siblings in the future.

Studies show that one is never too young to shape sibling experiences. Groundbreaking work by Judy Dunn observed siblings in the home environment. Dunn determined that children as young as one year of age were keenly aware of sibling disputes, able to assess the situation, and could side for or against a specific sibling in the argument—all while keeping an eye on their mother's interaction.[11]

Another unexpected double whammy associated with sibling rivalry is its impact on marriage. Apparently spouses inadvertently ascribe sibling roles to each other and deal with a marriage partner like a brother or sister—doting if the partner is older, seeking attention if younger. A New York–based psychotherapist shared a pithy patient quotation that summarized this phenomenon, "All these years I thought I was mothering him, when in fact I was sistering him."[12] For those who need help sorting out the complicated feelings associated with sibling rivalry and elder care, consider consulting the experts.

Outside Influencers

If it just seems like your family is getting nowhere trying to resolve outstanding elder care issues, it may be time to call in the professionals. Family therapists, psychologists, geriatric case managers, social workers, and professional mediators have been trained to help negotiate solutions in a diplomatic, collegial manner. Unfortunately, there is no single government agency that provides oversight or certifies these professionals, and even where they are licensed on a state level, there is no guarantee of quality or competency, which varies by person. This shifts the cost of search and the burden of quality control onto the family.

Two of the newer and more intriguing professional designations to emerge from the elder care conundrum are geriatric case managers and family mediators. The National Association of Professional Geriatric Care Managers defines its practitioners as "health and human services specialists who help families care for older relatives, while encouraging as much independence as possible. The professional geriatric care professional may be trained in any of a number of fields related to long-term care, including, but not limited to, nursing, gerontology, social work, or psychology, with a specialized focus on issues related to aging and elder care."[13]

Families need to be made of stern stuff to locate and identify competent professionals—take credentialing, for example. Three different nonprofit agencies certify case managers: The National Academy of Certified Care Managers (www.naccm.net), the Commission for Case Manager Certification (www.ccmcertifica tion.org), and the National Association of Social Workers, which offers two designations—certified advanced social worker in case management and certified social work case manager (www .socialworkers.org/credentials).[14] The search requires a fair amount of savvy and skill to investigate each governing body, its coursework and credentialing requirements, and to suss out the meaningful differences.

Mediators represent a very different alternative from geriatric case managers, focusing on dispute resolution and planning. What separates a mediator from an arbitrator? Carolyn L. Rosenblatt, a California-based lawyer and registered nurse at Aging_Parents .com who serves as an elder care consultant and mediator puts it this way: "Mediators don't make judgments. Arbitrators do."[15] Rosenblatt views mediation as a codification of what people have done for centuries when a dispute arises.

In the Native American tradition, tribe members stood before the chief who heard both parties and helped them work out a solution. In the federal court system, dating back for many years,

Rosenblatt noted that judges and magistrates would look at cases set for trial, sit down with the parties and try to help them work things out outside of the courtroom. It proved successful and earned the name mediation, which eventually got formally built into the legal system under the heading "alternative dispute resolution."

Call it what you will, mediation is a proven method for getting parties, especially those in emotion-laden situations, to reframe a dispute in an objective manner. A study of commercial mediation outcomes determined that the average settlement rate was 83 percent.[16] Although statistics were not available for elder care related mediations, it can be assumed that the success rate would be higher than going it alone.

It takes all this effort and all these disciplines for families to find someone who can help navigate the system and work through the communications problems that have been identified as a leading cause of disagreement across and within generations.

Talk About It

Dr. Brian Carpenter of Washington University in St. Louis has been developing a family-intervention program that uses facilitator-led exercises and a workbook to help families discuss elder care and end-of-life preferences. Carpenter's interest in the area dates back to his doctoral dissertation, which examined the relationships between middle-aged daughters and older mothers in caregiving. His work uncovered many issues surrounding elder care and end-of-life communications. It noted that there is a lack of agreement across generations about even fundamentals such as what topics should be discussed and when is an appropriate time to raise a subject.

Carpenter believes that the reasons we avoid such discussions rest deep in the American psyche. As a society, we're focused on youth and the future and extremely uncomfortable with the subject of death or frailty. Daughters in his study avoided the talk because it was "depressing" and "morbid." These are no doubt difficult conversations, but they are absolutely necessary. Sometimes the biggest roadblock is getting started, which is where Carpenter's current work comes in.

His elder care questionnaire is exceedingly thorough (some twenty pages long). Here are some of the topics included, which represent an excellent starter list for any elder care discussion: desired frequency of contact, help preferences for activities of daily living, housing preferences, financial planning, length versus quality of life trade-offs, and end-of-life planning regarding organ donation, cremation, and funeral preferences. Parents and children complete the forms independently and then a facilitator works with the family to achieve consensus around a topic.[17]

Mother and Father Know Best

Typical of the disconnect between generations that requires mediation is organ donation. When one daughter filled out Carpenter's questionnaire, she believed that Mom was 100 percent behind organ donation as a valuable contribution to society. Conversely, the form her mother completed made it clear that Mom is adamantly opposed to organ donation. Thanks to advance conversation prompted by the exercise, the family in Carpenter's program was able to resolve this potentially loaded issue and take it off the table.

Another hot-button area is end-of-life treatment. One mother's questionnaire showed that the mother would be willing to take an experimental drug that shortened her life but improved the quality of her remaining time. One son knew that she would value quality time versus quantity time. The other son not only vehemently denied that she would want the experimental drug, he added independently that he would "hold you down before I'd let you take that treatment. Sorry, Mom, but I know better than you." This man was in for two surprises—one, the divergence between his point of view and his mom's, and, two, the fact that he had no legal say in the matter as long as his mother was competent to make a decision and express it.

Get ready for sibling rivalries to simmer and explode. Carpenter forewarns that skeletons jump out of the closet during these discussions as seemingly rational fifty-year-olds dredge up old slights like, "You got to go to summer camp and I didn't!" or, "You gave her money when she bought her first house, so now it's my turn." The sibling balance sheet has been tallied, and siblings will use this process as a vehicle for airing grievances and seeking amelioration.

Meanwhile, parental needs are pretty simple. They want their children to be happy. They want to stay in their home and live independently for as long as they can. They want to be treated with the respect due adults with some history. Carpenter reminds us that people who are eighty are not children. Your parents will always be your parents, and adopting a paternalistic attitude toward them is both demeaning and insulting.

Touchy subjects all—and every penny paid to an impartial third party who can help resolve them is worth it. Know going into it that this is an incremental process. You're not going to have "the talk" after dinner on Thanksgiving when everyone is together and resolve things. That's just unrealistic. A more likely scenario is a series of discussions that introduce a subject, air views, and move people toward common ground over time. It's a process. It's an opportunity. With a gentle nudge from a skilled mediator, the family can become more cohesive, siblings less distant and more accepting, and parents more comfortable that their preferences have been made known and will be honored.

What We've Learned

Sibling rivalries wax and wane with time but never fully dissipate.

When things get heated, refocus on the core issue—doing what's right for Mom and Dad.

When you need outside help—ask for it!

5. WHEN HIS PARENTS BECOME
HER PROBLEM

My husband is an only child, so there was no question about who would take care of his mom. But, he travels a lot on business, so I became the caretaker, which I never, ever wanted to be. I just never saw myself as a caretaker. I would have loved the opportunity to be able to raise my kids and focus on my own life without the burden of caring for an aging, crazy person.

—Hannah, works at home, mother of two

"... And For Worse"

The Daughter Trap started out as a book about daughters caring for their own parents. However, once I began conducting interviews, the scope of the book immediately expanded. I never realized how many women were responsible for mothers- and fathers-in-law, not to mention close relatives who live nearby, and even aging neighbors who have no one else to look after them.

Last summer was a nightmare. Everyone was ill. His mother. His father. My mother. My father. My aunt. And oh yes, a lovely neighbor

who has no family to speak of. So guess how I spent my summer? I
felt like I was running some kind of health care agency, picking up
meds, going to doctors' appointments, visiting hospitals and nursing
homes, coordinating transport, double-checking discharge orders,
arranging for in-home care. The only question was who would stroke
out first—me or them.   —*Stephanie, schoolteacher, semiretired*

Americans are so focused on the nuclear family that the concept of extended-family obligations almost never enters the pre-
marital discussion. It's a nonissue until a parental crisis hits and
there is an immediate need to make arrangements for an in-law.

The marriage contract automatically imposes an elder care obligation on the wife. While rarely if ever discussed, the elder care
obligation is a very real expectation. It's why sociologists often
refer to marriage as an implied social contract between kin
groups. Although you exchange vows with an individual, you
marry into an extended family with established norms and expectations, some expressed and some implied, like elder care.

For most daughters, there is no question about the obligation
owed their own parents. If the relationship has been a good,
loving one, then the natural extension of those bonds is for the
daughter to ensure that parents are cared for, whether that means
delivering hands-on care or managing third-party caregivers.
And in the olden days, when a young wife often moved into her
husband's parents house, in-law relationships were so intimate
that similar obligations were automatically assumed. But in modern industrialized societies, where in-law relationships are often
developed long-distance, how has this scenario changed?

Academics who study the field of in-laws and family dynamics
have pinpointed a set of factors that determine who will assume
the caretaker role. These factors include social and cultural gender
roles, couple dynamics, physical proximity, and time availability—

Which is just a fancy way of saying that there are as many different reasons for choosing to become an in-law caregiver as there are people.

This chapter investigates the reality of in-law relationships and caring for the elderly. It determines how women really feel about caring for an in-law and why they sometimes agree to do so regardless of how they feel. It explores the impact of in-law elder care on a marriage. It also looks at the time, space, and energy needs that factor into the in-law caregiver decision, suggests ways to make the most of a difficult situation, and proposes some approaches for standing your ground when the possible negative consequences of elder care are too devastating to consider.

The Monster-in-Law Complex

My husband's mother started criticizing me the day we got married, and she hasn't stopped since.   —*Tanya, married, three grown children*

MIL [mother-in-law] is always around . . . she makes a big show over my grandkids when my kids are around so they think that she is just sweet. However, if there is a dirty diaper that needs to be changed, or one of them needs to eat or be corrected she wants no part of that!!! She does stuff on purpose to make me look bad and she always turns out smiling and turning on the charm to my kids.

—*Making Me Crazy [online name]*

That's not how we fix strawberries. We don't slice them. We mash them.   —*Mother-in-law to her daughter-in-law, conversation overheard*

Pity the poor woman saddled with caring for a monster-in-law. Those who saw the 2005 movie *Monster-in-Law,* starring Jane Fonda and Jennifer Lopez, know that demonized depictions continue to be the portrayal of choice for in-laws in the popular media. In part because it makes good theater. In part because this portrayal is sometimes accurate. Behind every stereotype is a kernel of truth.

You've certainly met her. The quintessential monster-in-law who simply refuses to be pleased by anything her daughter-in-law says or does. This mother-in-law is absolutely convinced that no one can take care of her baby or love him or nurture him like she can. And she's right. No one on the planet can do it exactly the same way. No one on the planet will ever be given the opportunity to do so if she has her way.

Then there is that small subset of narcissistic women who must be the center of male attention in every situation, at any cost. If her husband or sons compliment another female, it's viewed as a personal slight that merits correction or deflection. How exhausting it must be to constantly wrangle for the spotlight, to so desperately need validation and to do so at the expense of others!

As many of the quotations in this book attest, Internet chat rooms are full of daughters-in-law pushed to their limits by selfish or judgmental in-laws. How pervasive is the monster-in-law phenomenon? Ask a few of your friends how they feel about their in-laws and judge for yourself. Bookstores are full of books about in-law dynamics, from *I Heart My In-Laws: Falling in Love with His Family: One Passive-Aggressive, Grandkid-Craving, Streisand-Loving, Bible-Thumping In-Law at a Time* to *Toxic In-Laws: Loving Strategies for Protecting Our Marriage* to *The In-Law Survival Manual* to *Don't Call Me Mom: How to Improve Your In-Law Relationships*.

There's no question who both parties in a discordant in-law equation consider to be the outlaw—the other party! Because they have no choice in the selection of an in-law, the arrangement is viewed as inherently unfair out of the blocks. And complaining doesn't do much good, because there really is no "fix" available.

Are the average in-laws as bad as they're cracked up to be in our urban myths? Should the quality of an in-law relationship influence the elder care decisions that you need to make?

Living at the Edges

According to Professor Deborah Merrill of Clark University, who completed a 2006 study comprising fifty-three in-depth interviews with daughters-in-law and a subset of their mothers-in-law, relationships with the in-laws exist at the extremes and everywhere in between. When it comes to in-law dynamics, particularly dynamics between mothers- and daughters-in-law relationships can be very, very good or very, very bad.

Dr. Merrill asked her subjects to evaluate their in-law dynamics on a continuum of both affection and conflict ranging from extremely bad to extremely good. Considering the bad reputation of mothers-in-law in our culture, she was surprised to learn that most relationships between mothers and daughters-in-law were rated on the positive end of the spectrum and that most mothers- and daughters-in-law reported that they actually got along very well.

> My mother-in-law is great. She's a really upbeat, interesting person. I hate to say it, but she's a lot more fun to be around than my mom.
>
> —*Debra, newlywed*

Many daughters-in-law even went so far as to declare that their mother-in-law was more like a second mother to them than a distant or judging figure. Standing in stark contrast to these warm, filial connections were the alienated mother- daughter-in-law dyads, in-laws who simply did not like each other and reported a serious, longstanding estrangement.

According to Dr. Merrill's study, the quality of the relationship between mother- and daughter-in-law appears to be established, in part, at the initial meeting and is a function of whether a daughter-in-law felt that she was accepted and embraced as part of the family or whether she felt shut out. Even the smallest gesture can communicate a sense of inclusion: inviting the future daughter-in-law into a family photo, remembering her likes and dislikes, inquiring about her family and their holiday traditions and then incorporating several into holiday plans.

> It may sound dopey, but I was incredibly touched when my future mother-in-law made me a Christmas stocking that matched the rest of her family. She guessed that we were going to be engaged and wanted me to feel included from the jump.
>
> —Lindsay, feeling like part of the family

This isn't rocket science. Strong in-law relationships are forged by what Miss Manners or Dear Abby would view as basic etiquette: listening to the other person, hearing what they have to say, then demonstrating that you care enough to act on the information. Mothers-in-law just need to act like loving moms, which should be the easiest and most natural thing possible, since they've already parented their own sons. Mothers-in-law too need to feel welcomed by their daughters-in-law and, included in their sons' lives.

But if all it takes to get along with your daughter-in-law is a bit of goodwill, then why do so many daughters-in-law fight with their mothers-in-law? Some of the complicating factors uncovered in Dr. Merrill's research include the mother-in-law's attitude toward her son's marriage, social-class differences, divorce status, and presence of children. If the mother-in-law was pleased that her son was starting a family of his own, things were good. If not, not.

Major differences in social class posed big problems, especially when the mother-in-law was well-to-do, a so-called society lady, and the daughter-in-law came from a poor background.

Situational specifics aside, one thing's for sure: when the in-law relationship goes sour, it goes sour in a big way, and once the in-laws start needing additional care, the relationship dynamic takes another turn for the worst. Here are a few outtakes from a popular support group Web site called Aging Parents and Elder Care. To say the least, the comments were eye-opening in their candor and emotion:

> My partner's mother has been living with use for almost eight years now. I have regretted doing this from the day she moved in. She's [a] dependent, neurotic, needy, self-centered drama queen. It took a couple of years to get boundaries established so . . . she stays in her apartment and doesn't intrude on us so much, but in the beginning it was awful, in spite of her promises "not to live in our pocket." It's a horrible feeling to be waiting for someone to die so you can get your life back.   —*Linda, domestic partner*

> That's where I am now, thinking about moving, wishing I could move, realizing that I can't 'cause we made this "commitment" to take care of her, and now thoroughly resenting her because I can't move . . . because she is here! And every time I want to visit . . . and spend quality time with my grandkids, she has to come along.
>
> —*Terasita, married, doting grandmother*

> If she got an inkling that one of her children was planning on spending a holiday with his/her in-laws, she would plant her selfish butt in the hospital and lay a guilt trip all over everyone about how this is "probably my last Christmas and you won't be spending it with me. That's how much you love me."   —*Worn Out*

What's more surprising is that even women who have cordial relationships with their in-laws and willingly participate in their care eventually find themselves overwhelmed by the demands of running two families simultaneously and dealing with issues like wills, probate, burial services, and disposition of assets decades before their time.

> What will happen to my father-in-law, who, although in great health, cannot make a long distance phone call, because his wife does it for him? He doesn't pay the bills or make anything more sophisticated than coffee. He has led a coddled life. We need a DNR. We need a burial plot. You would think some of this would have been done before. But my in-laws like to live in denial, and frankly, up to now, it has worked for them.   —*Barbara, worried about the future*

Family F[r]eud

Why do so many women who have a dysfunctional or strained relationship with in-laws end up accepting primary responsibility for their physical care? The answer may be as simple as it's expected. It's viewed as a wife's duty as a woman. It's viewed as her duty as a daughter-in-law. It's viewed as her duty to her spouse. It's viewed as her duty to the family unit.

> His father asked for help, and it was denied by his other children. They told him he had to get up and take care of himself. He bottomed out and finally asked us for help. The guy is a depressive alcoholic with diabetes and completely unappreciative.   —*Jane, fiancée*

Current cultural norms and attitudes toward in-laws derive in large part from our agrarian roots. In those extended family settings, a woman's in-laws were critical to core functions from farming to herding to child and home care. Family roles morphed through time as people aged to accommodate changes in individual physical abilities and financial responsibilities, making in-laws a fact of life on the farm, part of the warp and weave of daily life. Quite literally, there was no way to survive without them.

Couple Dynamics

As with siblings who automatically turn to their sisters to take the lead with respect to elder care arrangements, husbands are likely to turn to their wives as a ready-made elder care solution. When this happens, the noise you hear in the background is the death knell sounding the end of a marriage, or at least marriage as they once knew it.

> Please, please, please, for the sake of your sanity and your marriage do NOT agree to have MIL [mother-in-law] move in with you. You WILL be her caregiver no matter what your husband says. Once you take her in, you will be trapped.   —Leslie, regretting her decision

One frequent mistake that evidenced during interviews involved emergency medical situations, where the husband spontaneously offered up his wife's services as a caregiver for the ailing in-law during a family meeting. The suggestion was tendered in front of the husband's siblings and medical professionals, leaving the spouse no room for a graceful exit strategy. The proposal was put forward without any prior discussion with his wife.

This does not make for a good situation on any number of levels. First, there is the subtle implication that the husband controls his wife's schedule. It presupposes that a husband's needs supersede those of his wife. It presumes that in-law needs take precedence over those of the son's wife and family. It makes the huge leap of faith that the daughter-in-law is physically capable of providing the needed level of care. And most egregious of all, it assumes that his wife is willing to care for the in-law, in spite or because of their prior interactions.

The relationship between mother- and daughter-in-law is a delicate thing. The two women didn't choose each other, nor have they grown up together, so when the ride gets bumpy, it gets really bumpy. Simmering under the surface can be the remnants of unresolved mother-daughter issues that color the adult emotional landscape, such as the struggle to establish independence and a separate identity. More delicate still is the marriage relationship, as two people jockey to accommodate each other and to grow as individuals, as a couple, and as a family with a resident in-law observing every move.

Despite the best of intentions, or even the best possible in-law relationship, drafting one's wife as caregiver is a simplistic attempt to resolve a complicated and unpredictable problem. The fact of the matter is that few people have the requisite skill sets to care adequately for their own parent, much less an in-law.

Cane Enabled

Elder care requires the patience of Job, the dedication of Mother Theresa, the physical strength of Arnold Schwarzenegger, the domestic skills of Martha Stewart, the nursing skills of Florence Nightingale, the negotiating skills of Condoleezza Rice, the therapeutic skills of Dr. Phil, the driving skills of Jeff Gordon, the management skills of Jack Welch, and the belief system of the pope.

Even with those admirable aptitudes and abilities, there are simply too many unknowns to be able to make an informed decision, because care needs can change in a heartbeat. Where the elderly are involved, what often begins as a straightforward problem can quickly cascade into a critical issue with long-term ramifications. Literal life and death decisions need to be made, often instantly, yet shouldering that responsibility can engender resentment and distrust among family members who view the daughter-in-law as an outsider. The situation described below is all too typical.

> Last summer, my father-in-law was in the hospital, and my mother-in-law fell in front of the elevator on his floor going home one evening and broke her pelvis. So she's on the orthopedic floor. Her husband is on a different floor. And I'm running between them both. Meanwhile, my father-in-law's nurse comes in and says "You can go home now." I went ballistic. How can he go home? There's no one there to help him, his wife just fractured her pelvis! Only then did my sister-in-law, his daughter, come in to stay the weekend until they both could enter the same rehab facility.   —Susan, mother, healthcare professional

A bad response to anesthesia can accelerate the progression of senile dementia. A cardiac catheterization can dislodge a piece of plaque that travels through the bloodstream, blocks an artery, and triggers a stroke. Medication mix-ups can send blood pressure plummeting or blood sugar skyrocketing. An urgent need to urinate can convert a walk to the bathroom into a mad dash, leading to serious falls, head injuries, and fractures. And the list goes on. These are not rare events or exceptions to the rule. It's simply what happens.

One of the first things to suffer as a result of this ramp-up in hands-on care requirements is the marriage. In interview after interview, chat room after chat room, the complaints share a common thread, beginning with phrases like "my husband travels frequently on business and. . . ." Whatever follows is never good. The caregiver feels abandoned, dumped on, and underappreciated by a husband who literally "got out of town" rather than changed his schedule or commitments to deliver care to his own parent.

> [H]e traveled a lot and wasn't really able to help out that much. It was almost all on me for the past five years. Now he's semi-retired, has more flexibility, and has started to see how much work caregiving is and helps with specific things.   —Harriet, might as well be single

> Things were quite hairy the first couple of years. He worked 60–65 hours a week and could only help on weekends. It wasn't equal in terms of responsibility. Now he realizes how hard it really is, and he's helping much more . . . spending more time with his mom. . . .
> —Denise, getting a reprieve

Read for yourself how daughter-in-law caregivers feel about the relentless pressure of having an ailing relative share their home. Unedited, these stories from the trenches resonate with the soul-searing pain of the bone-weary and emotionally depleted caregiver:

> Your household and your relationship with your husband will change! I know you love your husband and want to help him, but know what I know about elder care . . . I would do my best to encourage assisted living for your mother-in-law. Over time, your resentment at being a caregiver is sure to affect your personality and your relationship with your husband. As I have said many times in the past, the road to caregiving is surely a path to H*LL.   —Kathy, growing resentful

Another thing, Apprehensive, you and your husband value your privacy—you can forget about your privacy if she [mother-in-law] moves in. Even though my mother-in-law lives in her own area upstairs, we have to let her know every time we leave the house, we have to let her know when we get back. We have to call to let her know when we leave for work. There are so many little things you take for granted when you're free—you just don't realize how much you value them until you move that older adult into your home and lose all those little freedoms.   —*Linda, advice from the front*

As far as your husband and yourself—that one will be the worst. Especially if he doesn't want you to be her caregiver—you will be. There will be no more "family nights" that don't include Grandma, no anything that doesn't include Grandma. And there will be times that you and hubby just want to get away. And forget vacations. . . . And the tension when you finally tell him "enough" you told me I wasn't going to be her caregiver, now I am. I am NOT doing it anymore. How do you think he will react to that?   —*Laura, at the end of her rope*

Proceed with Caution

You're a reasonable human being. You love your husband. You love your children. You love your parents. You may even love your in-laws. But, to borrow a lyric from a favorite song, "What's love got to do with it?"

We're not talking about goodwill here. We're talking about the grinding practical, physical, psychological, and financial demands of caring for an in-law on a daily basis. Is your family in a position to take on that level of responsibility? This Readiness Assessment will help you make the call. Be honest with yourself, because if you're not, the whole family can end up suffering the consequences.

In-Law Caregiver Readiness Assessment

Question	Yes	Maybe	No
Has your in-law made you feel part of their family?			
Are you comfortable being alone with your in-law for extended periods of time?			
Is your in-law a happy person who will be pleasant to have around 24/7?			
Is your in-law willing to help around the house, perhaps dusting or watching the kids?			
Does your in-law have a good relationship with your husband?			
Does your in-law have a good relationship with your children?			
Does your in-law have many visitors or guests in their home?			
Does your in-law entertain often?			
Does your in-law smoke?			
Does your in-law drink?			
Can your in-law physically negotiate your house—e.g. hardwood floors, bathroom locations, stairs, etc.?			
Will your in-law be dependent on you for transportation?			
Does your in-law keep house the same way you do?			
Does your husband have siblings who can take over and give you a break on a regular basis?			
Does your husband have siblings willing to defray the cost of caring for their parent?			

Question	Yes	Maybe	No
Can you afford to support another adult who may require expensive in-home care and medications?			
Does your in-law feel obligated to weigh in with an opinion, even when no one has asked?			
Does your in-law have any personal habits that you find objectionable? (e.g. listening to the TV at ear-splitting volume, spilling drinks, passing gas)			
Do you and your husband have a strong enough relationship to deal with his parent being around?			
Are you and your husband up to the physical demands of caring for an elderly person?			
Can you afford and are you willing to make the physical changes to your home required to accommodate a senior?			
Does the layout of your home afford your family enough privacy if his parent moves in?			
Are there enough bathrooms for the number of adults who will be living together?			
Are you comfortable with having your in-law's belongings and furniture in your home?			
Will everyone living in the house have the ability to be alone sometimes, if they so choose?			
Will your children be able to adapt to having your in-law compete for your time and attention?			
Will having your in-law move in force you to drop out of any activities you enjoy?			

(continued)

Question	Yes	Maybe	No
Will having your in-law move in put a crimp in your social life?			
Will having your in-law move in impact your work?			
Are you confident you can supervise your in-law's care without getting stressed out?			
Are you able to ask for help when you need it?			
Do you have an exit plan ready for your in-law if living together does not work out?			
Are you comfortable having a very frank discussion with your in-law about the terms and conditions governing residency in your home?			
Are you prepared to ask your in-law to sign a contract that spells out your mutual financial obligations as well as the house rules?			

Now you have a pretty good idea of what's involved with the cohabiting decision and where you sit on the in-law-compatibility scale. If you think it can work for your family, great! Check out the section later in this chapter titled "If You Go for It" for specific suggestions about things to do and to keep in mind in order to make the new live-in-law relationship a success.

If you fear a live-in-law would be a complete disaster, it's time to prepare for the important next step: explaining your position and concerns to the person closest to you and to them, their son and your husband.

How to Have "The Talk" with Your Husband

There are only a few times in life when the subject of discussion is so fraught with emotion that it qualifies as "the talk." The first talk? Usually it's the birds and the bees with Mom or Dad. Next up? Perhaps the college-selection discussion. Or the losing-your-virginity discussion. Then, there's the getting-married discussion. Followed by the baby discussion. Eventually, there's the will-and-estate discussion. And sooner or later, the caring-for-the-in-laws discussion.

No one wants to have this conversation. But most of us will. All the standard ground rules for an emotionally charged discussion apply. Whether your spouse happens to agree with your position or not, the in-law discussion is guaranteed to dredge up psychological detritus dating back to childhood.

As my fifth grade teacher used to say, "Hope for the best. Prepare for the worst." Here are some ideas for approaching this loaded discussion in a way that will increase your chances of achieving the best outcome.

Pick your timing. You definitely want your spouse in a good mood for this conversation. Maybe after a workout when the endorphins are surging. Or after a light day at the office. Or following a great soccer or basketball game with the kids. Or with that final cup of coffee after a favorite dinner.

You want to be talking with a relaxed person in a positive state of mind so there is no spillover effect from work, family, or other situations. Plus, you want enough time together to really lay out the issues, even if you plan to broach the subject incrementally. Being rushed can spike the stress factor, so create a window of dedicated time adequate to the task.

Set the stage. Ask any meeting planner: environment can influence outcomes. Pick a room or location where you can focus on the subject at hand, review any pertinent background materials together, be comfortable for an extended period of time, and have a frank conversation free of distractions.

Introduce the topic, with the desired outcome in mind. From the jump, the tone and tenor of this conversation should presuppose that there is only one outcome—his parents will be taken care of, and it's merely a question of where and how.

You understand your partner's communication style and personal needs better than anyone. You know whether he responds best to an emotional argument or cold, hard facts. Whether the idea has to be his to gain acceptance or whether an expert third-party endorsement will sway the discussion. Think about your husband's hot buttons, his relationship with his parents and siblings, and what drives him crazy or makes him happy and use this information to shape a compelling case.

Anticipate objections and take them off the table. There is a pretty-consistent list of reasons that people proffer for taking on the responsibility of elder care. Chief among them are the following:

- *They gave me life, I owe them.* (There are lots of decisions adults make in life. Having a baby is one of them. Planning for retirement is another. If your parents failed to save adequately for retirement—it was their choice. If we decide to subsidize their care, that's our choice, but it is not an automatic obligation or solely our responsibility to support them.)
- *It's my responsibility because I'm the* _____ (insert oldest, youngest, favorite, closest, richest, etc.). (There is no cause and effect here. You may decide to provide care, but your status in the sibling pecking order does not obligate you to do so in any way. You have no control over the perceptions of others, and that perception should have no influence on your decisions.)
- *My parents took care of their parents and that's what they expect.* (It's an antiquated expectation. The world is a different place now. Families live far apart; adults typically work outside the home; there often isn't even anyone physically present in the home for most of the day to care for a pet much less a person.)

- *My parents are private people and don't want anyone in their home.* (While we'd all like to age in place, without any change in our daily habits or lifestyle, we have to adapt to the realities of life. There are just too many opportunities for accidents that could affect your parents and those around them.)

- *My parents want to live out their life at home.* (There's want, and there's need. Everyone wants to live as independently as possible for as long as possible, but the physical and mental limitations of aging often make that impossible or unsafe. It might be feasible for them to stay at home if they can afford the outside help to conduct activities of daily living and perform basic home maintenance.)

- *I'm not going to stick them in a nursing home.* (There are so many options for seniors other than nursing homes. Let's spend a weekend or two visiting continuing-care communities and see what senior apartments and independent-living units look like these days. What seniors tend to overlook is their need for social interaction with a peer group.)

- *What kind of person will people think I am?* (The kind who does what's best for his parents, instead of what's easy. You'll make the choice that is right for them and for your own family.)

- *We're family, and that's what families do for each other.* (That's what families did for each other in the twentieth century, when extended families lived and worked together on the farm and had lots of aunts, uncles, cousins, and siblings to lend a hand. It's not practical, feasible, or realistic given where and how we live. There is a different, equally good, set of options in the twenty-first century, from senior communities to live-in help to home health care to adult day care—options that didn't exist back in the day.)

- *Who else will do it?* (Let's take a look at all the possibilities available to help your folks as they age. It's not just about their physical needs, either. It's about their emotional needs, too. It would be much healthier for your parents to spend their days interacting with people their own age instead of being isolated in their home. They need to be with people who can share memories about families and Big Band music and World War II, who enjoy the same physical activities, who have the same physical restrictions, and who live life at the same pace as your folks.)

Paint him a picture. Move the conversation from the theoretical to the practical. Before talking, create a blank daily planner or download one from the Internet that breaks the day into fifteen-minute increments. Fill in a master form with your current obligations, then add those of your husband and children. Make a separate list of your in-law's daily schedule, with tasks and times, and be realistic about how much more time it takes a senior to perform one of the activities of daily living.

For example, a quick shower might take you five minutes. A "quick" shower can easily take an elder up to thirty minutes and require adaptive equipment like a transfer seat if there is a tub-shower combination or a special shower seat for walk-in versions. Most elders begin to shower sitting down to avoid slipping and falling. They can't just reach over to adjust water pressure and temperature. That will require the senior to hoist themselves out of the seat and step forward. Which means you'll need to retrofit bathrooms with grip bars so they can raise and lower themselves onto the shower seat. Or you can convert at least one shower head so it has a flexible hose.

Since it's probably not safe for an unsteady senior to shower while alone in the house that means that, unless you have an extra bathroom, someone else in the family will need to bathe the night before and get up thirty minutes earlier or be thirty minutes late getting their day started. Assuming thirty minutes is all the time it takes. If the senior has to blow their hair dry or set it, you can double the thirty-minute estimate.

You probably don't even include the time it takes you to dress on your daily schedule. You just throw clothes on, right? Not so for an inflexible senior or one with breathing difficulties, who must stop to catch their breath and recharge between every reach or stretch. Schedule another fifteen minutes for this activity.

Be sure to write in a doctor's appointment or test for the sample day, because there will be about one a week for a frail senior. Ask your husband to work through that with you. Who will drive them to the appointment? How long will you have to wait to be seen? Can your in-law walk from the car to the doctor's office unattended? Will they need a wheelchair, walker, or cane? Will that fit in your car? How much time do you need to allow for their transition from car to office? That fifteen-minute visit to the doctor's office just turned into a 2.5-hour ordeal between overcoats, drive time, waiting time, staff interaction, and transfer time.

For your in-law, this trip to the doctor is a social outing. They'll be taking every opportunity possible to stretch out their interaction with office staff, parking lot attendants, phlebotomists, X-ray techs, and the like. Meanwhile, who's missing an important meeting, trying to squeeze in a teleconference, picking the kids up at school or running them to music lessons and the orthodontist?

By the time you've worked through a day on paper, it should be fairly obvious what the impact of a single day can be on the entire household and just who (that would be you) will bear the brunt of the additional work and stress. It may be that your husband believes it is his obligation to care for his parents. That's fine. What he needs to understand is that there are many ways of providing quality care for his parent and ensuring their well-being that do not shift the burden to you.

Explain the options. Let him know that you agree it's important to make sure his parents are in a safe, comfortable environment. Then explain how you can achieve that without moving them into your home. There are any number of excellent books on the subject of elder care and nonprofit associations, such as the

National Council on Aging and the National Association of Family Caregivers, that can offer ideas and alternatives.

There is even an emerging group of professionals known as elder care consultants who conduct assessments in these very situations. Elder care consultants generally have a medical background—for example, they may be an RN or may have worked as a hospital-discharge planner or social worker. They will be familiar with everything from the support systems available in your community to the best home-care agency in town to financial subsidies or assistance available to how to access low-cost medications and medical devices. If you need, they can act as a third-party to negotiate the terms of your changing in-law responsibilities.

Stand your ground. Reassure your husband that you share his wish to provide for his parents but insist that it be done in a way that does not compromise your own family life and relationships. In fact, you can use his parents' situation as an object lesson to underscore your own need, as a couple, to plan for the future and retirement. As you talk about your desire to free your children from any financial-support obligation in your golden years, the analogy should be obvious.

This is more likely to be an ongoing series of discussions than a single conversation, but at the end of the day, your husband needs to feel that you explored every option, considered his feelings and needs, included his siblings and children in the decision, and presented his parents with reasonable options so they have a choice in the matter. A choice that you all can live with.

No Means No

You are hereby granted permission to say no to an elder care situation that is untenable for you. If the decision just doesn't feel right, it probably isn't. While it's okay to say no, it's even better to tell your in-law, "We have researched a couple of terrific options that we think you'll enjoy more and will keep you independent even longer." Give them a reason like "your friend x lives there/they have Texas poker games nightly/they have a musical revue and need dancers like you." Offer them a choice, but take residency off the table if it seems like a bad idea for your nuclear family.

Whatever you do, don't explain, rationalize, or argue about your "no" decision. Just tell your in-laws that it's not a workable option and focus them on the possible alternatives. Remember that having children does not obligate them to care for you in any sense, emotionally or physically. It is a gift of love, an act of charity, a benevolent mitzvah. Most of all, it is a choice.

The request to care for an in-law inevitably seems to coincide with the most inopportune times, when their children can least afford to deliver that care. Do not accept the responsibility lightly nor reject it automatically. As caregivers were quick to tell us, it is a life-altering situation for all parties, with ramifications throughout the extended family unit. Sometimes that's good. Sometimes that's bad.

Caregiving represents a continuum of activity and options— not just hands-on care in one's home. Develop a plan that benefits everyone involved and that accommodates the eventual physical decline and medical needs of the senior(s). Caring takes many forms. Emotional support is every bit as important as physical care, and while you can hire people to help with activities of daily living, you can't pay someone to love you.

If You Go for It

Hats off to those who decide to go for it and invite an in-law to take up residency. You are doing an amazing service for your entire extended family. You are demonstrating a remarkable generosity of spirit. You are about to undertake a life change of almost unprecedented proportions. You are about to enter the in-law zone.

There are lots of positive aspects to caring for an in-law elder, including the emotional and psychological advantages of having a resident archivist from your husband's side of the family, and perhaps even a doting grandparent, around 24/7. As caregiver or supervisor, you can feel good about your in-law's situation, confident that they are receiving loving care and social stimulation on a daily basis. You know that their clothes and person are clean. Their checkbook and meals balanced. Their medications taken at the right time, in the right dosage. Their minds engaged in helping with homework or meal preparation. You and your family have given your in-law a reason to wake up every day, an opportunity to take part in daily family life.

Your husband will be relieved to know that his parent is now comfortably ensconced in your home, embraced by family. Your children will have the opportunity to interact with a grandparent who can share history and stories about Dad as a little boy growing up or about their grandparents who may have migrated from another country or part of this country.

Achieving this state of live-in-law détente requires laying groundwork by managing everyone's expectations, as detailed in chapter 3. Your kids, your in-law, and your house need to be prepared. Most important, you need to formalize the arrangement with your husband, his siblings and their spouses, spelling out who will contribute what and when—in terms of cash, in-kind services, personal time and effort—to help you care for their parent or parent-in-law.

If your husband has siblings, don't let them off the hook just because the two of you have decided to undertake an ultimate act of generosity. Siblings-in-law need to obligate themselves contractually as a preexisting condition of the in-law move. They should ante up both time and money to help offset the added burden on your family. Detail the hours, days, and times when they'll pick up Mom or Dad so you and your husband can enjoy some well-earned alone time.

How much and how often will siblings contribute cash to defray the upkeep bill? Will they be willing to take the in-law into their home or make other care arrangements should your own family suffer a crisis? Will they be responsible for upkeep of your in-law's car? How will they become involved if your in-law has a health crisis? Will they take on administrative tasks like handling your in-law's finances or tracking the processing of health insurance claims?

Your husband's role in sibling negotiations is key. He needs to be the primary liaison with his siblings on establishing and enforcing a formal agreement. The "go to" guy who gets his brothers and sisters and their spouses on board, who negotiates terms and conditions. It's not your place or your role to handle those aspects of the transition. But you do need to agree in advance with your husband what constitutes an acceptable level of sibling participation. Like all good contracts, there should be periodic reviews to evaluate how things are progressing and renegotiate terms where necessary.

If your husband is an only child, either in fact or for all practical purposes, financial and free-time issues should be easier to resolve. But they won't resolve themselves without discussion. The rules of verbal engagement apply to any discussion with your partner—never assume that he knows what you're thinking; always articulate and be explicit about your needs and wants. Otherwise, you may find that your husband assumes you'll just handle things and take care of any problems that arise by yourself.

Cash for Care

An emerging trend in elder care called "cash for care" is a very pragmatic, businesslike approach that distributes the financial burden among the siblings, compensates the caregiver, and it is proving particularly relevant to the in-law scenario, where filial emotions don't override financial concerns. The emotional leitmotif for in-law caregiving involves the spouse relationship more than the in-law connection. Drafting a formal contract helps objectify and rationalize potentially charged issues, keeping the couple relationship separate and intact.

Most of us can't afford to just walk away from our jobs, even if we'd like to, in order to tend an aging senior. The "cash for care" approach takes the financial objection off the table by treating caregiving as a full-time job with requisite compensation and benefits. The family enters into an agreement with the caregiver (literally, a written contract) that specifies an hourly rate or salary; defines the roles and responsibilities of the position; measures the length of a shift; outlines when, how frequently, and for how long an outside professional will be needed to provide supplemental care; and details the amount of paid vacation time covered, of retirement contributions made to an IRA or 401(k) program, of health care benefits, and the like.

Sound crazy? Like a fox. This contract is analogous to what some women enter into with their husbands when deciding to become full-time moms. The process of negotiation serves many purposes. It forces people to monetize the time spent delivering care and to recognize that the caregiver could be spending that time in other ways. It preempts the so-called caregiver tax, a situation where opting out of gainful employment to care for a family member penalizes the caregiver's social security standing and ability to save for retirement.

Bear in mind that converting from mere in-law to true parent status is a tricky business. Moving in raises the intimacy ante. Your in-law will be in your space, but hopefully not in your face, on a daily basis. That slight edge of formality that may have characterized your prior interactions will need to go. For the live-in arrangement to work, you've got to be as spontaneous and honest with your in-law as you would be with your own parents.

Anticipate problem areas and forestall them. Embrace your in-law as one of the family. Assign kids a weekly task that involves the in-law. Set aside guest rules; have your in-law live by the house rules like everyone else. Hold regular family meetings where you can air out issues and fix them.

When it comes to in-law etiquette, the guidelines are simple. Keep it honest. Keep it real. Keep it respectful. Take the lead. State your case. Share the load. Share the love.

With Eyes Wide Open

Life expectancy has dramatically increased, but quality-of-life issues related to that extended life span are not addressed by our society in a meaningful way. Coping with aging, needy, and often demanding parents is a significant personal problem for dutiful daughters who are carrying an "obligation" laden with feelings of inadequacy, anger, or guilt.
—*Amien, insightful observer*

Whatever your decision about inviting an in-law to live with your family, only one rule really matters: Be true to yourself. Acknowledge your own needs. If you're not happy, no one else will be either. As much as you might want to acquiesce to your husband's wishes, as much as you might truly love your mother- or father-in-law, if your psyche demands control over your environment and a high degree of personal space, forget it. The best intentions will not countermand the impact of a constant presence in your home.

What is your vision for your family? How do you want to spend family time? Are you an active, on-the-go family where sports and physical activity are how you bond and blow off steam? How would a live-in-law adapt to that lifestyle choice? Is your home the social center for your kids and their friends? How would a live-in-law react to the constant noise and activity level? Are there special activities that represent "private time" spent one-on-one with each child and your spouse? How would a live-in-law react to being excluded from these outings? Do you have a pet that's literally one of the family? How would a live-in-law feel about sharing space with the family mascot?

What some people might see as a request for inclusion in an activity, others might see as an attempt at intrusion into family business. For coexistence with a live-in-law to work, you've got to honestly assess your tolerance for massive life change and for learning to accommodate the needs of an unrelated (to you) adult in family matters.

Before making the commitment to an in-law, reread the cautionary tales in this chapter. List all the ways your life and your family's life will change—for better and for worse. Think back to how tough it was to establish new boundaries with your parents as an adolescent. Now imagine going through that difficult process again as an adult, only this time negotiating with an authority figure who is neither your parent nor the alpha adult in the household.

Then consider the benefits, among them the opportunity to really get to know the amazing person responsible for bringing your spouse into the world. Helping your husband express his gratitude, and paying his parents back by caring for them. Allowing your kids to bask in the undiluted approval of an adult relative and to learn to consider the needs of another before their own. Other positive side effects include always having a willing adult around to air out problems, help with homework, walk the dog, make a meal, or share a favorite book or hobby.

Finally, ask yourself the overriding, determining question: Are you up for it?

What We've Learned

When you marry your spouse, you marry their parents as well.

In-law care comes with less emotional baggage than caring for one's own parents.

If you don't want to do it, just say no as often and as loudly as it takes.

This is a family obligation—incorporate your spouse and their siblings into the care plan.

6. IT'S OKAY TO FEEL BAD

Accept the inevitable. That's the advice offered by experienced family caregivers who have grappled with the day-to-day reality of caring for an elder and lived to share the tale. At best, caregiving is a mixed blessing, filled with the satisfaction of giving back to those who once took care of us, the joy of enriching and improving a loved one's quality of life, the opportunity to teach children a valuable lesson about family and obligation, and the prospect of bringing closure to one of life's most important relationships.

At worst, caregiving is a grinding drudgery, filled with the pain of presiding over a relative's decline, the physical depletion associated with 24/7 responsibility for a dependent adult, the conflict between people and priorities competing for a finite reserve of time and attention, and the financial drain of supplementing a senior's income. Even more unfortunately, what tracks across the digital ticker inside our head as we preside over this living exercise in decompensation is the subconscious daily reminder: Aging—it's in your future.

The whole thing just makes me depressed and anxious. Mostly because I can visualize me in that same position. And the overarching question: who will do this for me?   —*Dottie, divorced, no children*

It never changes. The stuff I worry about now, I'm going to worry about until the day I die or my father does. On a day-to-day basis, I worry about my husband, my sons, and my dad. Someday the boys will get married and have kids, then it will increase the scope, number of people, I worry about.   —*Cindy, married, two sons*

Quality of life is a huge concern. I want whatever time she has left to be great, to be rich with experience. My biggest fear is what happened to Ronald Reagan—that she'll live with increasingly severe dementia for ten years or so and that the remaining time will be horrid.

—*Nadia, single*

One Day at a Time

Coping with caregiving involves many of the same precepts embraced by twelve-step programs. Paraphrased, here are a few steps that apply to elder caregivers:

Admit that we are powerless over the situation. *Aging happens. There's no surgery, medication, or regimen that can reset the body clock. There is no "getting better."*

Believe that a power greater than ourselves can restore our sanity. *Whether we call it God, life force, karma, fate, chi, reincarnation, or some other dogma, caregivers cite the need to embrace a so-called higher power and accept what comes rather than rage against the unknown and unpredictable.*

Make a list of potential supporters. *Friends, neighbors, acquain-*

tances, church, school, and other social contacts in our sphere
represent potential links in a chain of support that can sustain
us through the caregiving process. *Find them. Use them.*

Make direct amends wherever possible. *Time is running out. If
you've got unfinished business with an elder, take care of it. Today.*

Take a personal inventory. *Determine what caregiving tasks you
can reasonably do yourself, and then figure out ways to get the
rest done through your support network, social service agencies,
purchased services, referrals, and fellow caregivers.*

Practice these principles. *Consider it tough self-love. Asking for
help isn't a crime or an admission of failure. Rather, it's a way to
protect yourself and your important relationships.*

Starting off, I was really pissed about how things turned out. But, this
is just how it works. I got over my tantrum. I have to be an adult. I've
got to admit it really scares me about my own future. I've been forced
to examine my own mortality. It makes me wonder, if that happened
to my mom, will it happen to me?   —*Peggy, single, two kids*

In the overall picture, it's like Nike. Just do it. It will become easier and
be less painful. In my daily life, all the answers will be more dementia-
driven anyway. If you've had it with the repetition or paranoia, it's your
clue for a break—take a walk, breathe deep, lock yourself in the bathroom and sing. Do NOT go until you drop or you'll hate your parent.

—*Brooke, single, two kids*

The steps just outlined should represent the first step in elder
care. Before agreeing to don the cloak of responsibility for a frail
senior, prospective caregivers need to take inventory to determine
if their marriage, children, career, friendships, lifestyle, and even
sanity, can survive the "big three" of caregiving: physical exhaustion, emotional turmoil, and financial sacrifice.

Physical Exhaustion

A friend of mine is just so run-down physically. She's always sick now . . . just completely depleted from devoting her life to caring for her mom. Meanwhile, her mother is oblivious to the damage. She just can't seem to see what she has done to her daughter. My friend would not even consider putting her mom in a nursing home. She didn't take a vacation for twenty-five years. Ironically, her mom had to go to a nursing home for rehab and absolutely loved it! She asked to be moved there. So my friend has sacrificed decades of her life for what turned out to be no reason at all. It's a modern-day tragedy.   —*Kate, divorced, two kids*

On airplanes, they instruct adult passengers to put on the oxygen masks first so adults can assist any dependents. The identical principle applies to caregivers: You must take care of yourself first in order to take care of others. While this may sound counterintuitive, it is a bedrock belief of the caregivers interviewed. Make a point of working working-out into your care schedule if you want to survive over the long haul with your health intact. Annual physicals and preventive measures like flu shots, pneumonia shots, and screening tests are a great idea. They'll keep you and your loved ones healthy.

If you wonder why that's so important, try assisting a two-hundred-pound person out of a chair or the bathtub. Let a senior with balance problems lean on your arm for stability. Count the number of steps you take running between the nurses' station and the hospital bed. Lift a wheelchair in and out of your car trunk five times in a row. Lug around a fifty-pound box of medical supplies.

For me, the worst was watching my mother suffer from not being able to help him. To physically decline as well. It was amazing. She lost thirty pounds in three weeks. She was emotionally and physically

disappearing before my eyes. The doctors did what they were licensed to do—treat. The system and the doctors were completely
working at odds with my dad's physical and mental state and the
family's needs.   —Beth, married, three kids

Caregiving in the United States, a jointly sponsored study by the
National Alliance for Caregiving and AARP, found that the major
determinants of caregiver perception of physical strain were their
general health and whether caregiving was a choice they embraced
or an obligation that was imposed. Typically, caregivers who felt
their health was negatively affected by caregiving were older (over
fifty) women, from a lower income bracket, those providing more
assistance at higher levels of care, and those who lived on-site with
the frail relative.[1]

Those caregivers providing the highest levels of care were also
those in the worst shape. More than one-third of persons providing intensive assistance, defined as a rating of 5 on the level-of-
burden scale, ranked their own health as fair or poor. At level 5,
caregivers are providing assistance with at least two or more activities of daily living (ADLs) and are involved with direct care
for more than forty hours per week.[2] ADLs include six functional
areas: bathing/showering, dressing, eating, getting in and out of
bed/chairs, walking, and toileting.[3]

I definitely resent all the personal sacrifices I made. The physical demands of caregiving. The stress. Sometimes what I wanted to say was
"I want to get my life back!" It can get pretty depressing. You'll need
to work on your own resiliency to survive caring for an elder. We, as
women, find ourselves in these situations and depression, anxiety, and
resentment come in. Create a network of support. Professionals made
a significant contribution to my feelings of self esteem.

—Blanca, divorced, one child

Tough. Really tough. I gave up my career when I did this. I moved cross-country. I started out doing it for my parents, but ended up realizing I was really doing it for me. For someone else, the caregiving burden would be a rude awakening. —*Stephanie, divorced, one child*

Caregiving is tough, physical, often dirty work. It requires physical strength and stamina as well as emotional resiliency. While seniors may sometimes act like kids, the physical requirements for handling them are definitely not kid stuff.

One word comes to mind when I think about caregiving: pain. I hurt everywhere, all the time. I'd clean my house, and then have to go clean my dad's house, too. If he needed help with maintenance chores, I'd be under the sink or on the roof with him yelling orders. If he wanted to take a bath, I had to help him in and out of the tub. Try that with a slippery old guy with a Santa Claus gut.

—*Margot, divorced*

Picture this. I'm trying to get my dad to a doctor's appointment. The front two wheels of his walker turned and got caught under the lip of the step. Then the back of it pulled off. It's freezing cold, we're on icy steps outside the medical building, it's snowing, his walker just fell apart. He started to fall. I caught him and went off balance and we both fell down. I remember thinking "Who's going to have a stroke first? Me or my dad?" —*Faye, married, one child*

Not Just Big Kids

Pediatricians are fond of pointing out that children are not just miniadults, that they have unique responses to everything from fevers to immunizations. Ask any caregiver, and they'll be equally happy to point out that adults are not just big kids. No matter how petulant or demanding they may act, senior citizens are not overgrown children.

Even the most obstinate, defiant child is still legally and physically subject to your will. Not so with obstinate, defiant elders. They are legally adults, independent in the eyes of the law until a series of egregious events brings them to the attention of the courts—and still, the courts will be reluctant to strip them of their rights and appoint a guardian.

It makes me really upset when she acts like a rebellious teenager. It's the tonality. I get angry and frustrated. I get so furious. I'll go "That's it. This isn't working. I'm out of this situation. I'm not going to do it anymore. Talk to your son." Mom says, "I'm getting on a plane and heading back." She did change her reservations, but in the morning, she changed them back.   —Jill, divorced

For me, the hardest thing is seeing the decline. From people who had been very active in their work life, their business life, their community life. To watch them physically and mentally decline. You wonder what you have to look forward to. When you see people on a fairly regular basis, you get used to who they are, how they are, and how they look. Every once in a while there were these moments when I would turn around and suddenly see them through different eyes. When did that happen? When did he get so old? Where did she get that scar? Bottom line is, you care about these people and it's difficult to watch   —Eden, married, one child

Dignity is the order of the day for caregivers, and everyone, including *non compos mentis* seniors stricken with dementia or Alzheimer's, deserves to be accorded respect and treated like an adult. A major mistake novice caregivers can make is to "talk around" or talk about the senior as if the person isn't present in the room. It's an easy pattern to fall into, but one guaranteed to spark both an immediate explosive reaction from the elder and, over the longer term, to foster simmering resentment. Besides, it's just plain rude.

> Overall, if I try to flash back to the big stuff that happened, I'm overwhelmed by a feeling of pure sadness for my parents. And for me as well. Get ready. Here you go. You're going to start the grieving process now. All the dignity stuff. It's sort of disgusting. My parents are just fighting to have their dignity. Nobody gives you a course on when to give up driving, managing your own finances, trying to maintain your home. When to know that it's time to throw in the towel. Some people handle it gracefully, some go kicking and screaming, but everyone has to give up something.   —Rena, married, two boys

> If I have any guilt, it's that I don't call often enough. I made a decision to move back east four and a half years ago. I wanted to be closer to my parents. I've seen more of them than I used to, but I feel badly that I don't stay in touch more by phone. It's never enough. My time is so limited as a single parent with two jobs. I could make a better effort. My parents don't call me, though. They have a computer and know how to use e-mail but don't do it. They see it as my job to call them.   —Catherine, single mom

Emotional Turmoil

The emotional impact of caregiving far outweighs the physical toll according to the study *Caregiving in the United States*. While only 15 percent of caregivers rated the physical strain of caregiving as a 4 or 5 on a 5-point scale, more than twice as many caregivers (35 percent) assigned those elevated numbers to the emotional stress factor.[4]

You reach that stage in life where the kids are gone, you should be
sailing along with less stress. There's more stress now than I've ever
had to deal with.   —*Geneva, married, two kids*

Life is so un-fun now. I guess I thought as you got older you got more
secure. Turns out, it's the opposite. I feel less secure, more tenuous
now than in my 20s or 30s.   —*Ginger, married, three kids*

Guilt. Stress. Depression. Anxiety. Resentment. Obligation. Ir-
ritability. Fatigue. Apathy. Withdrawal. All are signs of caregiver
burnout. The demands of caregiving can create a veritable geyser
of feeling, as cumulative tensions build and build over time.
Pent-up pressures sit dormant, ready to explode the minute that
physical exhaustion allows emotional barriers to fall. The pending emotional catharsis merges the visceral reactions of an over-
worked adult with the residual emotional baggage of childhood—a
most volatile mix indeed.

A lot of prayer got me through it. I was ready to crack. I got down on
my hands and knees and prayed.   —*Elizabeth, divorced, one child*

The best coping mechanism I found was talking to other people, getting some perspective. I was able to talk with other people with older
parents. That meant I didn't have to bear the burden alone or bore
my husband. I also found several online discussion groups where
people with similar problems would post.   —*Kyla, married, three kids*

Lost and found. Think of your emotional in-box as a more intimate version of the lost-and-found box. Only in this case, we're
collecting the series of losses that define aging as well as finding
the sentiments that enrich the elder care experience. We're los-

ing our parent. We're discovering a friend. We will soon be or-
phaned. We have reconnected with our roots.

> A friend told me a very wise thing. She said, "The hardest thing about
> a family member with Alzheimer's is you don't know when to breathe."
> She meant you need to relax along the way and enjoy what you can.
> You are losing parts of this person and it's sad. So I grieved as we
> went along.   —*Judith, married, three children*

In many ways, the physical and emotional aspects of caregiving are inextricable. Stress, depression, overwork—all can
suppress the immune system. Busy caregivers running from
commitment to commitment rarely make time for a personal
inventory to assess what's happening with them. Who can
blame them? It takes a strong focus on tasks and emphasis on
goals to navigate caregiving responsibilities along with family,
work, and social obligations. Caregivers are barely making it
through the day as it is and don't have time for what might be
seen as navel gazing.

> My husband grew tired of having Mom living with us after four years.
> We had no life at all. We moved her into a facility for the mentally
> impaired for fourteen months which put us $15,000 into debt. Then
> we moved her back into a special suite we built downstairs, complete
> with a baby monitor and locking door for safety. I had to help her
> bathe, dress, take her meds; even the simplest task was beyond her. I
> was on call, on edge and with her from 8 AM to 9 PM every day. Some-
> one suggested that I go to a support group. It turned into a horrible
> experience of shaming everyone. The facilitator thought she was a
> saint because she kept her husband at home for nine years. If you
> didn't do the same, the group gestalt was that you were a bad person,

that it was bad when relatives put people in a home. I could not dis-
agree more!   —*Bess, married, three kids*

Sometimes the signs of emotional turmoil are subtle. Difficulty sleeping. Forgetfulness. Preoccupation. Weight changes.
An undercurrent of anxiety throughout the day. A vague sense of
heaviness or fatigue. Trouble making decisions. Don't expect the
signs to be so debilitating or visibly manifest that even an outsider
would recognize them. Instead, they're more likely to be revealed as almost imperceptible nuances that even a spouse can't
detect. Just a feeling of being a little bit "off" pretty much all the
time.

Taking Stock

Recognizing the physical and emotional toll of elder care, the
American Medical Association and AARP have both developed
self-assessment tools for caregivers, which are available online.
Every caregiver should check in with themselves monthly using
these or similar exercises to stay attuned to any changes in attitude,
outlook, or physical status.

For those interested in logging on to complete the caregiver
self-assessments, here are the URLs: http://www.ama-assn.org/
ama/upload/mm/36/caregivertooleng.pdf and http://assets.aarp
.org/external_sites/caregiving/homeCare/managing_the_
stress_quiz.html. These provide a fast and painless way to take
stock and bleed off building pressure before it becomes a
problem.

Consider self-care a critical component of the elder care equation. Include "me time" in the weekly schedule and rejuvenate your
mind, body, and spirit. Meditation. Yoga. Exercise. Vacations. Spa
treatments. Painting. Massages. Music. Facials. Books. Movies.

Classes. Pottery. Therapy. Medication. Whatever it takes, get it or do it. Take care of you.

Financial Sacrifice

Not surprisingly, there is a direct correlation between family finances and caregiver stress. A 2007 study of family caregivers found "that the amount of out-of-pocket expenses was closely associated with reported stress, health, and overall well-being of the caregiver for the survey respondents underscores the importance of dealing with financial worries as a part of caregiver interventions."[5]

It costs to take care of someone. The typical caregiver estimated that they spent about $5,531 per year on average, which, relatively speaking, converted to more than 10 percent of the median income of $43,026 for the respondent pool.[6] That takes a huge bite out of a budget for families already strapped for cash.

To supplement their elders financially, families ended up dipping into savings (34 percent), putting off home maintenance and upkeep (32 percent), and reducing health- and dental-care spending to basic or essential care (23 percent). Long-distance caregivers ended up spending even more out-of-pocket annually ($8,728), because geography forced many services or interventions to be performed by hired contractors.[7]

Cutting Deep

How do they do it? How do caregivers manage to find not only the time for helping but also the money for necessities? Families do what they've always done. They band together to make it happen, working toward a common goal for the common good. In this case, it's to care for the titular, emeritus leader.

The Women's Institute for a Secure Retirement (WISER) guide, titled *Financial Steps for Caregivers: What You Need to Know About Money and Retirement*, explores the harsh realities of the unequal financial impact of caregiving on women. The cycle of care perpetuates the cycle of financial inequity. More women than men provide the intensive, hands-on care that conflicts with work requirements. Because they are unwilling to compromise quality of care, more women find themselves quitting jobs or cutting back on hours or bypassing promotions and associated benefits.

For women, the financial impact is the equivalent of a quick series of punishing body blows to their financial future. First, hours go down, resulting in reduced wages and pared-down benefits. With less money to invest, returns are minimized, along with the chance to leverage 401(k) matching employer contributions. It's a lose-lose-lose scenario that holds one person hostage to the fate of another. The average female caregiver will forfeit more than $566,400 in wages, $25,400 in social-security benefits, and $67,200 in pension benefits for a grand total of more than $659,000 in wealth lost in the name of caregiving.[8]

Works of Mercy

> For I was hungry and you gave me something to eat, I was thirsty
> and you gave me something to drink, I was a stranger and you invited
> me in, I needed clothes and you clothed me, I was sick and you
> looked after me, I was in prison and you came to visit me.
> —MATTHEW 25:35–36

Roman Catholics and many other Christians embrace a biblical directive to care for others known as the corporal works of mercy. These works provide a theological foundation that converted tribal convention into a religious edict. Where clan elders once were revered for their wisdom and experience, the works of mercy threw a protective blanket around them for less pragmatic reasons. The works of mercy include the six actions detailed in Matthew as well as one command from the Book of Tobit regarding burial.

Corporal works of mercy summarize the obligations of caregivers, and their moral force is in some part responsible for the guilt experienced by caregivers who feel they are no longer able to personally provide the level of succor detailed. The works exhort people to

> *Feed the hungry.*
> *Give drink to the thirsty.*
> *Clothe the naked.*
> *Shelter the homeless.*
> *Visit the imprisoned.*
> *Visit the sick.*
> *Bury the dead.*

Unfortunately, those works of mercy were written during a different time when women did not work outside the home in the way they do now. They thus presuppose that women would be available to serve as the front line of support and comfort for those in need. Those assumptions no longer hold.

Woman's Work

In its 2008 report *The Female Factor*, Americans for Secure Retirement (ASR) calculated that caregiving, whether serving children, elders, friends, or spouses, excises approximately twelve years from a woman's worklife.[9] Less work. Less money. Less savings. Less security. Of course, even if time at work and career tracks were equal, women still earn roughly $0.77 for every dollar men earn.[10]

Looking at median lifetime earnings, women employed full-time will bring home $10,000 less than their male counterparts. Expand that analysis to include women employed part-time, and the financial gulf widens to $13,000 less. Extrapolating from the salary differential, ASR was able to project that the median female income in retirement will be just 58 percent that of men.[11] The life expectancy of women is six years greater than it is for men, which means women will be living longer on less as their reward for caring for family members.

Caregiver Bill of Rights

Women take a hit on every front—personal, physical, professional, financial. They need to know that it's okay to say "enough" and that they have rights. Here is a caregiver's bill of rights adapted by Jo Horne from her book *Caregiving, Helping an Aging Loved One*. It's a great reference to keep handy when things get tough and perspective becomes difficult to maintain. It's an affirmation of the caregiver, recognition for their efforts, and a reminder to the caregiver that they should minister to their own needs as well.

I have the right . . .

- to take care of myself. This is not an act of selfishness. It will give me the capability of taking better care of my loved one.
- to seek help from others even though my loved ones may object. I recognize the limits of my own endurance and strength.

- to maintain facets of my own life that do not include the person I care for, just as I would if he or she were healthy. I know that I do everything that I reasonably can for this person, and I have the right to do some things just for myself.
- to get angry, be depressed, and express other difficult feelings occasionally.
- to reject any attempt by my loved one (either conscious or unconscious) to manipulate me through guilt, anger, and/or depression.
- to receive consideration, affection, forgiveness, and acceptance for what I do, from my loved ones for as long as I offer these qualities in return.
- to take pride in what I am accomplishing and to applaud the courage it has sometimes taken to meet the needs of my loved one.
- to protect my individuality and my right to make a life for myself that will sustain me in the time when my loved one no longer needs my full-time help.
- to expect and demand that as new strides are made in finding resources to aid physically and mentally impaired persons in our country, similar strides will be made toward aiding and supporting caregivers.[12]

You might add to Horne's list your own statement of rights and promise to read this list to yourself every day.

A bill of rights is needed because caregivers operate in a data void. Lack of information is one of the major problems associated with caregiving. Where to go, who to ask, what to ask are huge issues. No one trained us to care for elders and no one's helping us learn how.

Knowledge Gap

"Caregiver—this is not a role people prepare for," noted Diane Piktialis, a sociologist and Mature Workforce Research Working Group Leader at The Conference Board. "It's not like having children, where for years you do anticipatory socialization. As a child, you play house. You play wife. You play mom. Elder care very often takes us by surprise. If people have a child care question, they know where to turn for help. If people have an elder care question, they don't know what to do, what services are available, or how to pay for them. Sometimes they don't even know if something needs attention or whether a change is just part of normal aging."

Piktialis continued, "Exacerbating the situation is the fact that, with elder care, unpredictability is an important variable. You never know when something is going to happen. You don't know when your parent will go from well and independent to needing care. You don't know when somebody is going to be diagnosed with something serious, chronic or degenerative, physical or cognitive. It makes it very hard to plan."[13]

Family caregivers provide roughly 80 percent of the long-term care in this country for free and with virtually no formal training of any kind. According to an AARP study, family caregivers provide in-kind services valued at a staggering $350 billion, roughly equal to the total Medicare program budget in 2006 and more than total Medicaid spending in 2005.

On a state level, family caregiving ranges from 1.5 to 10 times Medicaid spending for long-term care.[14] These statistics become even more startling when we realize that even as patients are getting released more quickly and sicker from hospitals, there is no effort being made to provide family caregivers with thorough training or needed skills. Perhaps there might be a one-time in-room demonstration before release from the hospital about pain pumps or oxygen or suction machines. From there, family caregivers are on their own.

Training Tools

Training and preparedness are issues that Gail Hunt, the president and CEO of the National Alliance for Caregiving, feels strongly about. Simply put, Hunt believes that "the whole issue of training and education, or lack thereof, for family caregivers is nothing short of criminal."[15]

There are some excellent programs available on a regional basis, like Powerful Tools for Caregivers, but only a handful of people have completed the "train the trainer" course and are qualified to teach it. Hunt recalls that years ago the Red Cross had an effective nine-module series that covered issues like home safety, nutrition, bed baths, patient transfer, and caring for the caregivers, but internal sponsors left and the program went dormant.

Part of the issue is that caregivers don't self-identify as caregivers. It would be difficult for a program to seek them out to offer services and training. For family caregivers, caring for an elderly relative is just something they do. They don't think of themselves as caregivers; they think of themselves as relatives. With good reason. As Hunt explained, "Identifying oneself as a family caregiver changes the relationship with the recipient. It changes their point of view. They want to remain sons and daughters, not caregivers."

When I'm feeling like his daughter and not his keeper, it makes me sad that Dad's living without my mom. My husband was showing Dad something on the computer, some pictures of the kids. We put together a slide show. But on the same memory card were pictures of

Dad and Mom with my youngest at graduation. You could tell my dad
was very upset about that.   —*Miriam, married, four kids*

Single Sourcing

Another component of the training problem is that no one knows
how to find programs or where they should be housed. Several suggestions have been brought forward. One school of thought holds
that training responsibility should rest with the 660 branches of
the Area Agencies on Aging around the country. Another popular
training owner would be the network of forty-five aging and disability resource centers in the United States, which were conceived
as one-stop shopping, comprehensive resource centers on all aspects of long-term care for affected families.

What's needed, Hunt believes, is a national center on caregiving that addresses issues across the life span. It would serve as the
master database, collection point, curriculum developer, training
deliverer, referral service, counseling center, and mediation and
ombudsman source for everything having to do with caregiving.

Wayne Olson, the senior vice president of health care operations for Volunteers of America, concurs. He believes two of the
major problems with caregiving are access to information and a
general state of denial regarding the inevitable. "No one wants to
prepare for elder anything. Except, maybe, for going to the Web
and looking at financial retirement information. Nobody wants
to think about getting older, to plan for it, to educate themselves
about the options. Think of it this way," Olson continued. "It's
like starting out on a one-thousand-mile trip when you turn sev-
enty. There are two ways of trip planning—start to finish or incrementally in small day trips. Instead of looking at the total map
from start to finish, the family chooses to just deal with it in
thirty-mile segments. They don't want to plan because it's not

always the prettiest trip to take." Olson sees the solution in a cross-silo, integrated federal resource such as a department of elder services.[16]

Further confounding the elder care situation is the fact that the senior-services portion of the Medicaid budget is mixed in with every other Medicaid service for a wide range of constituents. Senior-service dollars are "hidden" from public view behind more visible budget chunks allocated to demographic segments that some may view (right or wrong) as less sympathetic or deserving than seniors, such as welfare moms, immigrants, or indigent disabled.

Based on the interviews conducted for this book, caregivers would be grateful just to have a starting point—a place to begin their search for information and assistance. A national center or department for elder services would be a superb jumping-off point. With a robust Web site and 24/7 hot lines staffed by social workers or case managers, this department could minimize the strain on caregivers and their families while maximizing the positive impact of available program dollars through coordination and consolidation.

There are few things as demoralizing as caring for a parent or relative with diminished capacity. The reality of their plight is driven home in the most visceral fashion possible.

What We've Learned

Training is the missing link in the health care chain. Caregivers should demand more training or hire it to avoid potentially deadly mistakes or injury.

Take care of you first, in order to take care of someone else. Embrace a holistic approach to wellness, addressing your physical, emotional, spiritual, and financial needs.

"Good enough" may just have to be good enough. Don't beat yourself up striving for perfection. Recognize that doing your best is awesome.

Acknowledge your limitations and those of your family. Develop a plan B if caregiving becomes overwhelming to the detriment of your life. Viable alternatives to home care do exist.

On a macrolevel, the federal government should investigate aggregating all elder programs, services, and dollars under a single umbrella entity such as a National Center for Elder Services.

7. BOY POWER

Props to the stand-up guys who take on an elder care responsibility. Admittedly, a growing number of men are stepping up and stepping into caregiver shoes, but a huge gender-equity gap remains. Part of it may be because the mother-daughter ties are stronger than mother-son relationships.[1] Part of it may be because many men deliver care in a different way from the way women deliver care. Men (sons and husbands) tend to compartmentalize, relegating caregiving to the category of task versus act of devotion and thus delegating hands-on care as they would any project. The orientation is function over emotion, task completion over personal performance. What is missing from this equation and the elder's daily interactions is the element of filial or familial attachment and love. While physical care is provided, the emotional connection goes absent. Even when a loving and dutiful caregiver relationship develops with an outside provider, it's still a case of kindred spirit not kinship.

It was exponentially more difficult to find male caregivers willing to be interviewed than female caregivers. Even when male caregivers agreed to be interviewed, they were less visible and less vocal about their contributions. They seemed less comfortable addressing the psychological aspects of caregiving and its impact on them personally. This may be a function of their acculturation in American society, which embraces the strong, silent male archetype with taciturn role models along the lines of Harrison Ford, Bruce Willis, Arnold Schwarzenegger, Wesley Snipes, and Keanu Reeves. Whether men will talk about caregiving might be in dispute, but the fact that they do act as caregivers is not.

When men do step up and take charge as the primary caregiver, whether as a hands-on or remote caregiver, they do an outstanding job of it. Generally, male caregivers fall into two very distinct categories: devoted spouse or dutiful son. Husbands typically find themselves cast into the caregiver role, often by default, as the vagaries of encroaching age take their toll on the physical or mental well-being of their wives. This is a dedicated group that deserves recognition for their unflagging, relentless daily devotion to a loved one. It is also a group that already has been much discussed and dissected in the literature as a result of their contributions.

The focus of this book is on the younger generation of caregivers who have no legal obligation of care but do so anyway out of love, gratitude, or duty. As the interviews conducted for this book revealed, caregiver motivation is a complicated thing, confounded by traditional gender roles, long-standing family dynamics, societal norms, residual hurts, parent-child interactions, and sundry secondary issues that color the relationship context.

Mothers Dear and Not-So

Mom is negative, sarcastic, and has intense anger that the world she has known is no longer available to her. It seems that as we age, our personalities become a distillation of who we are in a very raw form.

—*Charlie*

The party line in much of American cinema and literature portrays a loving mother at the center of her nuclear family who sacrifices all for the sake of her children, is fiercely protective of her offspring, and is devoted in all respects to their well-being. Unfortunately, this portrayal is not always reality, and even if it once was true for a given family, the positive feelings such a mother engendered can be corrupted by time and mental illness. Fortunately for many of these women, their children take up the yoke of caregiving despite current attitudes or childhood slights. Read on for what it feels like to grow up with Mommy Dearest and to then be thrust in the role of caregiver.

> Our relationship is completely one-sided. I give and they take. It's always been like that. I do it out of obligation. Out of responsibility. Mom's gotten crankier and meaner with age. She's always been a very selfish person. All she thinks about is herself. She treats my dad like shit. He bends over backwards for her and is very caring . . . very loving. Always asking what he can do for her, what he can get for her . . . and she's never satisfied. I wish I had this warm, loving relationship with her . . . that I could come into their house and she'd be nice to me. Half the time, I come into their house and she doesn't even bother to say hello to me. She just doesn't have a kind word to say to anyone.
>
> —Jim

> I shouldn't be surprised. I've always been the parent. It started years and years ago. I've always been responsible and very successful financially. I always made sure that they had what they needed and then some. I get a new car every year, and I give them my year-old car. I bought them a lovely home on the nicest street in a very prestigious suburb. I see other parents giving to their kids, doing for their kids, and putting their kids first. Me . . . I'm the parent and they're the kids.
>
> —Cliff

To make matters worse, instead of being grateful, my mom is jealous of my success. I'll get something nice and when they see it, she'll turn to my dad and say "How come we don't have that?" Sometimes I don't get them something I normally would because I don't want her to make my dad feel bad.   —*Steve*

Mom grew up poor in a ghetto in the 1930s. They lived nine people in a two-bedroom flat. The survival skills that served her so well as a kid or young adult—getting up in people's faces, going nose to nose— simply don't work for a woman her age in her situation. She's perceived as an angry, raging person. Because she is.   —*Evan*

My poor wife has been fantastic. She has had to hang around with the most negative person on the face of the planet. My mom is just extremely negative and bitter. She goes around asking ridiculous rhetorical questions like "Why aren't I rich?", "Where's mine?", or demanding "Take care of me!" We'd have her over for dinner and if the food wasn't to her liking . . . watch out! She was just really, really difficult. It was hard on my wife and on me. There were moments when I would take my mom aside and say, "If you can't say something nice . . ." and then she'd cry and weep and say she didn't know why she was so angry all the time. We didn't realize that it was an illness. To me it just seemed normal. I grew up in a house with screaming fights and dishes smashed on the walls. My wife marvels that I grew up OK despite all that negativity. Now, everybody pops a Prozac. It's what's for dinner, and I'm for it!   —*Luke*

The last month or so of her life, Mom made the comment, "It's just not fair. It's just not fair that I don't have a girl." I asked her what the difference was between a girl caring for her and a boy. She said "It's something that girls give each other." I think she was referring to comfort. Which is weird, because I can't ever remember my mom giving me a hug . . . the same comfort she was looking for now.   —*Ken*

By way of contrast with these hapless harridans, there are the amazing, loving, supportive moms who prove the stereotypes to be true. Salt of the earth, these "everymoms" retain their mental acuity and physical stamina, living independently and nurturing their adult children in a positive, healthy way. They gracefully yield the mantle of head of the family and cultivate new roles and relationships with successive generations. Wise women in every sense, they find a way to make peace with the vicissitudes of aging and embrace the freedom that comes with yielding responsibility to another.

One of the best gifts I've gotten was a lesson from an older friend. Her husband had passed before her and they didn't have any kids. She was such an amazing person, she taught me that there's the biological family, and then there is the family of the heart. I'll never forget that lesson.   —*Sean*

My mom doesn't need any help. She still sees herself as the caretaker and is able to live independently. If anything, we worry that she won't ask for help when she needs it. It's that self-sustaining, farmer's wife mentality. She doesn't put a guilt trip on us for not getting out to see her. She just says, "I know you have your own life and you'll come when you can."   —*Declan*

What's my mom like? Let's put it this way . . . she wore a gold lamé outfit to my daughter's baptism. Shy she's not!   —*Paul*

Taking my mom shopping was hilarious! If we were at a mall or department store, she would squeal like a baby when she found something she liked. I'd be in the men's section and I could hear her squealing. It was a little embarrassing and a little sweet all at once.

—*David*

This is both kind of funny and kind of sick. If I took you out to my mom's garage today, she has a miniature 7-Eleven in there. Why? Because she says she might need it someday. She feels the need to possess things, to store things. It's the Depression-baby outlook on life. You never know when the bottom is going to fall out, so you better stock up when you can. Oh—and did I mention that this hoard is uberorganized? Every purchase gets labeled as to when it was bought.   —*Brad*

Dear Old Dad

There is something to be said for male bonding. Especially as demographic trends take their toll and the male-female ratio becomes even more skewed in old age. One of the first questions many single male seniors ask when considering a move to a continuing-care community is the head count of current male residents. They hope that a large enough pool of fellow men exists to find a friend or two as a social outlet in what is traditionally a female-dominant setting.

Guy stuff. Taking in a game. Throwing back some beers. Hanging out with the boys. Men yearn for male companionship and often rediscover it as empty nesters after retirement. Sometimes, the companion they seek surfaces as one of their sons, when they become reacquainted as adults with shared interests. Often, merely the comforting presence of a male relative with a common history and belief system who is content to sit and watch television together suffices.

The difference in the styles of male and female caregivers has as much to do with financial disparity as physical ability or emotional competency. In general, men tend to write a check and pursue transactions with the elder at arm's length, while women tend to check in and handle the down-and-dirty physical delivery of care—not necessarily because women enjoy it or are better suited to it but because it's what they can afford.

According to the Women's Institute for a Secure Retirement, retired women receive pension benefits roughly equal to half that of men.[2] A 2007 Vanguard study of three million 401(k) participants showed an average balance of $56,723 for women versus $95,447 for men.[3] This finding was confirmed by a Hewitt Associates study of two million 401(k) plans, which determined that women averaged $56,320 in their retirement account versus more than $100,000 for their male counterparts.[4] That doesn't leave women a lot of latitude for underwriting elders' assisted-living expenses or purchasing a car for them. That's where male caregivers often enter the picture.

Whether senior men prefer a male caregiver for reasons of companionship, peer perception, purchasing power, cultural norms, or intimate personal-care tasks, they appear simply to be more comfortable with other men and crave their company. In any of these scenarios, the gender denominator tips the scales in favor of the male caregiver. As we discovered, many sons and male relatives are more than happy to oblige.

What I liked about taking over the caregiver role was, it grounded me a bit. Dad was always grateful for what he had, the people in his life, that he had been careful with his money and could afford to stay in his own home. He would always thank me for looking out for him.

—*Ethan*

My dad was never difficult to deal with. He was never grouchy or angry or belligerent. He was the nicest man you'd ever want to meet. He really was. He had a wonderful sense of humor.   —*Ned*

I was kind of flaky. I'd start these little art types of businesses that were doomed to failure. I watched myself transform into a responsible person for my dad. On a very simple level, this was something that I could do for him, especially after all he had done for me. I began, as frustrating as it was, to think of caregiving as a privilege. Something that I was fortunate to be able to do. So many people don't have that opportunity, don't have good relationships with their parents.   —Dirk

My dad went downhill fast. Scary fast. He's pretty frail now, but okay with everything that's happening. He's made his peace but is not ready to go. He told me that he wants to die when he can't be a contributor anymore. For now, he still glues stuff on wood, paints it, crafts every day. He gives them to people at the bank, at the grocery store.   —Brian

We're important to each other. I feel like I'm doing something for him that's tremendously personal. Christmas gifts are one thing. Springing him from the Alzheimer's ward to take him to lunch or church is the best thing I could ever do for him. He recognizes that and is tremendously thankful. He tells me it's the best time he's ever had in his whole life because it means so much to him now.
                                                                                          —Russ

The relationship with my dad has taken on an entire new significance. There's no way I could have done this when I was younger. I didn't care enough. I've started to understand what an impact I can have at this critical time for him.   —Ted

Talk about a heavy load, this role reversal. It makes me feel pretty good because I'm useful in his life. I can make a difference in how he sees life. That he knows somebody's there for him.   —Parker

Friends in the same situation don't want to talk about it. They're very
protective because it's so painful. I give myself permission to do what
I think is right for Dad. If something's in my way, I go around it. You
need to give yourself permission to talk about it.   —*Mark*

What I wish, looking back, is that someone had said to me, "Talk to
your dad! Understand what's going on from his point of view." Also,
help me understand how I could bring some value to the process. To
not kill myself trying to fix things. To not berate myself for things I
can't control. This doesn't have to be a horrible, stressful thing for
everybody. You control a lot of it. You certainly control how you feel
about it. Decide how you want it to be, and then make it happen.
                                                            —*Eric*

The True Meaning of Telecommunication

In boy land, telecommunication refers to a unique relationship
with the television, not the telephone. The television plays a
pivotal role in the masculine world. The size and quality of one's
big-screen TV speaks volumes about social status and income.
Then there are the delicate negotiations for parceling out command of the remote control that requires a skill set worthy of the
Geneva postwar efforts.

If you've ever observed a group of men watching a game on
television, you'll quickly realize that they talk to the screen, not
one another. That is, if they speak at all. In "Television and Gender
Roles," Daniel Chandler discusses David Morley's seminal work
Family Television, which finds that women perceive television viewing as a social outlet, so they multitask, watching and commenting
on programs. Conversely, men become deeply immersed in programs, focused on the show or game, giving it their full attention
in silence.[5]

This male mind-set transcends generational boundaries, socioeconomic distinctions, and ethnic divides. Age doesn't matter. These patterns persist into adulthood and old age. Quite literally, the television set is the focal point, the social hub, in many elder homes and apartments. A mechanical substitute for the absent spouse and children. The iconic value of a television apparently never wanes and often becomes a bone of contention among caregiver siblings. When a son (and it is almost always a man) antes up for a major gift for the elder, a big-screen TV is high on the list of possible presents. Daughters, out of practicality or penury, opt for more pragmatic gifts like clothing, food, or personal services and consider an oversized television to be a complete waste of money and space.

Morley's examination of television use explored gender differences and determined that social roles and power issues play a more important part in predicting usage patterns than sex.[6] For men, the home is a place of leisure; for women, the home is a place of work, irrespective of daytime work obligations. The battle for the remote control reflects what researcher Charlotte Brunsdon terms a "mode of power" versus mere gender roles and stands as precursor for sibling power struggles to come in the elder care venue.[7]

If the big-screen purchase wasn't a family decision, expect fireworks on delivery and a detailed accounting by female siblings of how that money could have been better spent as they rearrange the furniture to accommodate the behemoth—comments that will fall on deaf ears because Dad and the brother are thoroughly absorbed in the game playing on said television.

Pater Familias Silliness

Many male caregivers commented on how uncomfortable it felt to be living thousands of miles away, removed from quotidian tasks like attending doctor's appointments or handling real estate transactions, only to be called in at the eleventh hour to broker critical decisions. It might be speaking with a surgeon who is blowing off a sister's inquiry about an alternative-treatment protocol or procedure for the elder. It might be speaking with a realtor who refuses to negotiate requested concessions. The brother steps in, makes the call, issues the same request, and gets a reasoned response on a "man to man" basis for no reason other than gender. It might be the reallocation of an investment portfolio or the purchase of a condominium. Even if the daughter does all the footwork and research, tees up the contracts, and wraps up all the details, the senior often insists on getting a male opinion before proceeding.

> I'm a CPA with an MBA in finance from a top business school and a senior exec at a Fortune 50 company. Despite all that, my dad insists on talking to my brother about financial matters and getting his okay before signing anything. My brother is a schoolteacher.
>
> —Blythe, married, one daughter

Was the woman too soft in her approach? Perhaps. Was the woman too emotional in her phrasing? Perhaps. Was the doctor too busy when he took her call? Maybe. But it defies the law of random behavior when these situations arise on a near-universal basis. So, like it or not, regardless of birth order, geographic proximity, or emotional ties, men get dragged into the caregiving decision process whether they want to or not.

Worried and Waiting

Caring men worry about their elder relatives, about their physical and mental well-being. It's a silent, subtle concern that never wanes but rides just under the surface undulating with each shift in an elder's health status. Operating within societal constraints, men are less likely to openly discuss their emotions, but that doesn't make them less visceral or heartfelt. How they address them ranges from denial to stoicism to psychotherapy.

Watching them age makes me sad. At least I was able to quell my dad's financial fears, to take that worry off his shoulders.   *—Vince*

As a society, we don't deal well with death. It's all about fixing what's broken, about making someone better. You can't fix old age. Death is as much a part of life as birth. I find that spirituality gives some comfort.   *—Russ*

Supposedly I'm the ultimate Libra, taking care of everybody else. I came close to a meltdown a couple of times with certain friends in certain situations . . . where I felt safe. It surprised me when it happened. I was just really emotionally raw and with people who could handle it. What did happen was my temper would flare with my wife. Luckily, we both recognized what was happening and went to counseling. Everyone needs a tune-up now and then.   *—Nick*

Regrets? I wish I had expressed more love in the years when I could have. It was hard to communicate those types of things when they're that old. I wanted to tell her those types of things, but I just couldn't do it.   *—Sam*

The relationship is pretty much the same it's always been. I don't come from an extremely close family. We rally around when we need to, when Mom's in the hospital, to support her. That's how it's been my whole life.   *—Gene*

I feel sorry for her. I know that's not how I want to end my life, isolated and alone. I don't want that to happen to me.   —Lou

When she's gone, I'll miss Mom dearly. Right now, it's not an emotional experience. I don't like seeing her suffer. I have a tough time dealing with that. When she passes, I don't know how I'll feel.   —Mike

I'll tell you this. I'm learning what it means to be patient.   —Jason

What is, is. My wife, my sister, and I are on the same page, but my sister is a lot more emotional about things. Especially the prospect of a nursing home. I'm more pragmatic. Not sure if that's a gender thing or personality trait.   —Tom

Facing the Future

Dealing with an elder's issues today raises the specter of what a caregiver will face tomorrow. Male caregivers, watching the world shrink, the sphere of interest narrow, and the musings become more inner directed, were prompted to contemplate what their own golden years might look like. They expressed the opinion to an interviewer that helping out their parent somehow balanced the scales of equity and afforded them the chance to complete unfinished business. While there was little discussion of legacy per se, there was a profound sense that they were modeling behavior for their own children, leading by example.

My greatest fear is not being self-sufficient. The fear of having to rely on others, to have to ask for something to be done for me.

        —Steve

Lack of insurance is a huge issue. I wonder how we're ever going to have one-tenth of the coverage and support my mom has. Her last visit to the ER cost $10,000.
                                                              —*Matt*

I keep telling myself "don't be like him." Honestly, I am never going to treat people like that no matter how badly I might feel. I'm not going to be rude and uncooperative to people who are trying to help me.
                                                              —*Vince*

As I learn from this experience, I'm more prudent about finances. I want to make sure we have enough to maintain the kind of lifestyle we'd like. I feel like we're ahead of the curve because we recognize that assisted living is not the same as an "old people's home," but a wonderful environment with social interaction. It's not checking out of life, it's checking in.
                                                              —*Nick*

Keep active! Your body will atrophy sitting on the couch. There's a guy at the health club who is eighty-two years old. He's thin. He does push-ups. He works out on the machines. He's my hero. He's in shape. He doesn't just sit around and complain.
                                                              —*Stewart*

People in my family are long-lived. As a gay man, I don't have children or a large, extended family to count on. That's an issue. I worry that I won't be able to care for myself adequately and will wind up in some terrible place.
                                                              —*Bob*

Perhaps the most telling statement that serves as testament to devotion and expectation is this:

I hope that my son is as nice to me as I am to my dad.   —*Jack*

What We've Learned

There is no substitute for male bonding, especially for elders with limited opportunity to do so.

Men enjoy a cultural edge when dealing with patriarchal institutions and should use it to full advantage.

Just writing a check is only slightly better than writing off an elder.

Remote control only works for televisions—it's not a viable caregiving alternative.

8. THE DOCTOR IS IN

A surgeon should be young; a physician old.
—FRENCH PROVERB

Hospital systems are so inflexible. They're totally not designed with the family caregiver in mind. I ended up having to leave work early every day for a year, because if I didn't make it before shift change, it would be another twenty-four hours before I could get any information on my father's condition. That's just not right. As understanding as my employer was, eventually, people start resenting you. The work at work still needs to get done.   —*Helene, married, mother of four*

A geriatrician is the most wonderful thing that ever happened to us. A total saint. Mom probably had Parkinson's for five years before it was diagnosed, because she didn't shake. The world completely changed when a geriatrician entered the picture. This physician just "got it" and in turn, my mom got the care she needed. Our only question was, "Why was everyone else asleep at the wheel?"

—*Renee, single, no kids*

The worst part was the lack of information and the demand for immediate decisions. Big decisions. Pull-the-plug kind of decisions. These doctors would flit in and out of the room, ignore us other than to maybe nod in our direction, then return later, give us a thirty-second update and say, "What would you like us to do?" Well, how about more than thirty seconds to think about it? How about giving us some hard data, some trend info instead of this subjective, surface down-load?   —Cheryl, married, mother of four

Primary-care physicians are the lifelines, or the rip cords, of family caregiving. Boots on the ground in the fight for quality of life. But they represent just one element in a very complicated system. American health care sits poised on a precipice, staring down into the enormous gulf between the dwindling resources available and the burgeoning patient population. Advances in targeted pharmaceuticals, noninvasive surgeries, early detection of life-threatening conditions, and lifestyle management have combined to extend the average life span beyond precedent.

A statement of principles issued by the American Geriatrics Society noted that ". . . if we assume that life expectancy from age sixty-five will continue to increase at the rate seen in the 1990s, the projected population of people aged eighty-five and older will then reach an awesome 31.2 million by the year 2050."[1] While the United States may lag other developed countries on the longevity front, gains in life expectancy have been significant, rising from over forty-seven years in 1900 to almost seventy-eight years for a person born in 2005.[2]

It is no longer a rarity to encounter a person classified as one of the "old-old" (over eighty-five). Even according to the most conservative estimates, "superseniors" now number more than four million strong and will approach the six million mark around 2015.[3] They're alive and kicking but undoubtedly also managing multiple chronic health conditions. Consider that

- Eight out of ten seniors report at least one chronic condition.[4]
- Half of seniors deal with at least two chronic conditions.[5]

- Twenty percent of seniors over sixty-five have at least five chronic conditions.[6]
- The average seventy-five-year-old has three chronic medical conditions and takes five prescription drugs.[7]
- By 2020, there will be 157 million Americans with chronic conditions.[8] That's equivalent to more than half of the total United States population circa 2008.

We, as a society, do not deal with death well. It's all about making someone better, about fixing it. Death is as much a part of life as birth. At least in hospice, in palliative care situations, I saw working health care models where people didn't fear death, they embraced it as the next step in life.
                                                        —Seamus, single

I fear the nights now. You're at the mercy of the nightshift in hospitals. They're notorious for overmedicating patients so they don't have to deal with them. Or worse is the addicted doctor who "shorts" a patient in agony on their pain meds so he can get his own fix. I was shocked, but believe me, it happens more often than you think.
                                              —Meredith, married, three kids

Don't ignore the issue when your parents bring up health issues. Don't run and hide. Early on, I tried not to pay attention to that stuff. My mom would say "I don't think you understand how difficult it is becoming for me with my eyes." The next thing we know, she has macular degeneration and is legally blind in one eye. Head in the sand doesn't work.   —Morgan, married, one of three siblings

A Chronic Problem

Health care costs are exploding, driven by an increasingly older and sicker population. Sixty-five cents of every health care dollar spent in the United States today gets applied to patients with two or more chronic conditions, a disproportionate number of whom are over sixty-five years of age.[9] That means that two-thirds of health care spending benefits just one quarter of the population, according to a 2007 report on chronic conditions and associated spending prepared for the Robert Wood Johnson Foundation.[10]

The cost of chronic conditions is breaking the back of the health care system. Some 73 percent of private insurance dollars, virtually all Medicare spending, and about 80 percent of Medicaid outlays are allocated to chronic conditions.[11] Among the most common chronic ailments are hypertension (33.9 percent), cholesterol disorders (20.9 percent), respiratory diseases (20.0 percent), arthritis (15.8 percent), heart disease (12.5 percent), diabetes (12.3 percent), eye disorders, (11.1 percent), asthma (10.7 percent), and chronic respiratory infections (8.8 percent).[12]

Here's how the math of chronic illness works: a person with one chronic condition consumes four times more health care dollars than one with no chronic condition. A person with five chronic conditions consumes twenty-five times more health care dollars than one with no chronic condition.[13] One thing is for certain: It would behoove us as a society to spend more on prevention and avert the onset of costly chronic conditions.

Spending ramps up quickly, from an average of $994 per person with no chronic condition to $16,819 for a person with five or more chronic conditions,[14] who are ten times more likely to land in the hospital and will require twenty-five times more inpatient spending.[15] On average, we spend five times more money on people with chronic conditions than on the healthy segment of the population.[16] The cost of getting sick, especially with a chronic ailment, is enough to make you sick. If you're an elder, you might just stay that way, too, given the dearth of geriatricians in the United States.

Geriatricians Wanted

Who knew that there even was such a specialty as geriatrics? Most of the caregivers interviewed for this book, if they were aware at all of the field of geriatrics, discovered it serendipitously, as a by-product of extensive research or during conversations with hospital staff or when looking for a health care court of last resort—an expert whose knowledge is so deep and so niche that none dare contradict them.

> Listen. Listen. Listen. Listen. Listen. Listen. Listen. Listen to your parents. Listen to your patients.   —*Tierney, married, mother of one*

The requirements for geriatric certification are rigorous. They include a medical degree, a three-year residency in either internal or family medicine, and completion of a geriatric fellowship program. In the case of geropsychiatrists, the training requires a four-year residency in psychiatry followed by a fellowship in geriatric psychiatry.[17]

Knowing about geriatricians is one thing. Finding a geriatrician is a whole different story. There is a scary scarcity of geriatricians in this country. According to the American Geriatrics Society, as of April 2008 only 7,590 board-certified geriatricians were in practice, along with 1,657 board-certified geriatric psychiatrists.[18] To get a better handle on how this translates into accessibility to a geriatrician, consider that there is only one geriatrician for every 2,500 Americans over age seventy-five.[19] The society projects that ratio will become even more pronounced as the shortage grows and that by 2030 there will be only one geriatrician for every 4,254 Americans.[20]

Sadly, with 20 percent of the thirty-five million people over age sixty-five affected by either severe (two million seniors) or more moderate depression (five million seniors),[21] geropsychiatrists prove to be an even more singular commodity since there is just one geriatric psychiatrist for every 11,451 people over age seventy-five today and a completely unacceptable estimated ratio of one for every 20,195 older Americans by 2030.[22]

Depressing News

What makes this lack of trained geriatric psychiatrists so sad is the very fact that depression is a frequent by-product of the social, psychological, and physiological changes of aging. Many medical conditions common to old age—like heart disease, stroke, or cancer—require treatment with drugs that may cause depressive symptoms. Others, like ischemia or restricted blood flow, can literally reduce the amount of blood reaching the brain, prompting changes like depression.[23]

Life-stage events such as retirement, the death of a loved one, or a move from a familiar neighborhood can also throw people into a severe funk requiring treatment. While suicide among the young, especially teenagers, garners more headlines, in point of fact white males over age eighty-five have the highest recorded suicide rates.[24] What makes that statistic in itself depressing is that many of those senior suicide victims were seen by their doctors within a month of their death but no treatment was forthcoming.[25] For medical students, the choice of a specialty like geropsychiatry is really a choice of lifestyle. Kind of like marrying for love or money. You can have one or the other but almost never both.

The High Road or the "E-ROAD"

A very telling article in *Yale Medicine* magazine, penned by a recent medical school graduate, discussed the current trend whereby newly minted doctors opt into "lifestyle practices." This career trajectory is referred to as the "E-ROAD," an acronym for the five specialties that afford some quality of life by dint of controllable hours—emergency medicine, radiology, opthamology, anesthesiology, and dermatology.[26]

> Utterly ridiculous! My mom was seeing a gastroenterologist. He would examine her every three months. Actually, "examine" is being generous. All he did was take her blood pressure and tell her how nice she looked. Mom has good insurance, so I think he was just milking it.   —*Emma, divorced, one son*

If current trends continue apace, geriatricians will become rara avis in the medical world, with the geriatrician body count waning as the senior population burgeons. There are any number of clear disincentives to pursuing geriatrics:

- Geriatricians make less money ($161,188 on average, which is $2,133 less than the average family practitioner and a fraction of a cardiac or orthopedic surgeon income).[27]
- Medicare capitates reimbursement fees, limiting earnings potential.
- No one pays for the all-important task of coordinating care and services.
- Training takes one year longer for geriatricians than for primary-care physicians.
- Older patients are generally viewed as ugly, smelly, and difficult to handle.
- Medical schools steer promising young doctors into other more glamorous, exotic, and lucrative disciplines.
- Medical students become enamored with specialties that involve high-tech procedures.

Despite the barriers and biases, geriatricians reported the highest level of job satisfaction of any medical specialty researched according to a 2002 study published in the Archives of Internal Medicine.[28]

A Distinct Discipline

What exactly is a geriatrician? The American Geriatrics Society defines a geriatrician as "a medical doctor who is specially trained to meet the unique health care needs of older adults. Illnesses, diseases, and medications may affect older people differently than younger adults, and older patients often have multiple health problems and take multiple medications. Geriatricians prevent, manage, and develop care plans that address the special health problems of the elderly."[29]

> Now the way they reimburse, you get a number attached to a diagnosis and they don't move off that. Last month when my aunt went to the ER with dehydration, I tried to explain that this was how she presented when she had a stroke. The doctors didn't want to hear about it. They immediately went to dehydration versus stroke and only checked it out when blurred vision continued after rehydration.
>
> —Harriet, married, no children

Some of the ways in which seniors respond differently to diseases or ailments are unexpected and can mask the underlying condition. Unlike children or healthy adults, seniors rarely spike a fever when they develop an infection. This situation allows infections to grow unchecked and can result in much more serious conditions. They can have heart attacks without chest pain, instead showing signs of confusion. They can have acute appendicitis with normal white cell counts and no abdominal pain. They can have high thyroid activity yet appear lethargic instead of agitated. They have different systemic responses to extremes of heat and cold.

> Talk about the twilight zone! One doctor would walk in, shake his head, and say "It won't be long now." The next specialist would walk in and say "Hold a good thought. He's got a good chance at survival." Look for the doctor who can demonstrate that he shares knowledge, makes the effort to coordinate care, makes himself accessible to the family, and makes even the slightest attempt at being proactive with the family.   —Jody, married, mother of three

Take the case of an eighty-five-year-old female who began to exhibit signs of dementia virtually overnight. She was disoriented and unable to provide day and date information. This was not some sudden-onset dementia but, the effect of toxins from an undiagnosed urinary tract infection on her brain chemistry. It took a geriatrician just minutes to assess the situation after two general practitioners missed the call.

Patients and caregivers alike wax ecstatic when describing their experiences with a board-certified geriatrician. Many described the feeling of floodgates opening—that at last they found someone who understood the need to coordinate care across providers, who had hands-on experience with conditions affecting elders sufficient to offer very practical tips on coping, who readily communicated with caregivers and treated them as part of the health care team. In short, somebody who "got it." But getting an elder to be seen by someone who "gets it" is getting tougher.

> The doctors just weren't very helpful. Her GP gave us a book on Alzheimer's. The neurologist was totally worthless, really, just a me-

chanic. It wasn't until my mom went into a nursing home and we were able to see a geriatrician that things changed for the better. Finally, we had someone who knew what was going on and could give us good advice.

—*Pamela, married, one child*

Where do I start? My mom had what we thought was a bruise from a tennis ball on her chest. Turned into a growth. Her GP thought it was a hematoma. He just wasn't very vigilant or diligent about [her] health, so we switched to a geriatrician. The geriatrician took one look and said "That's breast cancer." First appointment, he caught it, but by then it was inoperable and had spread to her lymph nodes. It just seems like no one cares much about older patients.

—*Bridget, married, mother of two*

It was a wake-up call for me. I now know how imperative it is to find a primary care physician in a hospital network with an integrated approach to patient care. Now, when I've got the time, I've started to investigate and ask the right questions. How do you share information? How do you centralize files? Who is the point person on the medical team? How and how often do you update the family? Knowing all this in advance sure would have made life easier.

—*Letty, married, mother of two*

Who Will Care?

According to Dr. Robert Butler, CEO of the International Longevity Center, there are a number of promising initiatives on the state level that will encourage medical students to pursue geriatrics, including loan forgiveness.[30] The average doctor graduates from medical school with a debt load of roughly $150,000.[31] It's double jeopardy for those wishing to practice geriatric medicine; first, because their specialty requires an extra year of fellowship training with extra expense and delayed earnings. Then, when they enter full-time jobs, they'll be paying down those loans from a lower baseline income than a procedural specialty.

South Carolina is the only state with a loan-forgiveness program designed to help recruit geriatricians. Under terms of the South Carolina program, geriatricians qualify for educational-debt forgiveness if they agree to work in the state for five years. In return for serving the state's senior community, the geriatrician qualifies for debt repayment up to $35,000 per year of fellowship training.[32]

There is a bill pending in Oklahoma that would establish the Oklahoma Geriatric Medical Loan Repayment Program. The program is fairly limited, offering educational-loan repayment help to five physicians annually who have completed a fellowship in geriatrics, if they stipulate to working in high-need communities in the state. Qualified recipients may receive up to $25,000 per year for a five-year period.[33]

In California, the proposed California Geriatric and Gerontology Workforce Expansion Bill of 2008 was designed to bridge the gap in geriatric services by offering loan assistance to a spectrum of health care providers, including physicians, osteopathic physicians, dentists, psychologists, registered nurses, and social workers. Eligibility requirements include committing to three years of service in a geriatric-care setting. Financial assistance varies with profession on a sliding scale from a low of $7,500 per year to a high of $45,000 per year.

On the federal level, two acts moving through the legislature address loan forgiveness. The Geriatricians Loan Forgiveness Act of 2007 would extend the National Health Service Corps Loan Repayment Program to encompass geriatric training and would forgive up to $35,000 for each year of specialty training in geriatric medicine or psychiatry.

The Caring for an Aging America Act of 2008 combines career-advancement opportunities with loan-forgiveness benefits. Physicians, physician assistants, advance-practice nurses, psychologists, and social workers, in return for agreeing to fulfill a two-year term in full-time clinical practice serving older adults, can participate in the Geriatric and Gerontology Loan Repayment Program. Registered nurses who practice in home, community-based, or long-term care settings on completing specialty training in geriatrics or gerontology may enroll in the Nursing Education Loan Repayment Program.

Filling the Pool

Several ideas have been floated for addressing the geriatrician shortage. The Institute of Medicine's Committee on the Future Health Care Workforce for Older Americans recommended "an increase in payment for [geriatricians'] clinical services, the development of awards to increase the number of faculty in geriatrics, and the establishment of programs that would include loan forgiveness, scholarships, and direct financial incentives for professionals who become geriatric specialists."[34]

Geriatric medical education is an essential component of any solution to the elder care problem. The International Longevity Center looked at the issue of geriatric medical education and determined that staffing each of the 145 allopathic and osteopathic medical schools with just 10 geriatric academicians each, would effectively instill the basics of geriatric medicine in students. The cost: approximately $25 million per year for 20 years assuming a 16 percent faculty-attrition rate.[35]

The goal would be that no one graduates from residency without understanding the many physiological peculiarities special to aging and how they alter common conditions—for example, how drugs work in an older body, nutritional issues manifest, and heart attacks present. With this type of training, internists would be fully capable of serving seniors, reserving the small pool of geriatricians for the population over eighty-five or more medically complex patients.

One can't help but contrast the system in the United States, where some internists graduate with a microscopic six hours of exposure to geriatrics, with the system in the United Kingdom, where every medical school has a fully staffed department of geriatrics and where geriatric medicine ranks third among medical specialties.[36]

Yet progress is being made. Elder care is now integrated into the medical curriculum at more than fifty medical schools.[37] Private foundations are investing in geriatric medical education as well. The Donald W. Reynolds Foundation contributed $150 million to thirty medical schools to underwrite geriatric studies and the John A. Hartford Foundation wrote $40 million in checks to twenty-seven medical schools. Beyond the funding situation and the mechanics of education, there is a more fundamental health care issue, one that supersedes geriatric medicine. It is the issue of prevention versus cure.

> Doctors are oriented to treatment and cure. They can't handle, they aren't comfortable in, a setting they can't fix.
>
> —*Lily, married, mother of two*

> The doctors did what they were trained to do—everything possible. The health care system and doctors need to understand that life at any cost is often no life at all. They're not saving a life . . . they're destroying an entire extended family.   —*Darlene, married, mother of one*

> Get a good therapist. You're going to need one to get through this. Dealing with doctors like this is a business transaction. Keep it func-

tional. Keep it clinical. Keep it objective. If you're a woman and you get even the slightest bit emotional, they'll blow you off.

—*Sylvie, divorced, mother of three*

Fix-It Mentality

Robert Butler observed that in the United States only about 30 percent of physicians are primary-care doctors—the main point of patient contact, treatment, and information—while 70 percent are specialists. In Europe, the distribution is closer to 50/50. "Our health care system is based on perverse incentives for doctors," Butler noted. "If you're a specialist who owns a procedure, you make a fortune. If you're a primary-care doctor who takes care of people, you don't."[38]

There is virtually no money available under the American system to promote disease prevention in the medical community. Doctors and hospitals don't get paid to keep people well. They make money by letting people get sick and then fixing the problem. This will come as no surprise to anyone struggling to maintain the health status of a frail or elder person. The average doctor in the United States spends approximately one hour per year with each patient, even though multiple studies underscore the importance of a consistent source for care over time.[39]

What is needed is a sea change in attitude and outlook that will permeate the medical community and spawn new ideas about elder care and treatment. As with any organization or discipline, we manage what we measure. To effect change in health care, what needs to change first are the metrics used to measure patient-care outcomes. The medical-home concept is an attempt to do just that by redefining standards and objectives.

The Medical Home

A number of approaches focusing on wellness are being piloted with excellent results. Prominent among them stands the medical home concept that was first introduced by the American Academy of Pediatrics in the late 1960s. As initially conceived, a *medical home* simply meant a centralized location for archiving medical records, making a current, updated file available to all practitioners. It has grown to become much more than that.

Based on the success of the pediatric model, four medical associations (American Academy of Family Physicians, American Academy of Pediatrics, American College of Physicians, and American Osteopathic Association) banded together and issued a statement outlining the Joint Principles of the Patient-Centered Medical Home. The sponsoring organizations collectively speak for almost 333,000 physician-members who deliver primary care to children, youth, adults, and elders. Seven governing principles articulate the characteristics that define a medical home:

> *Personal physician*—each patient has an ongoing relationship with a personal physician trained to provide first contact, continuous and comprehensive care.
>
> *Physician directed medical practice*—the personal physician leads a team of individuals at the practice level who collectively take responsibility for the ongoing care of patients.
>
> *Whole person orientation*—the personal physician is responsible for providing for all the patient's health care needs or taking responsibility for appropriately arranging care with other qualified professionals. This includes care for all stages of life; acute care; chronic care; preventive services; and end-of-life care.
>
> *Care is coordinated and/or integrated* across all elements of the complex health care system (e.g., subspecialty care, hospi-

tals, home health agencies, nursing homes) and the patient's
community (e.g., family, public and private community-based
services). Care is facilitated by registries, information technology, health information exchange, and other means to as-
sure that patients get the indicated care when and where they
need and want it in a culturally and linguistically appropriate
manner.

Quality and safety are hallmarks of the medical home.

The principles go on to state that the "process [is] driven by a com-
passionate, robust partnership between physicians, patients, and
the patient's family," that "[e]vidence-based medicine and clinical
decision-support tools guide decision making," and that "[i]nfor-
mation technology is utilized appropriately to support optimal
patient care." The document continues:

> *Enhanced access* to care is available through systems such as
> open scheduling, expanded hours, and new options for commu-
> nications between patients, their personal physician, and prac-
> tice staff.
>
> *Payment* appropriately recognizes the added value provided to pa-
> tients who have a patient-centered medical home. The payment
> structure should pay for . . . coordination of care . . . between
> consultants, ancillary providers, and community resources . . .
> [and] support the adoption and use of health information tech-
> nology.[40]

A core value unique to the medical home program and critical
to successful elder care is the concept of coordination across
medical specialties and service providers. Ask anyone responsible
for an acutely or chronically ill senior and you'll find that the
complete and utter disarray of medical information ranks along

with finances as their first or second concern. You will hear stories about a relative sitting at the hospitalized patient's bedside as specialist follows specialist into the room, each with a different opinion, each unaware of the most recent change in care plan or medication. This situation undermines patient confidence in their physicians and most definitely can jeopardize the patient and course of treatment.

> One of the most annoying facets of the medical profession is they just do not communicate. I just sat in the hospital room with my dad for two weeks without much input from them.
>
> —*Pamela, married, one child*

> You know how they have suicide hot lines? They need elder care hot lines. Every time something happened, like a ministroke that would cause my dad to act really weird, we weren't quite sure what to do. Call 911? Go home? Take him to the hospital? You need someone who knows what's going on to talk you through it . . . You have to make critical, life-and-death decisions in a nanosecond without enough information.   —*Peggy, single, one of four siblings*

The only solution available today requires the patient/consumer to become his or her own case manager, mastering the nuances of the health care system, from medical records to drug interactions. To ensure that health information is exchanged and current requires a patient to take physical ownership of his or her records and personally hand them to a physician.

> Everyone needs what I call the "red file." You just hand it over to the paramedics or ER docs. It's got an up-to-date list of medications, a copy of emergency contacts including doctors with phone numbers

and pagers, family member phones, a copy of their living will, a copy of their health care directive, and the health care power of attorney.

—*Hailey, divorced, two kids*

I get "the call." Rush to the hospital. My dad is lying in bed in the intensive care unit with his eyes rolled up into the back of his head. My first thought was, he had a massive stroke. We come to find out he was being massively overmedicated instead. Here we are, at one of the finest medical centers on the planet, and they can't get meds straight.   —*Caitlin, married, mother of seven*

Communication at the hospital sucked. At any one time there were eight medical professionals working on the case. If they ever sat down and coordinated care, it sure wasn't evident to us. I can't count the number of times we had to say, "Whoa! Dr. A was just in here and switched that med." Then Dr. B would say, "I'm the blah-blah specialist, and I'm switching the med again." And so it would go. They didn't talk to each other and they sure as heck didn't talk to us.

—*Rena, married, mother of two*

Putting Theory into the Practices

That situation has changed for the fortunate 19,000 CIGNA members cared for by Dartmouth-Hitchcock primary care physicians. In June 2008, they announced a "patient-centered medical home pilot program, with the goal of improving care coordination and quality." The pilot program includes all the elements outlined in the "Joint Principles": a technology-enabled infrastructure, team approach, revised payment schedules, coordinated care, education, electronic appointment availability, and direct access to their personal physician.[41]

In the Philadelphia area, three insurers are investing $13 million in a three-year study of the medical home prototype, involving one hundred physicians and 8,400 patients. Participating offices are required to beef up their technology, commit to improved patient communications, and bring on board the necessary staff members such as patient educators or data analysts.[42]

Blue Cross Blue Shield of Michigan allocated $30 million of its 2008 budget to encourage primary care providers to adopt the medical home concept.[43] In fact, twenty-seven of thirty-nine Blue Cross Blue Shield plans are testing the medical home model.[44] North Carolina, among the first to participate in a test of this Medicaid-based concept saved 11 percent on health care costs, approximately $162 million in 2006.[45]

Follow the Money

As with so many issues surrounding elder care, conventional wisdom and standard practices fly in the face of hard facts. The Future of Family Medicine Task Force undertook primary research that determined that "[i]f every American used a primary-care physician as their usual source of care, health care costs would likely decrease by 5.6%, resulting in national savings of $67 billion dollars per year, with an improvement in the quality of the health care provided." Some of the financial changes that would be required to effect this result include an "annual per-patient fee, a chronic care bonus," and an annual outcomes-based performance bonus, as well as compensation for telemedicine, "e-visits[,] and chronic disease management," of particular importance in geriatric medicine.[46] But that's not what medicine in America is all about.

The United States system rewards health care providers based on visit frequency, tests performed, procedures completed, and specialist referrals given. What doesn't get compensated is the mission-critical function of care coordination. For time-strapped physicians, there is little room with back-to-back fifteen-minute appointments to reach out across a network to harmonize medications and care strategies. In the forward-looking visions of alternative medical models, there are two strata of workers who may make that possible: nurses and allied health professionals.

Staffing Shifts

Under the medical home model, the titles on the staff roster at your doctor's office will look much different. They may include nurse practitioner, physician assistant, MIS specialist, patient educator, group facilitator, social worker, care team leader, patient coach, or data analyst. The underlying philosophy of the medical home calls for more frequent communication between patient and provider and more opportunities for improved aftercare and for learning about managing chronic conditions.

Another alternative care-delivery model, called guided care, inserts a nurse with specialized geriatric training into a primary-care practice, where the nurse works exclusively with the older patients who suffer from chronic conditions.[47] Many patients are intimidated by their primary-care physician and afraid to "bother" them with questions. Guided-care nurses in one pilot study report that patients are much more open and willing to ask questions. Part of the reason may be that frequent contact makes patients more comfortable with the nurse, which relaxes them, allowing them to remember questions and issues.

Other aspects of guided care include a comprehensive, personalized care plan that includes vigilant monitoring of health status and tracks preventive measures like tetanus shots, flu shots, and colonoscopies; medication management; counseling around chronic conditions like diabetes and obesity; and proactive outreach such as regular check-up calls to patients and home visits.

The most exciting aspect of movements like the medical home and guided care is that they offer patients a viable alternative to a system that's too costly, too invasive, and too passive to work.

What We've Learned

The medical home may provide every consumer with a health homeroom where a dedicated team focuses on wellness and pursues a holistic, patient-centric approach.

Just as the need for geriatricians is set to explode, the number of geriatricians is contracting. Incentives need to be developed to encourage medical students to pursue this specialty.

Allied health professionals will serve a pivotal role in the medical home and guided care models, enabling more efficient, effective health delivery.

Technology will empower the entire caregiving team, from physician to patient, putting essential information at their fingertips.

THE SOLUTION

9. IT TAKES A VILLAGE

Today's global village is missing something. Make that missing somebody. If you scan foot traffic on Main Street, audiences taking in a weekend movie, diners at a family-style restaurant, exercisers at a local gym, checkout lines at a clothing store, there will be a decided lack of wrinkles and gray hair in your field of vision. Albeit sometimes willing accomplices, America's seniors have either aged in place but withdrawn from the public eye or opted into "senior shtetels" where they are surrounded by peers of similar age and background.

Beginning in the 1960s with the founding of Del Webb's Sun City in Arizona, many middle-class and affluent seniors removed themselves from their communities of long-standing residence and migrated to active adult communities. Despite the many physical amenities, social opportunities, and enrichment programs available, these age-restricted communities became tantamount to "gray ghettos," isolating residents from multigenerational interactions.

As a result, there are children growing up in America today who will never interact with a person over sixty-five until they become adults. Staggering thought. But in our nomadic culture, where tightly knit nuclear families readily relocate away from extended families to satisfy a career need or lifestyle choice, it is a growing reality. It is also a social travesty, because it steals life-enriching experiences from young and old alike and may engender unacceptable bias or fear of the unknown in children who already operate in an ageist society.

Children are exposed on a daily basis to images in entertainment media and commercial advertising that are blatantly ageist. Forged in childhood, these ageist attitudes can persist into adulthood and operate subconsciously on a multitude of decisions. The popular book *Freakonomics* presented a real-world example of age discrimination at play, downloaded directly from the small screen: voting patterns on the television program *Weakest Link*. Older players were consistently voted off more often than younger counterparts, even when the performance of older players was statistically better and when retaining them would benefit the voting contestants.[1] The reason? Older contestants were perceived as less competent because of a cultural bias against age, the actual facts notwithstanding.

Stereotyped

The negative stereotypes about aging and the old are pervasive in our society and extend beyond imagery. In a culture that cringes when a black person uses the *N* word, derogatory statements about old farts, geezers, or Q-tips get tossed off without comment, as if they are socially appropriate in any way.

The medical community is hardly immune from the practice either. Interns quickly learn the lexicon of health care ageism that evolved to describe elderly patients—bed blocker, crock, fossil, gerry, gogy, and GOMER (get out of my emergency room).[2] This is hardly the sympathetic language one anticipates hearing from hands-on care providers, but it is an accurate reflection of a system that bases rewards on curing acute conditions and that avoids dealing with chronic conditions that typically afflict the older population.

The same negative stereotyping holds true for the workplace, where anyone over fifty who loses a job will find it extremely difficult to find a new one and will rarely be able to match the income or status of their former employment. In a 2008 study of more than 2,200 adults, 52 percent of respondents rated ageism as the most prevalent form of discrimination in the workplace, outranking gender (43 percent) and race (32 percent).[3]

Because children absorb attitudes and beliefs about the elderly from their parents and other adults, it becomes increasingly important to stay connected to the extended family or develop proxy relationships with people of varying ages to avoid forming biases.

Learning by Example and Exposure

Depending on how emotionally connected parents are to the grandparents, it is entirely possible for children to associate seniors exclusively with negative perceptions regarding their physical or mental capabilities. Without positive personal experiences to offset the insulting and demeaning portrayal of older people in our society, we are raising a generation that will inherit an inherent disdain for elders. And we will all be the poorer for it.

A 1998 study by the National Association of Secondary School Principals (NASSP) concluded that the limited nature of intergenerational interactions in daily life, lack of exposure to grandparents or older relatives, and lack of awareness of the contributions of elders to family and society lead children to form misconceptions about seniors. As a result, children perceive being old as a negative state of being and, further, express a dislike of the physical manifestations of old age.[4]

Conversely, studies of intergenerational programs ranging in nature from pen pals to crafts, music, reading, or tutoring programs sited at senior centers underscored the benefits of multigenerational mingling. Participating children registered improved academic performance and demonstrated better social skills. The NASSP study thus concludes that informal exposure to seniors imbues children with an enhanced awareness of life and allows them to develop a textured understanding of elders as contributing members of society who have value and deserve respect. Older adults opting into multigenerational programs come away with a stronger sense of attachment to their community, while their self-esteem enjoys a well-deserved shot in the arm. Both groups reported improved empathy toward and understanding of the issues facing the other generation.[5]

The Drama of Life

Massachusetts has become a veritable hotbed of innovative concepts about aging. Home to one of the first large-scale naturally occurring retirement communities (NORCs), Beacon Hill Village, the Boston area also has spawned a number of other initiatives including an intergenerational film project titled *Act Your Age*. The producer/director Peter Rhodes began with an idea, that of "a special magic spell that could turn seniors into kids and kids into seniors." He recruited the playwright Marcy Goldberg to write the play. Making the fifty-minute movie required the talents of more than eighty local people and a combination of public and private support. Pretty much everyone got into the act.

Area businesses kicked in with in-kind services and donations fueling cast and crew. Generous supporters entrusted the production with expensive equipment.

But it was family, friends, and the production staff in front and behind the camera who benefited most from the production. The result of the filming can best be appreciated by reading comments by cast members of all ages as they describe the experience. What the cast and crew members took away from the experience of working with people of another age is detailed on the film's blog:

Catie, age twelve, writes:
They weren't as creepy and old as I thought they'd be. They were nice. It was fun to make friends with the seniors and talk to them. I really enjoyed working with Mildred. She was cheerful and friendly. It was really fun to talk and work with her. It was really uplifting to see her on those hot, hot days. She just kept on going when I thought I was going to pass out.

Peter, forty-four, admits:
Our very first workshop with the seniors was an eye-opener for me. I discovered that seniors are worldly people who may be frail physically but psychologically can be just as open to new ideas and a good rowdy joke as anyone. At that point I knew we didn't have to make a serious, sensitive film—we could make a wacky comedy and the seniors would have a great time doing it.

Sam, age thirteen, remarks:
What surprised me about working with the seniors was how much energy they had and how much passion they had for working on this movie. It's like you would walk onto the set and they would be so happy and ready to go.

Rachel, age nine, was interested in:
Seeing how me and Evelyn (the lady that I turn into) had to relate to each other. It was interesting seeing how a kid acts as an old lady. What I enjoyed the most was I think knowing that I'm in something and having that feeling that I'm famous even though I'm not . . . really.

Leah, nine years old, writes:
I thought me and Jean, she was the senior I turned into, got really close. I went over to her house a couple of times, and I just think she's amazing—she's so much fun to be with and we got a really good connection going. And I think that's really cool. I didn't think that most seniors would be so energetic. The funnest thing about working on this project was working with so many people that you never knew and making so many new friends.

Morey, who is seventy-four, had the following to say:
I think a movie like this is important because it promotes a better relationship between children and adults and helps us to understand each other more and be more tolerant and to be respectful of each other. I think the kids learned that too. They learned that we are not ogres and we're not old fogeys (well, some of us may be but I'm not, for sure). I loved it. I haven't had this much fun since I was drafted. These kids are just so damn smart. There's no difference anymore in the ages. In the film we were going back and forth, and we found that in working together with them for so long, that this was really turning out that way.

Celia, ninety-one, comments:
In my script I say "It helps me stay young"—and it does, being with children does help me stay young.

Evan, eight years old, thinks:

It was fun because I met a lot of new people and I'm good friends with a lot of them now.

Ilana, who is eleven, recounts:

You see them walking with canes but a lot of them like just bounced around sometimes. They were so lively . . . I felt like they were jumping off the walls just as we were because they were so excited. I have grandparents but I had never really spent time with other seniors. It was really nice to work with the senior who I was supposed to have been changed into because she was really nice. Also just working with everyone it was really nice and seeing how everyone acted and everything.[6]

There you have it—the benefits of multigenerational activities and environments at work, in a filmed play. How much better it would be for all concerned if multigenerational interactions were a fact of daily life instead of an artifact of a purposeful program. One of the easiest ways to achieve that is by adopting new or adapting old forms of housing for today's environment that create natural opportunities for interface.

Village Confines Defined

Old-school thinking about housing for seniors unable to remain at home was centered on a medical model that emphasized functional delivery of services in an antiseptic, institutional setting. If you've ever had a discussion with an elder about housing options like assisted living or nursing homes, even continuing-care retirement communities, more likely than not you'll hear the disdain in the senior's voice as he or she talks about "those places." As in,

"I don't belong in one of those places," or "Don't make me move to one of those places," or "I don't want to live in one of those places." It's pretty clear that "those places" aren't cutting it with today's seniors.

Fortunately, a number of exciting new options for aging in place are emerging. With some 90 percent of adults over age sixty expressing the wish to age-out in their familiar neighborhoods and homes, these enterprising solutions are just in time.[7] The list includes: virtual villages; NORCs; in-law units or granny flats, more formally known as secondary or accessory housing units; intergenerational housing; home sharing; and co-housing options.

Virtual Villages

Home sweet home. Love it and never leave it. The passionate desire to remain in their homes spurred founders to create Beacon Hill Village, which serves as an operating model for other nascent consumer-directed support communities. Beacon Hill Village serves residents in the Beacon Hill section of Boston, the Back Bay, West End, and adjoining neighborhoods. Anyone age fifty and over residing in the service area can become a member by paying an annual fee of $600 for individuals or $890 for a household. Low- and moderate-income households enjoy identical services for a reduced fee of $100 per year with the assurance that they will receive $250 back toward services. The core tenet of the model is that a village be developed and run by the elders themselves.

In return, privileges of membership include access to a wide range of concierge-style benefits at reduced rates 10–50 percent below retail, negotiated by the village with vetted providers, as well as free offerings available through volunteers. Services typi-

cally include information and referral assistance, help with errands like picking up prescriptions and dry cleaning, home-office
aid, financial planning, legal advice, cleaning services, weekly
grocery shopping, home-delivered meals, furniture arrangement,
bringing the car in for repairs, dog walking, packing boxes, wa-
tering plants, and picking up mail.

At Beacon Hill Village, members also enjoy expedited access
to the Massachusetts General Hospital Senior Health practice, a
discounted prescription-drug card that complements Medicare
Part D; special rates on long-term care insurance; geriatric care
management for a member or elder anywhere in the United
States; fitness classes; assisted-living help at home; and wellness
seminars.

Social Ties

The glue that binds the village together, though, is the social
aspect. The executive director, Judy Willett, believes that
"[c]ommunity-building is one of the core essences of the Beacon
Hill Village model. The founders and those who run the Village
are the consumers as well. They have no interest in being isolated
in their apartments alone. We offer everything from life-essential
programs to life-enhancement programs. The goal of Beacon Hill
Village is to engage members in life and help them to connect."[8]

Many residents join to gain access to a group of like-minded
folks who share interests such as the theater, music, travel, dance,
literature, and art or to enjoy field trips, special celebrations, community service, and home visits with others. In our increasingly
isolated society, this not-for-profit network provides a mechanism for creating a new type of urban village, a safe and effective
way to become acquainted with neighbors and peers so the bonds
of interdependency can be established.

Beacon Hill Village operates three service segments: information and referral, also known as concierge services; assistance in living in the home, the volunteer services portion of the program; and community building. A foundation concept is the idea of connectivity. Willett is quick to point out that aging in place only works when residents can stay connected to the outside world. Otherwise, home quickly becomes a prison instead of a haven.

A Model Program

Interest in the village concept has grown exponentially, and Beacon Hill Village staff members field more than three thousand inquiries from fifteen countries, including Germany and Japan. There were forty-five fully operational virtual villages in the United States as of fall 2009, and an additional eighty on the drawing board. To handle the overwhelming response, Beacon Hill Village has developed a detailed how-to manual addressing every aspect of start-up through operations and offers consulting services to prospective villages.

The popularity of the village concept is undeniable and begins with the membership. Willett noted that "Beacon Hill Village enjoys a more than 85-percent member renewal rate, and those who don't renew typically have either moved or died. Virtually no one leaves because they're unhappy." One reason for such high satisfaction levels are village policies to keep it personal and follow-up. That means regular check-in calls to gauge satisfaction with services provided and see how members are doing.

"The phone call is critical," Willett added. "Although more than half of our members are online, it's the personal interaction that makes the difference." Sensing a hesitation in the conversation or an emotional break in a voice can tip off village staff members to the need for a neighbor visit or invitation to participate in an upcoming event. Members are devoted to the village, and who wouldn't be when the informal motto is to provide members with true "One-stop shopping—anything and everything you want and need"?

Change Agents

Intentional communities like Beacon Hill Village represent the first phalanx in a movement toward what Professor Victor Regnier of the University of Southern California School of Architecture dubs a "new urbanism."[9] Instead of selling the homestead and migrating out to geographic retirement centers in Florida and Arizona, boomers are moving back to city centers, reengaging with urban environments where services are within walking distance, and cultural-enrichment opportunities abound.

Naturally Occurring Retirement Communities (NORCs)

Sometimes referred to as virtual retirement communities, NORCs work because they evolved organically in answer to the need of residents in a given area. NORCs were a first-response effort to accommodate the desire to age in place, and they coordinate and deliver services to the aged in the home setting. In a dramatic reversal of the typical care-delivery model, NORCs bring the services to the elders instead of making them travel to service providers. NORC characteristics include a service portfolio encompassing four areas:

- Social services such as case management, home assessments, and other assistance directed at helping both the elder and caregiver navigate the programs and entitlements available

- Nursing services with an emphasis on managing chronic conditions and maintaining wellness through preventive testing and activities, as well as on working directly with physicians to coordinate medical care
- Community-engagement opportunities to introduce senior skills into the neighborhood through volunteer efforts such as tutoring, mentoring, and organizing fund-raisers
- Ancillary services that reflect the unique composition of the community and can range from transportation to dog walking, from plumbing work to handyman help, from voice lessons to adult day care

A New Hampshire–based study of NORC pilot sites detected a rank order of services "most wanted" versus those "most needed" by participants.[10] The most-wanted services, in priority order, were: transportation, help with heavy household chores, service coordination, access to a personal emergency-response system, shopping assistance, aid with light household chores, meal preparation, and personal care. Most-needed services were similar in nature but different in order: heavy household chores, shopping, service coordination, transportation, light household chores, personal emergency-response system, meal preparation, and personal care.

Folks of a Feather

In 1984, Michael Hunt, a professor at the University of Wisconsin School of Human Ecology, observed a social behavior in the city of Madison. College students came for an education but found a vibrant community and never left, remaining in the area through retirement. He dubbed this phenomenon a naturally occurring retirement community. Two years later, another innovator, Fredda Vladeck, brought the NORC idea to life by organizing supportive service programs at the ten building cooperatives known as Penn South Homes in Manhattan.[11] Thus a concept and trend were born.

According to the Web site www.norcs.com, a NORC is defined as a

> demographic term to describe neighborhoods or buildings in which a large segment of the residents are older adults. In general, they are not purpose-built senior housing or retirement communities and were neither designed nor intended to meet the particular health and social services needs and wants of the elderly. Most commonly, they are places where community residents have either aged in place, having lived in their homes over several decades, or are the result of significant migrations of older adults into the same housing constructs or neighborhoods, where they intend to spend the rest of their lives.[12]

Basically, wherever there is a high density of older adults, the opportunity exists for a NORC. As originally conceived in New York state, a neighborhood qualified for NORC status if more than half of the residents were age fifty or older. Today, funding sources are much more flexible in their definitions and may classify an area as a NORC if 40 percent or more of households are headed by persons age sixty-five or older, as long as there are at least two hundred qualifying individuals in the locale. NORCs can be vertical, administering to residents in a single apartment building or a multiple building complex with a shared management structure, or horizontal, encompassing a neighborhood of single-family homes or two flats.

Funding Issues

Unlike virtual villages, which are driven and operated by consumers, NORCs are generally initiated through government agencies; rely on federal, state, and city funding supplemented by private grants; and target low- to middle-income seniors. For example, the Baltimore NORC Senior Friendly Neighborhoods is financed through a combination of United States Administration on Aging (AOA) grant monies and funding from the Jewish Community Association of Baltimore, Baltimore County, and local foundations. Philadelphia's STAR NORC relies on AOA dollars as well as grants from the Pew Charitable Trusts and the Connelly, Tuttleman, and Clayman Foundations.

The 2006 reauthorization of the Older Americans Act reempowered the AOA to supervise a wide range of initiatives, including competitive grants to NORCs under Title IV, Activities for Health Independence and Longevity, which offers grant programs under section 422 to community innovations for aging in place.[13] Funding for the Older Americans Act in 2008 was $1.935 billion, with roughly 0.8 percent earmarked for Title IV programming.[14] While that sounds like a big number, the advocacy arm of the National Council on Aging is quick to point out that by 2008, the act was underfunded by more than $400 million when adjusted to reflect the impact of inflation and the increase in the senior client base.[15]

Private-sector funding for NORCs has been relatively sparse for several reasons. Chief among them is the lack of consistent performance metrics for evaluating success. The most definitive assessment conducted to date, a 2004 study by the Department of Health and Human Services, straddled the fence, stopping short of a full-out endorsement of concept efficacy. Another issue compounding the difficulty of measurement is the unique nature of NORCs—each delivers a basket of services calibrated to its specific clientele, making meaningful comparisons across programs more difficult.

Initiatives like NORCs hold great promise and appeal for the baby boomer generation. A transformational age cohort since birth, by dint of sheer size, boomers will leave their imprint on adult housing, demanding more plentiful and more creative options as they age to senior status. NORCs are just one of the evolving scenarios. Another concept is an updated rendition on the classic in-law unit.

In-Law Units / Granny Flats

While it hasn't been proved that absence makes the heart grow fonder, distance can sure help maintain civil relationships in extended families. That was the original theory behind the granny flats so popular before the 1950s, also known as mother-in-law units, secondary units, accessory dwelling units, or elder cottages. The motivation behind today's revival of the concept may have as much to do with the environmental orientation of families attempting to limit their carbon footprint as with a "good fence, good neighbor policy."

Characteristically, granny flats are composed of an apartment separate from and smaller than the primary dwelling and feature a private entrance. The flat is built on the same lot as, above the garage of, or attached to the main house. The nuclear family and the elder maintain privacy and independence but remain involved in each other's lives, sharing meals, helping with chores, and enjoying companionship. The suburban flight associated with post–World War II affluence and optimism put an end to the granny-flat movement, and city planners sounded the final death knell by outlawing coach houses or secondary units in single-family neighborhoods.

Modern Update

Fast forward to the twenty-first century, and everything old is new again. Even states like California and Colorado, bastions of restrictive development and environmental-protection laws, are reconsidering their position on granny flats. City planners in Cary, North Carolina, promote granny flats as a vehicle for attracting more people to the downtown area.[16] Santa Cruz, California, which boasts some of the highest real estate values in the United States, goes so far as to post architectural blueprints for secondary units on the city's Web site and waives up to $6,000 in permit fees as an incentive to build such a unit. In turn, Santa Cruz realizes more property-tax income and eliminates the need to erect affordable housing. One city councilman estimates that one thousand in-law units would save the city something on the order of $100 million.[17]

Form, Function, and Families

Requirements and restrictions for accessory-dwelling units vary by city and country. Elder Cottage Housing Opportunities, or ECHO housing as it's known in Australia, is a more transitory approach than stick-built apartments: a rented modular unit is parked on the family grounds. Some areas require that the ECHO dwelling occupant be at least sixty-two years old and/or a relative. Other cities address the rental fees rather than resident relationships as a means of controlling density and property values. Another popular approach is to dictate rigid zoning specifications regarding lot setbacks, square footage, roof lines, amenities, and egress points. In a sense, granny flats are a precursor of intergenerational housing, since they often revert to flats for a son or daughter after college.

Intergenerational Housing

We have artificially segregated age cohorts in the United States and need to remedy that situation. While communities have mounted major initiatives to address racial, ethnic, economic, and handicapped discrimination in housing, no equivalent effort has been directed at age discrimination in housing. Part of the rationale for that is market driven; opponents argue that physical needs and accommodations force clustering by seniors who seek similar features. In truth, that's a handy cop-out and flies in the face of universal design principles.

HOME (Housing Opportunities and Maintenance for the Elderly) in Chicago has championed the cause of intergenerational housing while serving its primary constituency of indigent elders. Its success with multigenerational housing is a model and inspiration to other groups around the country and offers proof that such efforts can be financially viable. Roughly one hundred seniors now live in intergenerational housing situations thanks to HOME, which also provides home-repair services to more than 650 additional senior households.

The HOME mission began in 1983 with Pat Crowley House, a renovated six-flat unit now home to twelve seniors, four resident assistants (usually college students interested in inexpensive housing), and a nuclear family with young children who function as a de facto extended family sharing cooking, laundry, and housekeeping duties to support the elders.

Next came Nathalie Salmon House, a state-of-the-art, purpose-built structure a block from the shores of Lake Michigan that offers assisted living to frail elders on the dedicated fifth floor, as well as apartments for independent elders, resident assistants, and live-in families. Paul Dean, the HOME executive director, touts the upside of multigenerational living, sharing an anecdote from one of the resident dads, who reflected that the major benefit for his kids growing up in an intergenerational situation was that "it's like growing up with all these grandparents."[18]

From the mature-resident point of view, multigenerational housing is literally just like home. Dean told the story of a senior named Mary who didn't know where to go after release from a nursing home. She was referred to the HOME system and, fortuitously, there was an opening at Nathalie Salmon House. On moving day, Mary cried as she hung pictures on her walls. When asked why, Mary said, "I've never owned pictures to hang before. I needed the money for food instead of pictures."

The latest addition to the HOME multigenerational real-estate portfolio is Blackhawk Manor, an eight-unit brick apartment across from a huge public park in Chicago. Independent seniors occupy the six one-bedroom units and one of the two-bedroom apartments, while an on-site maintenance person and his family reside in a second two-bedroom unit. Convenient to public transportation and enrichment programs at the field house of the nearby park, residents keep an eye out for one other and lend a hand with homework and babysitting.

A Recent Resurgence

When counted in the 2000 census, approximately 4 percent of households in the United States were defined as multigenerational, with three or more generations residing under one roof.[19] Multigenerational housing is more popular in states like Hawaii and California that have large immigrant populations. In 2004, thanks in large part to a strong Asian influence, 8 percent of Hawaii's housing was multigenerational. California's Hispanic residents account to a significant degree for the 6 percent of housing that is intergenerational.[20]

Another rendition on the multigenerational theme now gaining traction is the planned multigenerational community. Companies like Del Webb that built their reputations by developing age-restricted senior communities are undergoing a paradigm shift. Del Webb's Anthem prototype in Arizona, Colorado, Florida, Nevada, and North Carolina combines retirement housing with regular homes using a "separate but adjacent" model that offers residents the best of both worlds—access to their peers and age-specific features and ready proximity to family members, especially grandchildren.

Some credit the credit crunch and residual overinflated housing prices with spurring interest in intergenerational housing options. The economics of multigenerational housing are undeniable if residents also embrace some of the quasi-communal aspects that represent the natural outgrowth of geographic closeness such as sharing responsibility for preparing meals, running errands, performing child care, and doing maintenance chores. For those seniors adamant about staying in their home and hungry for companionship on a more regular basis, home sharing might be an even better option.

Home Sharing

Share the spare. That's the premise underlying home-sharing programs, where a senior with a spare bedroom and bath hosts a housemate. Home-sharing programs tend to be operated by local nonprofits, city departments of aging, and religious organizations serving the elderly.[21]

Just like it sounds, home sharing describes a situation where a person over age sixty or sixty-two, who owns a home or condominium, registers with a service to find a roommate willing to share the premises. These "guests" undergo extensive screenings, including personal interviews and reference, financial, and criminal-background checks. The final step is a facilitated introduction between host and prospective guest for a gut check on personal chemistry and accommodations. If all goes well, host and guest sign a written agreement spelling out terms and conditions of the shared living situation.

Typically, the housemate enjoys a much-reduced rent in a prime neighborhood in return for contributing to household expenses like utilities and for lending a hand with yard work, shopping, driving, food preparation, and some light housekeeping. Host benefits include a modest income, improved security, social companionship, and the kind of upkeep help that enables one to remain in the home.

Taking the Temperature

Before taking the plunge and inviting a stranger to take up residence, it's always a good idea to run through an internal checklist and assess your ability to accommodate a roommate. Things to consider include lifestyle issues like smoking, drinking, exercising, snacking, daily schedule, pet preferences, housekeeping expectations, overnight visitors, entertaining habits, technology needs, and privacy requirements.

Recognize that this is an adult moving in with adult habits, needs, wants, and issues. Your best bet is to discuss both your and your prospective guest's lifestyle issues and concerns during the intake interview and write them into the contract. Mutually agree on a set of predetermined house rules along with a process for addressing any violations. In this case a little formality goes a long way to forestalling conflict and misunderstandings.

Group Homes

In some cases, home-sharing situations occur in residences designed to provide affordable housing to seniors. Group or shared homes enable seniors, particularly single seniors without children or extended families, to live in a family-style environment. At the Senior Home Sharing properties in DuPage County, Illinois, each resident occupies and decorates a private bedroom, receives three home-prepared meals a day, and enjoys access to the services of a live-in manager as well as the benefits of a knowledgeable case manager who can secure and coordinate additional services.

Interested in pursuing a home-share arrangement for your loved one? If they're not comfortable with an unsupervised, electronic option like posting an availability on Craigslist or a similar service, check out the National Shared Housing Resource Center (NSHRC) and its online directory of match-up services and shared-living residences at www.nationalsharedhousing.org. If your interests are more global in nature, query Homeshare International at www.homeshare.org for opportunities in eight countries.

With an increasing population of seniors, astronomical home prices, ever-rising taxes, and an economy that is rapidly eroding life savings, home sharing makes it financially possible for elders to remain connected to their community of choice.

Co-Housing

One of the most intriguing concepts to emerge from the alternative housing fray is that of co-housing, a purpose-built neighborhood that combines private homes with shared or common spaces as well as retrofit communities created by using existing structures. Retrofitting presents more options for more people who could potentially introduce a co-housing community to where they live now. A Danish invention, co-housing traces its roots to a movement from the 1970s, when the primary stimulus was the need to share child care duties.

Two American architecture students, Charles Durrett and Kathryn McCamant, both enrolled at the University of Copenhagen, were intrigued by the concept, and imported it to the United States. In its country of origin, co-housing is known as *bofaellesskaber*, which translates as "living community," a wonderful way to think of these developments.

Fast forward three decades, and co-housing has successfully transitioned from an untested, unorthodox idea to a mainstream housing alternative. At present, there are more than 112 of these intentional communities operating in the United States. Each shares six characteristics, according to Craig Ragland, the executive director of the Co-Housing Association of the United States:

Participation. *From inception, future residents either direct or actively participate in the design of the community, establishing the overall aesthetic, signature elements, recreational amenities, pedestrian orientation, green-space allocation, common-area locations, and any other special accommodations or dedicated-use areas.*

Neighborhood focus. *Site plans for co-housing developments take great care to create communities that foster engagement and interaction among residents. Cars are often relegated to the sidelines to encourage walking so residents enjoy frequent casual encounters with neighbors. When possible, front doors face the common house, an orientation that reinforces the literally central role of shared space and activity. Homes tend to be massed together to maximize open space and allow proximity to build relationships.*

Common facilities. *Although every co-housing development is unique, they encompass a few core beliefs. One of which is the idea of living in community. A common house, or common space in some cases, is a must. Typically, the common space will house a kitchen, dining area, sitting area, playroom, and laundry, as well as a multipurpose room for music, exercise, or performances. Some even include guest rooms for visitors. All residents are expected to participate in communal activities such as shared meals, governance, and entertainment. Ragland explained that co-housing "helps people live in authentic relationships with people beyond the single-family household. In co-housing, you share parts of your lives and you make some decisions with others about your life together."*

Resident management. *Everything about the shared aspects of co-housing is resident directed. They are not run by management companies. Resident management begins with the design and extends to daily management and maintenance. Residents take care of themselves and their neighbors in co-housing. As owners, they control and manage the community, embracing the principles of consensus.*

Nonhierarchical. *Consensus rules. That's a second core belief of living in community. It can be cumbersome, and at times frustrating, but consensus is a natural outgrowth of the founding principle of shared experience. While leaders often emerge within a community, no one occupies a position of authority over another. Each resident contributes to the best of their abilities.*

No shared economy. *The community is not a business enterprise. Even if the community design incorporates for-profit retail and service companies, they exist to serve, not to profit, residents and to enhance the experience. If the community raises vegetables or creates functional artifacts, they are typically for the enjoyment of members, not for commercial sale.*

Ragland believes that much of the appeal of co-housing stems from a fundamental human need for connection:

> The idea of the Lone Ranger . . . of the Maverick . . . is a myth.
> Everyone lives in community. However, in the case of co-housing,
> it's a different quality of community. As a species, we've lived
> more tribally for millennia. It's our natural state of being. In truth,
> single-family homes are a comparatively new phenomenon. We've
> only taken to isolating ourselves relatively recently in evolutionary
> terms. It's a modern-day version of the small town where every-
> one knows each other and rallies around when there's a problem.[22]

Here's another way to think of co-housing: as a technology-enabled
version of Grover's Corners, redesigned for the new millennium.

A Natural Affinity

As with NORCs, co-housing developments begin with one or
two prime movers—passionate advocates for the concept who
stimulate discussion, generate interest, and proactively recruit
potential members. Many co-housing situations form around
shared affinities or values such as a commitment to environmen-
talism or a devotion to vegetarianism. There are some that share
a defined philosophy, such as the thirty-home Christian Elder-
spirit development in Abingdon, Virginia, one of the first designed
exclusively for seniors. Trillium Hollow in Portland, Oregon,
was organized by members of a local Unitarian church, but is
populated by people of all faiths. KitsHarbour in Bremerton,
Washington, is a self-planned community for single women, particularly lesbian women, who wish to age in place together.

Investment in Living

From a financial perspective, co-housing functions along the lines
of fee simple title arrangements where families own their own

homes and are free to sell them on the open market. The organizing principles determine whether the community has a right of first refusal to purchase the property before listing on the open market.

Co-housing developments generally adopt conventional homeowner association, condominium association, or cooperative covenants and restrictions. Individual units qualify for traditional mortgage financing and, as evidenced by resale prices around the country for co-housing listings, manage to retain their value regardless of volatile real-estate and financial-market fluctuations.

Green House Project / The Eden Alternative

In long-term care, love matters.
And the heart of the problem is institutions can't love.[23]
—DR. BILL THOMAS, FOUNDER, GREEN HOUSE PROJECT,
THE EDEN ALTERNATIVE

Isolation. Loneliness. Fear. Depression. That's the refrain of aging alone in America, especially for the oldest and most frail segment of the population. By dint of their comparatively intense care requirements, vulnerable seniors find themselves sequestered in sterile, institutional environments designed to promote efficiency for care providers rather than succor for patients. Without regard for patient preference or comfort, baths are taken, linens changed, medications administered, and meals served on a schedule convenient for shift workers.

Say the phrase "nursing home" to just about anyone and watch their body language. Depending on age, it will range from a physical cringe to a wrinkled nose. Universally, the phrase conjures up images of long, linoleum-limned corridors with wheelchairs diagonally calibrating the hallways, the air redolent with the stench of urine and decaying bodies. Residents locked into a fuguelike state, staring vacantly at unseen images, their limbs mechanically tracing a repetitive gesture, disengaged from their surroundings or neighbors. These images are the reason that only 1 percent of the United States disabled population over age fifty expressed any interest in moving to a nursing home.[24] Clearly, the system is broken and new thinking is required.

A Healing Spirit

Most physicians are trained to treat the body but not necessarily the soul of their patients. It's a certainty that insurers, public or private, are not going to compensate for ministering to the ailing spirit of an aged patient. Dr. Bill Thomas, a Harvard-trained geriatrician, begs to differ with that conventional wisdom after experiencing a personal epiphany while acting as medical director for a New York nursing home in the 1990s. His conclusion: "What we want are gardens that grow people."[25]

As a gentleman farmer / physician, Thomas was unusually connected to the earth and growing cycles, so it was only fitting that he turn to the natural world for solutions. His concept: integrate living beings and things into the very fabric of the nursing home in the form of birds, dogs, cats, and plants, symbolically bringing the physical building to life while readjusting priorities to place residents first. Acknowledge that a person's interior world is every bit as, if not more, important than their external bodies.

The eighty-bed nursing facility that served as the Eden Alternative posted remarkable results. A New York State Health Department audit reported that the facility had a 71 percent decline in daily drug cost per resident, a 50 percent decrease in the rate of infection, and a 26 percent drop in personnel turnover.[26] Unexpectedly, it turns out that a humane environment prompts humane behavior at all levels—among residents, staff members, and management personnel—leading to higher satisfaction with the workplace and lower likelihood of leaving.

An idea was born, succeeded, and began to propagate, and it was based on a core set of principles that would guide a movement that now numbers more than three hundred registered Eden Alternative nursing homes and long-term care facilities and some fifteen thousand certified Eden associates to carry out the work.[27]

The Ten Principles of Eden Alternative

Central to its mission is a belief that aging represents one stage in a continuum of development and growth rather than a period of slow, inevitable decline in body and mind. The following philosophical principles govern every aspect of the Eden Alternative:

1. The three plagues of loneliness, helplessness, and boredom account for the bulk of suffering among our Elders.
2. An Elder-centered community commits to creating a Human Habitat where life revolves around close and continuing contact with plants, animals, and children. It is these relationships that provide the young and old alike with a pathway to a life worth living.
3. Loving companionship is the antidote to loneliness. Elders deserve easy access to human and animal companionship.
4. An Elder-centered community creates opportunity to give as well as receive care. This is the antidote to helplessness.
5. An Elder-centered community imbues daily life with variety and spontaneity by creating an environment in which unex-

pected and unpredictable interactions and happenings can take place. This is the antidote to boredom.

6. Meaningless activity corrodes the human spirit. The opportunity to do things that we find meaningful is essential to human health.

7. Medical treatment should be the servant of genuine human caring, never its master.

8. An Elder-centered community honors its Elders by de-emphasizing top-down bureaucratic authority, seeking instead to place the maximum possible decision-making authority into the hands of the Elders or into the hands of those closest to them.

9. Creating an Elder-centered community is a never-ending process. Human growth must never be separated from human life.

10. Wise leadership is the lifeblood of any struggle against the three plagues. For it, there can be no substitute.[28]

Green House

The success of the Eden Alternative yielded another, related concept, where the ten principles could be applied to the physical plant itself. Instead of merely humanizing large, institutional-style nursing homes, Thomas envisioned the Green House Project—small, home-style facilities housing ten to twelve residents, each with a private room and bath, and able to enjoy the companionship of communal meals and programs.

Relationships between people and nature are the connective tissue of Green House. Those relationships are enhanced and enabled by the three characteristics of Green House design: a warm environment, where aesthetics complement functional needs; smart technology like computers, electronic ceiling lifts, and adaptive devices that enhance daily life; and green aspects that include patios, gardens, and environmentally conscious design choices.

The design goal was to create a look and feel that would let you drop a Green House home into any neighborhood and have it fit right in. Perhaps even more important to residents is the fact that they have the freedom and control to dictate their own schedules—to determine when they eat, sleep, and interact—and the option to partake in communal meals with staff members, residents, and visitors, a concept called convivium.

Practical Matters

As with any new idea, there are skeptics who want their doubts to be proved right and the idea proved wrong. The major barriers to replicating the Green House Project around the country are twofold: economic and administrative. Since the basic model for existing nursing homes is a clinically driven formula based on economies of scale, it is difficult for entrenched nursing-home management to grasp how Green House can be financially viable. Yet these are the very corporations that need to replace the crumbling infrastructure that grew out of the seeds of the 1965 Medicare and Medicaid programs.

Fortunately, Jane Isaacs Lowe and her cohorts at the Robert Wood Johnson Foundation saw the light, embraced the Green House vision and committed to a $10 million, five-year investment to encourage model adoption and measurement.[29] The goal of the grant is to achieve critical mass by nurturing fifty new Green House start-ups by 2010.[30]

Operators can take heart from the experience of Saint John's

Lutheran Ministries in Billings, Montana, which runs both a traditional nursing home and Green House homes. After tracking comparative costs, administrators determined that the Green House homes were 22 percent less expensive per resident and per diem, costing $150 a day versus $192 a day at the nursing home.[31]

The other, more daunting, barrier is administrative roadblocks as the Green House Project navigates turbulent regulatory waters while trying to maintain the residential feel of its homes. Designed to provide all necessary care to very ill patients, Green House must comply with life-safety regulations, rigid building codes, and extremely detailed health-system rules regarding everything from privacy to infection control. Regardless of the obstacles placed in their path, Green House homes represent an idea whose time has come, and whether they prove to be launch pads for a more refined solution or the prototype of nursing care to come, succeed they will. Because Green House celebrates the most important aspect of life: the human spirit.

Innovation Continues

Dissatisfied with the traditional aging options currently in place, enterprising boomers are exploring new ways to age in place, retain ties to the community, and build their own microcommunities in a way that keeps them connected to the world at large. Instead of an introspective, exclusive experience, boomers are looking for housing solutions that anticipate the changing physical requirements of an aging body and that generate opportunities to promote interaction with neighbors.

There is an emerging recognition of the importance of *community* in the truest sense of the word, according to Merriam-Webster online, "an interacting population of various kinds of individuals in a common location." There is also a growing appreciation for the contributions that elders can make to a social fabric by imparting skills, knowledge, values, and (quite literally) the wisdom of the aged.

10. IT TAKES A COMPANY

Elder care: Is it a corporate imperative or a corporate prerogative? There are those who would argue that providing elder care benefits is simply good business. And those who would argue that providing elder care is the job of government. And those who would argue that providing elder care is the responsibility of the family. And those who would argue that providing elder care falls into the purview of nonprofit groups. And those who would argue that providing elder care is a function of religious organizations. And those who would argue that providing elder care is a community-based activity. And those who would argue that every one of those positions is correct—to a degree.

Elder care is the inevitable and overlooked by-product of improved health care and consequent unanticipated longevity. It is also the elephant in the living room—the enormous problem that everyone can see but no one wishes to address. Working couples struggling to make ends meet, who put the younger kids through college and tolerate the return of recent graduates unable to cut the economic umbilical cord, find themselves further strapped when something happens to their aging parents. And it always does. Elder care is in fact a question of when, not if, something will happen.

Visibility Problem

Out of sight, out of mind. Take a quick scan of desktop photos the next time you're in an office and check out who takes center stage and who is missing from the photo array. In corporate America, as in our society as a whole, children are the focal point of social networks, while elders are the invisible members. Discussing one's children is considered socially appropriate and in fact encouraged by many companies. Yet while kids make good water cooler conversation, no one talks about parents or grandparents, and their images are missing from desktop arrangements.

Why is elder care overlooked by so many firms when putting together benefit offerings? For some 70 percent of companies responding to a Families and Work Institute survey, the major obstacle cited was perceived cost, but this is an erroneous assumption.[1] Despite all the recent articles and television segments about aging boomers and their parents, it's just not a front-burner issue. While most major companies offer some elder care assistance, generally in the form of information and referral services, most small to mid-sized companies do not, and those are the firms that traditionally employ 51 percent of Americans.[2]

Dr. Marcie Pitt-Catsouphes, with the Center on Aging and the Workplace, believes a large part of the cause is associated with the transformational impact of the boomer demographic. In the early 1980s an unprecedented number of younger women were in the workforce, and as they contemplated starting families, they initiated a corporate dialogue around work-life issues. As a result, the work-life movement traces its roots to child care concerns. Now those same women have aged into elder care responsibilities and are just beginning to lobby for an expansion of corporate benefits to encompass this need. But cultural and financial obstacles remain.

Security Threats

In an uncertain economic climate, and for employees over age fifty, elder care represents a double threat to financial security at a time when they can least afford it. There is the perception, correct or not, that those caring for elders are unreliable employees because of the demands of care, which places them at the top of the expendable list for downsizing. Additionally, many older workers are rapidly depleting personal retirement savings to care for parents who outlived their pensions or retirement reserves.

> Prepare yourself for a bumpy ride. It would be great to feel that I wasn't alone in this. If there was someone who could guide me through all the paperwork and hassle. To make sure that I'm making the right decisions. Everything has to be done yesterday.
>
> —*Amber, divorced, two kids*

> I just take it day by day. When Dad's happy, I'm happy. When he's not, I'm not. And when something goes wrong . . . well, let's just say I'm not "all there" at work. —*Noelle, single, no kids*

Why are people so hesitant to talk about elder care? When we posed that question to the experts and to firms that do offer robust elder care services, there were two predominant answers: first, the most frequent answer was the reluctance of employees to self-identify as a caregiver for fear of potential retribution or repercussion by their supervisor or colleagues, and, second, many caregivers believe it is their moral obligation to take care of the parents who cared for them without outside assistance or interference.

Once a caregiver "outs" themselves in the workplace, there may still be a stigma of sorts attached. One negative is the possible perception of being tied to a parent's apron strings. Another negative is the subtle undercurrent that the employee will become undependable, subject to unanticipated absences and erratic work habits in response to the elder's needs. Fears of such stigmas are justified. In a Society for Human Resource Management (SHRM) study of human resource managers, fully 45 percent strongly agreed with the statement that "elder care issues can inhibit an employee's career growth/advancement opportunities."[3]

The wellspring for these concerns is related to the concept of a so-called "ideal worker," an archetype that remains part of the employer mind-set, believes Dr. Jacquelyn James, the research director at the Sloan Center on Aging and Work at Boston College. "The 'ideal worker' is the employee who gives heart, mind, and soul to the corporation, or who at least acts like they do. There is a healthy skepticism about whether or not you'll still be viewed as a good employee if you have to leave early or come in late. A concern that you'll be passed over for promotion, or viewed as less committed to the job."[4]

A Personal Commitment

Any reservations employers hold about caregiving and employee engagement are unfounded and unfortunate given the empirical evidence. According to one study, employees who stated their company provided work-life support (including elder care services) and ample flexibility scored 14–20 percent higher on the commitment measures that translate into improved output and efficiency.[5] The study findings were used to design a commitment pyramid that ranks and ordinates the elements of employee engagement. "Flexibility" and "work-life support" sit at the top of that pyramid, the section containing commitment drivers responsible for true employee engagement.[6]

The reason employee engagement matters is its direct, positive correlation with total shareholder return, enhanced productivity, reduced turnover, and higher customer satisfaction and loyalty levels. Truly engaged employees represent 90 percent of a company's productivity. Over a four-year interval, companies with the best employee-engagement results enjoyed a correspondingly high total shareholder return almost three times that of companies with less engaged workers.[7] These impressive results speak to the quantifiable economic value of work-life accommodations that cost a company relatively little to implement.

For the employees challenged by elder care duties, reliable help of any kind is hard to find and harder to afford. Sometimes, the quintessential American ethic of independence and self-reliance imposes unnecessary hardship on a caregiver by foreclosing available avenues of assistance.

Private Lives

Elinor Ginzler, senior vice president for Livable Communities, Office of Social Impact at AARP, observed that for "someone engaged in this part of life's journey, they think of caregiving as personal, private and individual, not political or social"[8]—certainly not as something to be bandied about the workplace or revealed to coworkers.

While many similarities exist between the demands of child care and elder care on employees, the differences are vast and significant. The cycle of life for a child is pretty predictable. The cycle of life for an elder is much less so. Prospective parents have nine months to prepare for the birth of a child and evaluate care-giving alternatives. In a sense, we spend our youth preparing to become parents, using role-play games as anticipatory socialization.

The same is not true for elder care. There is no anticipatory socialization. There are few role models to pattern after. There are few examples embedded in popular media or entertainment offerings. We're not sure what to expect or what is expected. Elder care needs crop up unpredictably and can rapidly rise to the level of life-threatening events. Thanks to the longevity revolution, no one is prepared for elder care.

> I was lucky because the current management regime is nice and they liked me, so they were really good about it when I had to leave early or come in late. But they so totally didn't understand. When my contract was up, they said "Let's wait until your mom gets better to discuss renewal." I had to point out that she'll never recover from old age and dementia, so let's talk now.   —*Darcey, divorced, one kid*

> Advice. What I needed most was someone to set expectations. To walk me through procedures. To say "Here's what you need to know." There was no one to do that for me. I was completely shell-shocked and struggling to process her situation.
>
> —*Madge, widowed, three kids*

In a way, it's almost counterintuitive. Everyone has parents, but not everyone has children or a spouse. Yet almost every firm has policies addressing special consideration for the latter two categories, while fewer companies have formal policies with respect to elder care. What will it take to get equal play for elder care? Perhaps just a look at the numbers and a change of perspective.

The Business Case

First, the numbers. According to the *MetLife Caregiving Cost Study: Productivity Losses to U.S. Businesses*, the total annual estimated "all in" cost in lost productivity associated with full-time employed caregivers is $33.6 billion per year.[9] This takes into account the cost of replacing employees who leave, absenteeism, workday interruptions, elder care crises, supervisor time, unpaid leave, and a switch from full- to part-time employment. The burden rests equally on employer and employee alike. The average employed elder caregiver forfeits in excess of $650,000 in lifetime earnings potential because of family obligations.[10]

> How do you keep the job going when you take time off to care for your folks? It's a real issue. I called myself Miss Donut because I was caught in the middle. Frankly, at my company it all proved to just be lip service . . . not real help.   —*Leigh, divorced, two kids*

The AARP believes that as many as 30 percent of employees are elder care providers, with 40 percent of that number sandwiched between generations and responsible for children at home.[11] A privately funded study of ten thousand employees confirmed the figure, with 30 percent of employees anticipating some elder or adult care responsibility in the next few years.[12] The AARP projects that almost half of the American labor force will become caregivers by 2013.[13] Elder care is reaching a tipping point based on the sheer number of workers affected. Businesses either will be forced to respond or will seize the opportunity to use elder care as a differentiator in the marketplace.

The Simple Things

The really good news for businesses looking to become employers of choice is that the type of elder care services people rate highest also happen to be among the least expensive services to provide. Dr. Sandra Timmermann, the executive director of the MetLife Mature Market Institute, notes that in study after study flextime seems to be the top-ranked elder care benefit.[14] The ability to come in a little later, leave a little earlier, or work from home relieves a tremendous amount of stress for the caregiving employee when support systems break down.

Without the safety valve of flexibility, employed elder caregivers have a tough time fulfilling all their obligations at work and at home. A SHRM study on elder care and the workforce determined that "44% of respondents report workday interruptions as a result of eldercare issues; 41% report mental/concentration problems; and 37% report excessive personal phone calls/business during work hours."[15] Lack of infrastructure forced six of ten working caregivers to reduce hours, take unpaid leave, or make another change in employment status to juggle responsibilities according to the MetLife Mature Market Institute.[16]

For businesses trying to make the call on adding elder care support and resources to their benefits portfolio, the math is simple: AARP estimates that for every dollar a company spends on elder care resources, the firm will realize a return in the range of $3 to $14.[17] These days, that's one of the best rates available on any investment. Surprisingly, given its significant impact on shareholder value, productivity, and other key performance metrics, elder care proves to be very affordable.

Ceridian, a leading provider of health and productivity solutions, offers employers access to in-person elder care management services at a cost as low as $2 to $5 per employee per year, with a minimum threshold of $3,000.[18] Yet in 2007, only an estimated one-third of large companies and one-quarter of all other businesses offered elder care benefits to their employees.[19]

Ginzler asserts that this approach may help corporate America rethink elder care by framing it in terms of a productivity issue rather than a benefit issue. Setting up the elder care discussion around the bottom line and resource optimization makes it more palatable to executives with sharp pencils. However, elder care availability alone may not solve the problem if employee awareness and supervisor support are lacking.

Best-Kept Secret

Unexpectedly, even when progressive companies offer elder care benefits and implement detailed policies, employee awareness may be low, and use of the benefits even lower. Ceridian estimates the typical use of services for in-person adult and elder care managements between 0.15 percent and 0.25 percent of the total employee population, varying with company demographics and program promotion.[20]

The SHRM fielded a two-tier study of employees and human resource (HR) managers and found that "only 6 percent of (employee) respondents said that their organization has a specific policy or policies addressing elder care issues." In actuality, according to the HR managers at the same set of firms, 25 percent of the companies had such policies.[21]

In a different study at three Fortune 500 companies with particularly deep elder care offerings, fully two-thirds of employees had no idea that their employer provided elder care programs.[22] What accounts for this? In part, information overload. Since the majority of employees either have no immediate elder care needs

or already have resolved them, the information gets filed or ignored. Or poor internal marketing could be to blame.

It seems pretty clear that companies need to do a better job of
proactively communicating elder care benefits to employees at
regular intervals so these benefits are at the top of a caregiver's
mind when a senior health crisis does occur. Employees' blind
spot to elder care is a perfect reflection of the passive system of
elder services in the United States.

Everything is left up to the individual—the research, the outreach, the analysis, the contacts. Individuals and families are expected to ramp up to expert level, becoming amateur geriatric
case managers virtually overnight when they get the "twenty-four
hours' notice" call from a hospital discharge planner. It is only the
lucky few who can afford or who work at firms that provide on-
the-ground geriatric case management, where a qualified nurse
or social worker conducts an assessment of the elder to determine assistance needs and makes specific recommendations as to
the resources and suppliers best equipped to meet them.

Marketing Principles

GlaxoSmithKline (GSK) operates a very comprehensive elder care
program and is an acknowledged innovator in the field. After
twenty years of experience with some form of elder care services,
GSK is still tweaking and enhancing its programs based on
employee feedback.

Caregiving itself is an intimate experience, and as it turns out,
caregivers also appreciate the personal touch. Annette Byrd, who
administers the GSK elder care program, observed that service
use jumped when they changed the pathway to information and
access. Today, GSK brings an elder care consultant to multiple

company locations, enabling employees to schedule an individual appointment for a private consultation with a case manager. As a result of the personal attention, the use of both in-home assessments and facility monitoring went up.

To fill the pipeline, one very smart strategy GSK instituted was the mounting of a targeted marketing campaign directed at members of an affinity group for employees over age fifty. While many people requiring elder care assistance are younger than that demographic, the limited campaign proved to be an efficient mechanism for spreading the word to likely service users. The strategy paid off by getting people in the door for consultations with a specialist, which bumped up the rate of use.

The company learned very quickly in the early years that elder care is not just child care on steroids. For starters, while dependent children reside with their parents, elders may live hundreds or even thousands of miles away from their adult children. Young children are under parental control: they can be told what to do and physically managed as necessary. Parents are legal adults who must be convinced or cajoled into cooperating and into giving permission for service delivery to take place. Not every adult child has developed those negotiating skills, and those delicate conversations are sometimes better conducted by a trained professional. *Training* is the operative word in the workplace as well.

Supervisor Support

After the primary-care physician, the next most important person in the elder care support team may well be an employee's direct supervisor. In virtually every interview, caregivers said that their boss made all the difference. If the boss was supportive, life was manageable. If the boss was not supportive, life was miserable. Thus in the absence of formal elder care policies, the interpretation and implementation of flexibility rests with the supervisor who can rally the team in support of the caregiver or choose to be obstructionist.

Despite the all-important role of supervisors, only 11 percent of employers claim to educate supervisors about elder care demands and how to work with employees using support services.[23] The same SHRM study found that, for 16 percent of respondents, the unpredictable demands of elder care placed a strain on employee-manager relationships.[24] At a minimum, even the most basic management training course should include a unit dealing with work-life issues and managing around the company's flextime policies.

Another mechanism for removing the onus from employee assistance is to keep things confidential by using a third-party vendor. There is no need for an employee to self-identify unless they choose to do so. Although we have been specifically referring to elder care in this discussion, most companies correctly cluster elder care services under the more comprehensive work-life umbrella on the theory that every life stage has its own equally important challenges. Under most flextime policies, employees must explain how and when they intend to get the job done, but not the reason behind the request for nontraditional work hours.

Help Is at Hand

In the Internet age, the information and referral services once so popular with HR departments now deliver only marginal value to employees, since almost everything, from provider Web sites to caregiver quality reviews, is available on the Web at the touch of a button. What families need is immediate direction and specific guidance, as well as a detailed road map of what needs to happen and how to pull it off.

Each elder care case is as unique as each family situation, involving a different mix of services and a different approach.

This requires a portfolio of options including services such as the following:

Geriatric case management
Flextime/telecommuting
Health care coverage/extension to seniors
Discounted products/services
Lunchtime "brown bag" support groups
Caregiver affinity groups
One-on-one counseling
Referrals for dependent-care services
At-home assessments
Leave sharing
Legal services
Emergency backup care

The last item on the list, backup care, is one of the most desirable and fastest-growing employee benefits, with 14 percent of employers offering some type of backstop help for associates.[25] One study proved that backup care resulted in lower employee stress and absenteeism.[26] Knowing that a crisis can be resolved with a single phone call enables employees to get to work and concentrate on work-related tasks, confident that their elder is safe and comfortable.

No Time Like the Present

Without the assurance that there will never be a gap in elder care, workers can readily fall prey to presenteeism. It's one of the hot topics in productivity discussions these days. Distilled to its essence, presenteeism refers to an employee who comes to work too impaired physically or mentally to do the job. Elder care is a major mental distraction, and even the best-intentioned and most highly motivated employee can't control the emotional seepage when a loved one needs help.

> There was a time when I just started to lose it. Not productive. Missing details. Too consumed by what was happening to my dad to care. I needed time off, and they said sure—but it was unpaid and I couldn't afford it. My husband had just lost his job.
>
> —*Esther, married, one kid*

Presenteeism is much more difficult to quantify than absenteeism, because the employee is physically present but underperforming. Findings from a 2007 survey revealed that 38 percent of companies believe presenteeism is a problem.[27] In an attempt to quantify the issue, one company discovered that productivity consequences were greater from presenteeism days than from sick days and calculated the cost of presenteeism at $180 billion.[28]

The Payoff

Why should companies offer elder care benefits and what's their incentive to do so? Because elder care pays off big-time. Consider the case of elder care corporate leaders. Regardless of its role in the mortgage-market implosion, Fannie Mae has sterling credentials as an employer. The organization spends an estimated $100,000 annually in elder care assistance[29] and asserts that as many as 28 percent of employees who tapped into those benefits would have been forced to leave the company if such help was not available.[30] For every dollar in elder care benefits paid out, Fannie Mae recaptured $1.50 on dimensions such as improved productivity, employee retention, and lower turnover and absenteeism.[31]

Baptist Health South Florida calculated savings of $65,000 in just nine months directly associated with not having to replace absent employees.[32] Backup-care services were added to the health provider's benefits portfolio in response to employee requests. More than five thousand hours of backup care were used in six months, 32 percent of which was for adult or elder care.[33] And the list goes on. Intrinsic benefits. Extrinsic benefits.

Get Busy

> Employers shouldn't be in the caregiving business. They would do a bad job of it. But they can sure make it easier for workers to take care of elders by adding options to a cafeteria plan and hooking up with companies that are expert at care management.
>
> —*Mariel, divorced, one kid*

There's no time like the present to enhance a company's competitive advantage and recapture waning productivity by incorporating low-cost, high-yield elder care programs into the employee-assistance plan. For details on best practices and how to pull off a truly flexible work environment, consult the Boston College Center for Work and Family, which published a comprehensive study in 2008 titled "Overcoming the Implementation Gap: How 20 Leading Companies Are Making Flexibility Work."[34]

The research describes programs, associated benefits, drivers, obstacles, success factors, and recommendations. Categories include part-time and reduced workload programs, job sharing, telecommuting, a compressed workweek, alternative work schedules, phased retirement, and the implementation of flexible work arrangements.

Elder care is not a matter of sensitivity. It's a matter of sensibility. Or better put, "cents ability," a bottom-line issue that can return the best financial results available in today's financial markets.

11. IT TAKES A TECHNOLOGY

Science fiction writers in the 1950s envisaged a world where helpful electronic devices saved the day for the hero, his sidekicks, and the planet Earth. Among the first entries in the pantheon of space conquerors was Captain Video, who stormed across the galaxy in his rocket ship dubbed, appropriately enough, *The Galaxy,* along with his companion Tobor the robot.[1]

At Captain Video's disposal was a veritable war chest of exotic gadgets with nonsense names like the opticon scillometer, which enabled the user to see through anything; the cosmic-ray vibrator, designed to paralyze its victims; the discatron, which functioned as a two-way radio;[2] an electronic straitjacket; atomic rifle; solenoid assentuator; and the atomic collection screen, which acted like a television in reverse mode.[3] In the twenty-first century, those early projections have proved remarkably prescient as technological advances are converted into practical applications ranging from robots to talking medicine bottles to autonomous wheelchairs that help elders adapt and adjust to physical limitations. The age-in-place goal voiced by so many seniors, once affordable only to a few, will be achievable by all who seek it.

Yet another engineering vision of the future from early sci-fi works was pounded-tin robots with bucket-shaped heads, frozen faces, accordion-pleated rubber joints, staccato movements, and garbled, synthesized voices, stuttering in random patterns. With the passage of time, those early predictions of robot usefulness have proved remarkably accurate, although the packaging has changed dramatically.

Relatable Robots

Today, that android dream has been realized in the form of social and personal robots that perform a variety of operations from health monitoring to housekeeping to companion duties. The robots vary in physiognomy from the smooth white planes of ASIMO, Honda's walking humanoid robot, to Paro, a robot designed to look like a soft, furry baby seal.[4] Japan has led the way in assistive robotics, in part because of the size of that country's aging population and its dearth of caregivers.

In the twenty-first century, robots will play just as important a role as their more primitive predecessors, but they will have much more elegant and relatable carapaces. One of the more intriguing categories of robots is the therapeutic-companion group, which includes Paro the baby seal and Huggable, the bear, made at MIT. For movie buffs, Huggable will look remarkably similar to Teddy, the animatronic bear friend of Haley Joel Osment's character in the movie *A.I. Artificial Intelligence*.[5] A teddy bear was selected because of its status in the childhood pantheon of comfort creatures and because it doesn't exist in nature and thus carries no predetermined behavioral expectations.

Furry Friends

The realistic seal and bear design concepts both capitalize on the unique relationship between humans and their pets in an effort to achieve the benefits of caring for a pet, such as improved self-esteem, enhanced mood and outlook, facilitated socialization, reduced heart and respiration rates, as well as lower stress-hormone levels. The many benefits associated with pets account for the growing popularity of animal-assisted therapy in settings such as the Green House, hospitals, and nursing homes.

Unfortunately, in many situations, animals are verboten for reasons ranging from hygiene to allergies to infection control to personal safety. Additionally, live pet interactions must be scheduled in advance and occur with an animal handler present, which alters the nature of the relationship.

Enter the ersatz animal, fabricated to respond to handling and programmed to capture a full range of sensory input, albeit in a mechanical way. In the case of Huggable, that means a supple, plush synthetic fur exterior covering a silicone-membrane layer that overlays a sensing skin with more than fifteen hundred embedded electric sensors.[6] Here's what the developers had to say about their sensory goal:

> One important and novel capability we are developing for the Huggable is its ability to participate in active relational and affective touch-based interactions with a person. Social-relational touch interactions play a particularly important role for companion animals in their ability to provide health benefits to people. Touch can convey a wide variety of communicative intents—an animal can be tickled, petted, scratched, patted, rubbed, hugged, held in one's arms or lap just to name a few. To be effective,

therapeutic robotic companions must also be able to understand and appropriately respond to how a person touches it.[7]

A robotic companion that features touch capabilities is crucial not just because of the all-important huggability factor but because it can convey data about grip strength, tremors, and body temperature that imparts important information about general health. Cameras behind the buttonlike eyes, microphones implanted in the pricked ears, and voice-coil actuators that detect positions help the ursine critters interact in a more lifelike way, making eye contact and responding to a vocal source by shifting shoulders, neck, and head. The overall effect is so lifelike—and, well, huggable—that the "robobear" was voted one of *Wired* magazine's fifty-best robots ever.[8]

The Seal Deal

Viewing Paro the baby seal from a distance can be very disconcerting, prompting reactions like, What's he doing indoors? On dry land? In that lady's lap? Created by Takanori Shibata of the Intelligent System Research Institute in Japan, Paro was the talk of the COMDEX computer show when the prototype debuted and has been in commercial production since 2004.[9] The physical attributes of Paro were selected to foster bonding and acceptance, from the luxurious, white coat that encourages touching and stroking to the button nose and oversized, black eyes with long lashes that convey a childlike sense of innocence and interest. Far more than a stuffed toy, Paro interacts with people in the same manner as a real pet, responding to physical touch by swishing its tail and flippers, blinking its eyes, and squealing with pleasure at the attention.

Unlike the natural seal, Paro's circadian cycle has been readjusted to better match that of human beings by switching sleep time to evenings instead of days. The Intelligent System Research Institute refers to Paro as a "mental commitment robot," a genre of machines whose prime directive is to foster emotional attachments with people on three levels, defined as: "1) psychological—relaxation and motivation, 2) physiological—improvement in vital signs, and 3) social effects—activation of communication among inpatients and caregivers."[10]

To facilitate human interaction, Paro was outfitted with five types of sensors: the ability to detect and respond to light, which triggers sleeping patterns; touch, which initiates a physical response such as purring; sound, which enables the seal to swivel its head and appear to look at the sensory-input source; temperature, which indicates the health of the human being; and posture, which allows the seal to recognize when it is being held.

Another eerie point of differentiation is that Paro can learn. When an action by Paro elicits a desired response such as petting or a kiss, the robot will repeat the catalyst action in an attempt to evoke the same response. Tweak its whiskers and Paro will pull away or shake its head. If punished, Paro will avoid repeating the trigger movement. Paro simulates emotions such as surprise, sadness, or happiness through blinking, moving its head, or twitching flippers.

To get a look at Paro in action, check out a number of video clips on YouTube. Footage ranges from a laboratory demonstration of Paro "eating," which consists of plugging a pacifier-appearing charger into its mouth, or interacting with residents at a nursing home, who treat Paro like a favorite infant grandchild. Anecdotal evidence suggests that interacting with Paro can soothe and calm agitated Alzheimer's patients.

Less-sophisticated, less-natural-looking precursors to Paro and Huggable include AIBO, which resembles a small plastic dog; i-Cybie and Robo Puppy, other versions of a robodog; QRIO and ASIMO, both humanoid entries from Sony and Honda, respectively;

and Pleo, a robotic dinosaur that rolls its eyes, coos, and begs for attention when ignored for too long.[11]

By design, the simulated pets have been crafted with physical characteristics such as round faces or big eyes and with behavioral capabilities like purring or smiling, which deliberately evoke positive associations for human beings. As a result, many people become quite emotionally attached to their mechanical pets even while fully aware that they are inanimate machines.

A Leg Up

Robots take many forms, some more functional than others. Cyborgs are already being produced and made commercially available. As of October 2008, Japanese citizens could rent a robotic suit called HAL (hybrid assistive limb) capable of interpreting brain signals and instructing the suit to move the indicated arm or leg.[12] The artificially powered exoskeleton uses a portable computer unit that straps around the user's waist and a battery pack that provides more than 2.5 hours of operating time. Bioelectrical sensors pick up brain waves through the skin and act on them.

The wearable robot exoskeleton can enhance strength by as much as 80 percent, enabling a person who normally can perform a leg press with 220 pounds to lift 396 pounds.[13] For elders with weakened muscles, the suit should prove a boon as a rehabilitation tool and assistive device. It has been tested under a variety of climatic conditions and in daily activities such as standing up from a chair, walking, climbing stairs, lifting, and holding items.[14]

Virtual Assistants

The global robot population will reach more than eighteen million units by 2011. Robots in personal or private service made up some 3.4 million units for domestic applications such as household cleaning or gardening chores and another 2.0 million units for entertainment purposes such as toys or education. Although still a relatively small segment of the robotics picture, the number of assistive devices and prostheses for disabled persons is expected to double in the next four years.[15]

Mechanical assistants will be able to assess changes in gait, behavior, and vital signs; perform breath, blood, and urine analyses; detect trips and falls; remind people about appointments and medication schedules; enable remote video viewing and monitoring; locate and transport items; administer physical therapies; shop for groceries; play games; call relatives or care providers for a chat; and even dial 911 in emergencies.

The University of Massachusetts at Amherst advanced the robot cause with the introduction of uBot5, a very mechanical-looking device with exposed armatures, servitors, Segway-style wheels, and a video screen at eye level. Sensor arrays proximate human senses such as sight and sound and can differentiate between normal activities such as walking or sitting and unusual events that require investigation such as a fall.[16]

Although uBot5 is not as endearing looking as other robots, its programmers opted for function over form, and it works. Family members living far away and the primary-health-care team appreciate the remote-access feature that enables them to traverse the home locating the elder, who might not have heard the phone ring or who may be in trouble. Using the robot video feed, physicians can walk the patient through a quick evaluation such as the smile, reach, talk, and walk series for strokes and even use a digital stethoscope to get a quick read.

With an emphasis on dexterity over strength, the uBot5 can perform household chores like cleaning house or grocery shopping, although its load-bearing weight limit for packages is around

2.2 pounds.[17] To achieve these remarkable results, researchers studied neurology and mimicked human anatomy, designing an inner ear to facilitate balance and joint and muscle analogs that allow the unit to right itself if knocked over.

Human Is as Human Does

A curious thing about human-robot interaction: The more human robots appear, the more humanly they are expected to behave. Victoria Groom recounts research showing that people anthropomorphize robots, responding to them as social entities by assigning names and gender and by observing the rules of polite interaction.[18] An early indicator of this trend was the phenomenal response to electronic toys called digital pets like Tamagotchi that required owners to provide periodic care such as food, water, or sleep.[19]

Next up in the humechanical relationship arena came Roomba, the robot-vacuum. Findings from a 2006 detailed ethnographic study determined that fully half of all owners formed some type of social bond with the robot, assigning it a personality, often naming the unit, and at the behavioral extremes arranging play dates with other vacuums or dressing it up.[20]

A later study assessed nine noncleaning Roomba activities and discovered that roughly three-quarters of owners simply watched the Roomba for fun. Almost 60 percent enjoyed demonstrating the vacuum to visitors. More than one-third played or experimented with Roomba and assigned it a gender. While the people who viewed Roomba as a social being were in the minority at about 20 percent, they reported higher product satisfaction levels.[21] Even in situations involving task-specific robots like search-and-rescue or bomb-disarming robots, the human operators formed an emotional attachment and expressed grief when the units were damaged or destroyed.[22]

It is clear from these early observations that human beings crave a relationship with robotic entities that display a form of artificial intelligence and coexist in a home or work setting. However, not all machines need to have a personality to be appreciated. Sometimes, they just need to work.

Scrubbing Bubbles

One such device earning high marks for efficiency and user satisfaction is the human washing machine or robot bathtub from Sanyo Electric.[23] Similar to a human car wash, a wheelchair-bound patient is rolled into the unit and remains seated while the tub closes around them like a clamshell, leaving the patient's head exposed. An attendant operates the tub, which runs through wash and rinse cycles. Advocates see the assisted-care bath as one solution to the elder care crisis in Japan, where the population over sixty-five is expected to peak at 36 percent of the population by 2050.[24]

Caregiving often entails repetitive, mind-deadening tasks of an intimate nature that can strain muscles, fray nerves, and throw out backs. These activities of daily living represent perfect applications for robots who are indifferent to monotony and impervious to tedium and that have no construct for impatience. There are no muscles to get sore, no feelings to get bruised. Automatons are uniformly pleasant and diligent in completing their tasks, which they perform with inhuman precision.

Just ask ERNIE (Evergreen Robot Noticeably Improving Efficiency), a $3 million robot pharmacist responsible for packaging 93 percent of prescriptions at Evergreen Hospital Medical Center, resulting in a 25 percent reduction in medication errors. ERNIE works tirelessly, twenty-four hours a day, and over one nine-month period dispensed an estimated 400,000 doses of medication.[25]

The largest such robot can be found in the United Kingdom, at Norfolk and Norwich University Hospital, where a pharmacy features four robots dispensing medication. The system reportedly is 100 percent accurate and can handle 40,000 different drugs, far exceeding the speed and accuracy of its human counterparts. In addition to dispensing drugs, robot functions include accepting returns, restocking, storage, and crediting medications, all using bar codes.[26] Allowing robots to handle routine dispensing duties frees up human pharmacists to consult with clinicians and patients.

Distance Doctoring

Now the doctor is in even when out of town, as long as there's a webcam nearby. Thanks to electronic medical records and Internet-enabled video, physicians and surgeons will find it easier to fulfill their clinical responsibilities from virtually anywhere around the world. Patients in rural or remote areas unable to travel to world-class medical centers can now tap the expertise of leading specialists by using video Internet connections and robot assistants that probe, sample, analyze, and monitor key metrics.

The eICU is one such model that focuses on the needs of critical patients in intensive-care units (ICUs), who tend to crash or develop serious complications quickly. Their unique requirements could benefit from the attention of "intensivists," physicians who specialize in treating critical-care patients in the hospital setting. While it is estimated that full-time ICU coverage by intensivists could save as many as fifty thousand lives each year, as with many medical specialties, a physician shortage exists.[27] There are approximately six thousand practicing intensivists working in the United States today, who support just 13 percent of ICU patients.[28]

Enterprising hospitals looking for a workaround to the intensivist shortage that improves outcomes and patient care are opting for an electronic solution. These systems electronically link multiple ICU rooms to a centralized monitoring location where highly trained staff members conduct virtual rounds, track vital signs, vigilantly compare physiologic results for deviations from normal ranges, and supervise the medical response in an emergency situation.

Many hospitals use the eICUs as a supplement to, not a replacement for, the human touch of medical staff. Videoconferencing capabilities allow on-site staff members and off-site specialists to consult on a case in real time or, in the case of an emergency, immediately at the touch of an alert button. Manufacturers estimate that the eICU video monitors are in off mode for approximately 90 percent of the time, activated as needed and turned to face the patient. Visual clarity and resolution are good enough to allow eICU staff members to evaluate pupil size, skin color, and respiratory activity.[29]

Nerves of Surgical Steel

Carrying a price tag upward of $1 million with maintenance costs in excess of $100,000 per year, surgical robots represent a significant expense for a health care system.[30] But patient outcomes suggest that hefty bill might be well worth the investment, according to a University of Maryland Medical Center Study of robotic heart bypass surgery. The Maryland researchers determined that robotic heart bypass patients spent anywhere from three to seven fewer days in the hospital, required one-third as many blood transfusions, and presented with 25 percent fewer complications than conventionally treated heart-bypass patients.[31]

One of the main reasons for the differences in patient response is the minimally invasive nature of robotic-bypass surgery, which allows doctors to operate through a few small incisions placed between the ribs, rather than to crack the rib cage and expose the chest. Intuitive Surgical, manufacturer of the da Vinci Surgical System, cites the following patient benefits of robotic surgery:

> Reduced trauma to the body
> Reduced blood loss and need for transfusions
> Less post-operative pain and discomfort
> Less risk of infection
> Shorter hospital stays
> Faster recovery and return to normal daily activities
> Less scarring and improved [physical appearance][32]

Researchers at institutions like the University of Washington BioRobotics Lab are experimenting with ways to convert these large, cumbersome, complicated systems into more portable, lightweight, rugged versions that can help save lives in combat situations or be used in harsh climates and nonsterile environments.[33] Soon, however, virtual medicine may become accessible to every family as a part of smart home technology.

Telemedicine Trends

Health help is now literally just a phone call away for the average person. While telemedicine has been available for years in institutional settings like hospitals and nursing homes, its footprint is now expanding to the home front. One example is the Intel Health Guide, a multipurpose system charged with tasks like performing medical checkups, educating patients, and monitoring vital signs, then transmitting the information digitally to medical providers, who can schedule a video conference. Other companies getting into the home-telemedicine game include Honeywell HomMed, McKesson Health Hero Health Buddy, and Phillips Healthcare.[34] These virtual physicians have been dubbed the ultimate version of a "doc in the box."

One consulting firm placed demand for home-monitoring products of all types at a robust $2.5 billion as soon as 2012.[35] Its predictions are predicated on the number of chronically ill persons in the United States, a segment that accounts for eighty cents of every health care dollar in the country.[36] Telemedicine has already gained a foothold in the United States, with a patient base in excess of 200,000 being actively monitored for conditions like high blood pressure, diabetes, and a host of heart issues.[37] Data-monitor analysts who looked at the broader telemedicine industry, including home monitoring products, estimated the market would expand at an astounding 56 percent compound annual growth rate over five years, with a global price tag of US$8 billion by 2012.[38] All of which begs the question: What exactly is telemedicine?

The American Telemedicine Association defines *telemedicine* as

> the use of medical information exchanged from one site to another via electronic communications to improve patients' health status. Closely associated with telemedicine is the term "tele-health," which is often used to encompass a broader definition of remote health care that does not always involve clinical services. Videoconferencing, transmission of still images, e-health including patient portals, remote monitoring of vital signs, continuing medical education and nursing call centers are all considered part of telemedicine and telehealth.[39]

Despite proven success in field trials and institutional installations, experts are divided on just how fast telemedicine will gain traction. On the plus side: Telemedicine is efficient, quick, delivers up-to-the-minute data for diagnostic purposes, facilitates a team consultative approach, provides access to remote experts, enables early trend spotting to interdict condition declines, reduces costs on multiple levels, and promotes patient involvement in health maintenance.

The major barriers to uptake appear to reside in the financial and psychological realms versus the technological arena. On the minus side: Many doctors remain skeptical and concerned about the potential for communication errors when standard body language cues are missing, as in an e-mail exchange. Others object to the expense of installing technology and the associated need for changes to office protocols prompted by a near-continuous virtual data stream. Another faction cites the possibility of further social isolation among the frail or elderly, for whom doctor visits represent a significant interaction.

Professional resistance aside, telemedicine appears to be gaining momentum, especially after major insurers such as Aetna and CIGNA extended pilot programs and now pay for cyberhealth services on a national basis.[40]

Home Smart Home

Overwhelmingly, older Americans express a desire to age in place. Elinor Ginzler, senior vice president for Livable Communities, Office of Social Impact, at AARP assessed the situation this way:

> Most people, the vast majority, like where they're living and really want to stay there. Literally, they want to stay in the actual house they're in. Almost 90 percent want to stay at home in the 50-plus age category. That number goes up with age. The older

you get, the more pronounced the trend gets. If you look at 75-plus year-olds, about 95 percent want to age in place. It's the power of the familiar at work. Our homes are where we invest on many levels: financially, emotionally, familiarity. It's where we put our roots down. A correlating statistic is that they like their house and their community. The house is viewed as part of that community. It's all about connections with others, a sense of place; it represents independence, choice and control.

Technology will make that aging-in-place preference a practical possibility, even for the very old or physically frail. Companies are clogging the development pipeline with an array of support systems and services, ranging from the types of telemedicine options just discussed to personal-security systems, smart in-home appliances, sensor clothing, wearable computers, prepared home-delivered meals, and entertainment and tracking systems. These devices not only will be able to monitor behaviors but also will be tied in to computers with predictive algorithms that alert the care team to potential issues in the making. Early intervention can stave off or slow down declines that once were viewed as inevitable by-products of aging.

Prototypes for the house of the future are being researched at Georgia Tech (Aware Home), the University of Florida (Gator Tech Smart House), MIT (House N Place Lab), as well as by for-profit enterprises such as Procter and Gamble and Intel. Tricked out with context-sensitive technologies, the houses interact with users, measuring physical and sedentary activity and offering up healthy options at areas of the home where key decisions are made, such as the kitchen.

There will be medicine cabinets that check for drug interactions, remind residents when to take a drug, track compliance, order refills when supplies run low, provide education about a disease state, and suggest additional enhancing therapies such as exercise tips. There will be "smart" everything—toilets, picture frames, pill bottles, cabinets, kitchen appliances, gaming systems, cars, clothing, you name it.[41] They will remind, track, manage, cajole, encourage, alert, stimulate, and assist older consumers in a friendly, intuitive way. And they will communicate with users, families, and caregivers to deliver a holistic, preventive health care experience.

One of the first such devices on the scene was the personal emergency response system (PERS). Popularized by the once-ubiquitous "I've fallen and I can't get up" ad campaign, PERS are slowly gaining in popularity, although market penetration is estimated in the very modest 2–4 percent range.[42] Typically, a PERS consists of a transmitting unit and some type of wearable trigger device such as a bracelet or lavaliere that can be activated by users when they're feeling sick or vulnerable. The alert ties in to a call center that can check with the patient and decide on an appropriate course of action, whether that's a call to emergency services or to a designated family member. Not all aging-in-place issues involve physical accommodation. Sometimes, mental issues take precedence and represent a major area of concern.

Brain Training

So-called brain games will help seniors stay mentally alert, stimulated, engaged, and continuously learning while providing enriching social-networking opportunities. We can expect an explosion in the number of brain-game options entering the marketplace as aging baby boomers try to exempt themselves from the dementia candidate pool. According to a 2007 report from the Johns Hopkins Bloomberg School of Public Health, the dementia incidence rate is expected to quadruple, affecting as many as twenty million people in the United States and 106 million persons globally by 2050.[43]

Andrew Carle, who coined the term *nana technology* to encompass offerings "designed, intended, or that can otherwise be used to improve quality of life for older adults" evaluated a number of popular brain games and has a few recommendations based on his informal analysis:

- Brain Fitness Program 2.0—in a sponsored study, participants achieved a ten-year improvement in memory, with results that lasted three months after completion.
- MindFit—a double-blind study of outcomes detected an 18 percent jump in short-term memory among participants age fifty and over.
- [m]Power—Media and medical skills merge in this entry developed by Disney executives in concert with the UCLA Center on Aging that targets early to midstage dementia patients.
- My Brain Trainer—offers thirty-nine exercises for a three-week brain "boot camp" that allows players to measure performance against others based on age, occupation, or other criteria.[44]

Slow Going

As with all technological enterprises, achieving compatibility and integration between disparate systems is a major concern. Ask any business PC user with a Mac at home. Manufacturers, designers, and other industry participants have formed the Continua Health Alliance, "a group of technology, health care, and fitness companies dedicated to establishing an ecosystem of personal health and fitness products and services, making it possible for patients, caregivers, and health care providers to more proactively address ongoing health care needs."[45]

Another entity serving as a clearinghouse for innovative

technologies is the Center for Aging Services Technologies (CAST), charged with the responsibility to "expedite the development, evaluation and adoption of emerging technologies that will trans-form the aging experience."[46] The CAST Web site includes case studies detailing practical experiences and outcomes from ground-breaking technologies as well as commercially available products. The CAST product roster lists an array of advanced tools such as telemedicine products, PERS systems, remote-presence robots, online education, wander-prevention units, intelligent pill bot-tles, activity monitors, smart wheelchairs, monitor clothing, and more—all available today, just in time to help the thirty-four million unpaid caregivers supporting families and friends, pro-viding assistance that would cost in the neighborhood of $375 billion if purchased.[47]

The big technology questions remain: Will consumers em-brace these new technologies? Will seniors be able to interact with them? Will health providers adopt them? Can they be of-fered at a reasonable price? Will they work in emergency situa-tions? Because PERS and other innovations have been slow to catch on, the MIT Age Lab sponsored a focus group among thought leaders to identify barriers to acceptance and reasons for delayed adoption.[48]

Issues surfaced in the MIT brainstorming clustered into four areas: technology design, ethical considerations, user percep-tions, and the role of markets and policy.[49] Design issues focused on function, reliability, and usability. Ethical concerns centered on privacy (of paramount concern), trust, and dignity. User per-ceptions involved safety versus independence and the stigma of or off-putting associations with products designed for the elderly. Public-policy considerations included equitable access to technol-ogy, affordability, and the lack of any cohesive policy at the state or federal levels.

Thanks to the target-rich environment of a burgeoning baby boomer population, we can expect to see increases in the number of technological-assist devices and services coming onto the market, enabling users to live longer, healthier, more productive lives through early prophylactic interventions. Given their long-standing history as a transformational generation and their facility with computers, cell phones, PDAs, and other technologies, expect boomers to clear the tech hurdle and eagerly embrace anything that fuels their drive to remain active and relevant a reality.

12. IT TAKES YOU

The one thing is, there are no "do-overs" in life. Remember what's important and spend your time wisely. You just never know what's going to happen when. You have to appreciate every day. We didn't know how fleeting those good moments were going to be.

—Louise, married, mother of three

Caregivers, make your presence known! Shed the cloak of invisibility, grab the headlines, and tell the world what elder care is all about. The good and the bad. The happy and the sad. The pretty and the ugly. Go big. Go bold. Go public. Bring elder care out of the closet and engage others. You're only in this alone if you choose to be. Make a decision to become the face and the voice of what many see as one of the major global issues of the twenty-first century.

Borrow a page from the movements that have come before, from civil rights and women's rights and gay rights. Elder care is a bigger issue than any of them, because it cuts across every line that exists, be it gender, age, race, income, religion, sexual preference—you name it. Everyone has or had parents. Elder care is a human issue, not just a woman issue.

What elder care needs is a superhero—a high-profile person willing to champion the cause. To make it important. To garner media attention. To alter perceptions. To raise funds. To galvanize the politicians. To change the tide of public opinion. To lead. To inspire. While we're waiting for that inspirational advocate to emerge, here are other actionable suggestions—some institutional, some individual—for radically redesigning the care, feeding, and loving of our elders.

Mainstream Elders into Society, Media, and the National Dialogue

The Face of Aging

In America, elders have become our version of "the disappeared," virtually missing in action from neighborhoods, streets, and stores; from advertising, film, and music; from positions of influence, impact, and import. There is an aversion in the media to depicting anything less than cosmetic perfection, which immediately rules out the physical evidence of aging like wrinkles, age spots, soft bodies, and hair loss. When elders are shown, it's usually in concert with a "cure" to prevent or fix the perceived aging problem, be it Viagra, Rogaine, or Botox.

Our culture has devolved from one that values experience and wisdom to one that worships youth and beauty at the expense of all else. Despite a growing green movement, disposable products are still popular because they're convenient. That throwaway mentality has extended to our treatment of senior citizens, who find themselves dissed and dismissed, rendered virtually invisible because they are old and no longer deemed attractive. Regardless of energy, regardless of accomplishments, regardless of potential, our seniors sit on the sidelines. Ageism is one of the last bastions of acceptable prejudice in our society. This needs to be addressed—now.

Generate and Finance New Solutions and Concepts for Healthy Aging

Bright Ideas Welcome

What's missing in elder care circles is an organized mechanism for surfacing, testing, and funding great ideas. There are glimmers of hope in the ether, however. In late November 2008, the MacArthur Foundation announced "a new inter-disciplinary research network to help America prepare for the challenges and opportunities posed by our aging society" and funded it to the tune of $3.9 million over three years.[1]

The MacArthur Research Network on an Aging Society has a member roster that reads like a "who's who" of distinguished authorities: Dr. John Rowe of the Columbia University Mailman School of Public Health and the former Aetna CEO; Dr. Robert Binstock, Professor of Aging, Health, and Society at Case Western Reserve University; and Dr. John T. Cacioppo, professor and director, Center for Cognitive and Social Neuroscience, the University of Chicago, to name a few.[2]

The Robert Wood Johnson Foundation also has been instrumental in funding many innovative programs, notably underwriting expansion of the Green House Project conceptualized by Dr. Bill Thomas and providing $10 million over five years to it and other senior health and safety initiatives.[3] The John A. Hartford Foundation took on the cause of elder health by funding the $70 million Hartford Geriatric Nursing Initiative to build specialized nursing capacity and, through a grant to the Association of Specialty Professors, to inject sorely lacking geriatric knowledge into the internal medicine curriculum.[4]

More funding, more cross-pollination, and more frequent exploration of innovative alternatives are needed to even begin to pace the explosive growth in the elderly population. The government is overwhelmed and the populace is already overtaxed trying to support existing programs, so this needs to be a private-sector initiative. What's called for is a fast-track, deep-pocket, no-holds-barred effort on the order of magnitude of the Manhattan Project to prevent an infrastructure implosion. The best bet for identifying new concepts and approaches is to tap into that endless resource of innovation known as American ingenuity through privately funded research and development and nontraditional outreach vehicles like Internet-based crowdsourcing, or "mass collaboration" an "open call" on the Web asking all interested parties to submit ideas and solutions to a specific problem.

Use Technology to Stimulate Creative Thinking About and to Simplify Elder Life

Getting Creative
A note on creativity. Thanks to recent work by Professor David Galenson of the University of Chicago, it appears that boomers will indeed be able to help themselves. Galenson's research began with an exploration of visual artists, age, and creativity, then expanded to fields as diverse as poetry and economics. His conclusion: there are two types of creative minds. "Conceptual innovators" are the bold and brash youngsters who make giant leaps of faith in their fields leading to breakthrough work. The other type, "experimental innovators," exercise a more incremental approach to creativity,

perfecting their craft through trial and error over time, peaking later in life.[5] We need to activate, incent, and reward both types of innovators to create pioneering aging solutions. Fortunately, technology tools can accelerate the process.

Ideas Wanted

Wouldn't it be amazing if we could harness the creative capacity of the geniuses of our time from around the world and put them to work 24/7 problem solving aging challenges? We can! Worldsourcing is happening as you read this, through Internet sites.[6] These sites promote "crowdsourcing" and "open innovation."[7] The model is simplicity itself.

Here's how the InnoCentive model works according to Wikipedia:

> InnoCentive, started in 2002, crowdsources research and development for biomedical and pharmaceutical companies, among other companies in other industries. InnoCentive provides connection and relationship management services between "Seekers" and "Solvers." Seekers are the companies searching for solutions to critical challenges. Solvers are the 125,000 registered members of the InnoCentive crowd who volunteer their solutions to the Seekers. Anyone with interest and Internet access can become an InnoCentive Solver. Solvers whose solutions are selected by the Seekers are compensated for their ideas by InnoCentive, which acts as broker of the process. InnoCentive recently partnered with the Rockefeller Foundation to target solutions from InnoCentive's Solver crowd for orphan diseases and other philanthropic social initiatives.[8]

For millennials, the generation most comfortable with digital groupthink, crowdsourcing is a chance to work in concert with their parents and address elder care issues. For Gen Xers unhappy with the anticipated resource "draw down" by retiring boomers, crowdsourcing represents a terrific opportunity to generate new ideas and resolve issues affecting aging populations without tapping into reserves or penalizing wage earners. Boomers can get into the act as well, brainstorming through these innovative research and development Web sites to deliver short-term fixes for parents and to create the architecture for new aging options for themselves.

Going proactive in the search for solutions is a great way to offset and ameliorate the impact of a prospective run on Social Security under an already-battered national economy—not to mention a wonderful pathway to engage the collective brainpower of boomers who are on the cusp of retirement and in search of enriching and rewarding experiences. Boomers have rallied together, addressing every significant cause of their life span, and we can expect more of the same on the elder care front.

Talk to Me
One of the greatest boons of technology is connectivity among people, resources, and ideas. Self-help has long been the boomer mantra. Let it be so again. Talk to one another. Attend a support group. Text each other. Blog your life. Join an online social network. Post to the Internet like crazy. Use consumer-generated media to share key learnings, to empathize, to sympathize, to distribute solutions in the hopes of preparing those who come after for what lies ahead. Full disclosure is the order of the day.

No Time Like the Present
The Daughter Trap was intended as a call to action, an editorial spotlight to illuminate the fundamental imbalances in elder care.

More important, it was designed to begin an earnest dialogue and serve as an avenue for surfacing solutions. We invite everyone—caregivers, grandchildren, doctors, lawyers, psychologists, case managers, senior-care advocates, academicians, sociologists, researchers, entertainers, politicians to log on to www.daughter trap.com and make their voices heard:

Submit your creative ideas about fixing common elder care problems
Share your proven survival tips with fledgling caregivers
Vote for your favorite candidate for "caregiver superhero"
Download information about experts and helpful resources
Reveal best practices from other areas and countries
Connect with other caregivers who walk in your shoes

In the 2008 election, the voting populace demonstrated that it was ready for a profound change. Let's seize the momentum and start an initiative to change elder care. An initiative that will benefit our parents in the near term and in the not-so-distant future will benefit us more directly.

Everyday people have effected profound social change before. Rekindle the drive; harness that expertise and energy and direct it like a laser at the elder care problem. The days of delegation or abdication to government agencies are over. There's just no money available to expand existing programs or even fully fund legislation that's been passed. It's time for a private-sector solution. One unfettered by bureaucracy. One that leverages the power of the collective creative consciousness. One with obvious incentives for fast-tracking implementation. One that begins today.

Establish a National Clearinghouse as a One-Stop Shop for Senior Solutions

Change Agents

What we learned in researching this book is that the current system of elder care is inaccessible, disorganized, and expensive, modeled after institutional health care paradigms instead of user-friendly alternatives. Each acute incidence of elder care drives a costly, time-consuming, one-off solution because people are hesitant to share experiences and discuss what they perceive to be a private matter and a family obligation. They struggle through the research and analysis alone, scouring the Internet and social networks for tips on how to evaluate elder housing and home aides, assuming they're lucky enough to afford either.

Boomers have been called the transformational generation because the overwhelming size of the age cohort forced change as boomers flowed through the pipeline, influencing and shaping demand for everything from housing to cars to education. Now, boomers face the toughest challenge yet—redefining elder care and retirement options, molding them to the unique requirements of a generation that demands the best, expects the most, and makes it happen.

Help or Hindrance?

Anyone who has tried to gain access to government help can relate to the frustration of navigating layered bureaucracies and swimming through red tape. If you've spent the ridiculous number of hours required to comprehend the Medicare prescription-drug benefit program, you probably agree that it's time for the government to get out of program and service delivery. If we think it's tough on consumers, pity the poor provider organizations attempting to comply with reporting requirements.

Government documentation is backbreaking and regulations can approach absurdity. In the words of one newly credentialed participant in the highly touted Programs of All-Inclusive Care for the Elderly (PACE), "It's virtually impossible to start a PACE program. Our total start-up costs were close to one million dollars, and we're a well-funded organization. The barrier to entry is very high. Too high. We anticipate an additional operating loss of one million dollars in the first year. The paperwork alone is daunting enough to preclude start-up—it could fill a minivan!"[9]

Yet PACE represents a terrific single-source approach to wellness, functioning much like a mini-HMO. Participating seniors sign over their Medicare or Medicaid benefits to the operating agency and in turn have a centralized point of coordination for all services. Case management is a core value of the program, and the service mix is comprehensive, ranging from adult day care to meal programs to help with the activities of daily living to home health aides.

It's a holistic framework with a genius financial model—administrative bodies get rewarded for keeping clients healthy. If members are in the hospital, the entity loses money. If members are healthy and independent, the entity makes money. As straightforward and logical as that may seem, it is the exact opposite of today's health care system, where providers get paid more the sicker you are and the longer you're sick.

Two of the frustrations many nonprofits cited about dealing with the government were the burdensome reporting requirements that cripple operations with inflexible rules and the fragmented way in which funds for senior programs are housed and distributed. For example, a nursing-home administrator cited a recent facility audit where there was not a single correction order related to care but nineteen correction orders associated with documentation issues.

An example of how ridiculous the rules are follows: A nurse took a blood-sugar reading on a Sunday but did not call the doctor to follow up because the result was normal and it was the weekend. The doctor was called on Monday instead. This was an infraction deemed worthy of a write-up, but it had no material impact on patient health.

As for disparate distribution, it takes a skilled and persistent researcher to identify the senior programs available and where they reside in the network of government programming. For example, the seniors' portion of the Medicaid budget is mixed in with every other service you can imagine that target a myriad of other constituents.

Single Source

What's needed is to simplify the route to elder care information access and retrieval, to create a single, well-organized, current database warehousing all qualified senior programs and suppliers, including for-profits, that has very robust and forgiving search capability. Ownership should be vested in a private-sector company or nongovernmental organization that understands concepts like customer-driven and user-friendly. As an assist to potential searchers, a feedback system much like the eBay star ratings would keep vendors honest and provide an outlet for frank, candid reviews. The Web site could become self-liquidating by either charging a nominal search fee to consumers, billing companies on a per-referral basis, or invoicing for controlled advertising on the site.

Some would argue that the Eldercare Locator (www.eldercare .gov or 1-800-677-1116) performs this function, but it is at best a three-step process: access the locator Web site or hot line, get transferred to or served up local agency names, then contact those groups for specific referrals or provider companies. It's cumbersome, time-consuming, and inefficient, especially for employed caregivers who may be reaching out during the wee hours of the morning when local agencies are closed.

While a good start, the Eldercare Locator remains an agency-to-agency solution, injecting a sometimes unnecessary intermediary into the process and adding to the length of search. In a personal test of the system, the automated Eldercare Locator operator efficiently handed off the call to the local branch of the Area Agency on Aging, where we were kept on hold for more than fifteen minutes and never did connect with a specialist who could answer our question.

Build a "Family of Choice" and Consider Fostering or Adopting an Elder

Pick and Choose

Consider recruiting peripheral players into the elder care game. In fact, you can even recruit an elder to join your family! Think of it as analogous to a foster or adoption situation, where there is a formal commitment to a dependent person. Blood relationship isn't a necessary requirement for offering care and support to a frail senior. It used to be called being a good neighbor and keeping an eye out, checking in to make sure all was well if an elder's daily patterns were broken.

Now we have the "Levittown effect," suburban-style living where neighbors pull into a garage and enter the house without any opportunity for friendly exchange. Mom and Dad likely both work, and children are tightly scheduled around play dates and lessons when not in school. There are no stoops or porches on today's mini-mansions where neighbors can hang out and talk in good weather. Urban silo culture prohibits even making eye contact on the street or an elevator. The net impact on elders is a culturally enforced isolation. Countermanding that seclusion takes effort, but it can be done.

Elder care was once an extended family phenomenon. We can make it a "family of choice" phenomenon by enlisting interested tangential parties like friends, neighbors, church members, health-club contacts, local seniors, and coworkers onto a care team. The interesting by-product of proactively caring for a nearby senior is that it reestablishes a sense of community since cooperating parties connect to coordinate services. The concept of family of choice is long overdue because, while we wait for a national long-term-care solution, life and caregiving problems continue unabated.

Publicize Available Programs and Resources

The caregiving landscape is both replete with macrodata and starved for helpful information. As pointed out above, elder care problems often arise unexpectedly, and the need to identify support services is immediate and intense. One quick fix that would accelerate access to necessary information is readily available: publicize what already exists.

One Ph.D. with fifteen years of experience in the elder care field laughed with exasperation explaining how she spent hours sitting with her brother, who holds a masters degree in social work, poring over the Medicare drug-benefit brochures, trying to figure out which plan and which pharmacy to choose. With almost forty years of education between them, they found the government-issued material obtuse to the point of indecipherable. If two acknowledged experts have difficulty understanding federal elder care materials, how can the average person be expected to digest them?

Agencies need to borrow a page, literally, from consumer marketing and spread the word through an integrated marketing communications campaign that uses the entire portfolio of print, broadcast, and digital media available. Campaign duration and coverage should be enough to ensure that a minimum awareness threshold gets met for the target caregiver audience. Pretest messages and creative concepts to guarantee message resonance and overall impact. In short, sell available programs! The task is a marketer's dream—proactively package and deliver the goods to an already-receptive audience with an absolute and profound need and no alternatives.

Excellent campaign templates exist within the federal infrastructure. The army does a great job of marketing itself. The federal government has made impressive strides in the past with antilittering, antismoking, and antidrug campaigns. Now we need to apply that expertise to the issue of elder care.

Let caregivers know who and what's already out there. It almost seems as if Congress remembered to fund programs but forgot to fund the marketing of those programs. In an administrative corollary to the "if a tree falls in the woods . . ." conundrum, we ask, If a program is funded and functioning but nobody knows about it, is that money well spent?

What is the Area Agency on Aging, what does it do, and how do you find a local agency? What is the Eldercare Locator all about? How does a caregiver connect with other caregivers for hands-on pointers? Where does one go for elder-specific information about diabetes? How does one check out a home health aide someone recommended? As structured today, the elder care network is a passive system. It's up to the individual to figure out. Under the proposal to publicize what exists, monies would be earmarked to proactively communicate the features and benefits of elder care programs, in addition to their operational requirements.

As an adjunct to publicizing existing senior programs, there is a need to educate families about planning for elderly relatives. Such prophylactic planning could ultimately minimize or possibly alleviate the need for government-sponsored elder care programming.

Make Life-Stage Planning as Common as Financial Planning

There are two problems with elder care in this country: the lack of a long-term government policy and the lack of individual planning for the eventuality of the need for care. We are a nation in denial about aging. Granted, as boomers age into the system, the dynamic and the dialogue have begun to change. By 2050, fully 20 percent of the world's population will be over the age of sixty, twice the current rate.[10]

Who is responsible financially for an ailing elder? Pose that question to a group and the discussion quickly becomes mired in the detritus of ethics, morality, religion, and family obligation. Interestingly, in the United States we assume a personal responsibility; in countries like Scandinavia, they assume that issues like elder care are too overwhelming for families to manage alone.

Learning from the errors and omissions of our fathers, let's not repeat their mistakes. Instead of expecting that the government or our children will take care of us in our dotage, let's plan ahead. Prudent adults usually perform some degree of financial planning to put money aside for a house, the kids' college, and retirement. Holistic financial planners will also invite clients to articulate their medical treatment and burial preferences. Life-stage planning represents a natural progression in financial planning by following it through to the final stage of life.

Senior life-stage issues are varied and demand a passing acquaintance with moral and ethical issues. How do people want to live—in their own home? as part of a naturally occurring retirement community? independently in a continuing care community? in a co-housing development? What kind of help will they likely need and how will they pay for it? What level of care represents a logical point at which to move into an assisted-living setting? When and what type of medical interventions are sanctioned, and which are not? Will family caregivers be given any compensation? If so, how does that impact division of inheritance?

Long-term-care insurance represents a great first step in life-stage planning. Evaluating policy options forces buyers to walk through choices and to consider the various levels of care and associated health issues. The process also reinforces the fact that adults are responsible for their own endgame—not just how they lived life but how they will live it out.

Elder care is fundamentally a simple matter involving a simple principle. It's a matter of equity. It's a matter of rights and what's right. For men. For women. For families. For society.

Mobilize a Miracle

The new millennium brings with it new opportunities. The chance to forge a new social order. To introduce a new civility. To fashion new connections. To form new relationships. To close generational divides. To bridge societal chasms. To develop new bonds. To connect in person. To reach out virtually. To interact virally. To weave a new tapestry using the tools of today while honoring the wisdom of the ages.

Reject the past. Cast off outmoded norms. Rewrite your personal history. Redefine what it means to be a neighbor, a friend, a family, a community. Rebuild the foundation of society. Reaffirm the moral imperative that values the human spirit at every age.

Let us declare a new American Revolution; a revolution of the spirit. Declare war on the loneliness and isolation of old age. Embrace the enabling technology that can unite us across time, across geographies, across capabilities, across generations. Let us be more by involving the many. Let us lead by example and live to instruct. Let us applaud initiative and inspire by action.

All it takes is you.

RESOURCES

AARP	www.aarp.org
Age Lessons	www.agelessons.com
Alzheimer's Association	www.alz.org
American Association for Home Care	www.aahomecare.org
American Association of Homes and Services for the Aging	www.aahsa.org
American Cancer Society	www.cancer.org
American Health Care Association	www.ahca.org
American Heart Association	www.americanheart.org
American Society on Aging	www.asaging.org
Beacon Hill Village	www.beaconhillvillage.org
Boston College Center on Aging and Work/Workplace	www.agingandwork.bc.edu
Center for Aging Services Technologies	www.agingtech.org
The Center for Social Gerontology	www.tcsg.org

The Conference Board/Mature Workforce Initiative	www.conference-board .org
The Daughter Trap	www.daughtertrap.com
Eldercare Locator	www.eldercare.gov
Families and Work Institute	www.familiesandwork.org
Family Caregiver Alliance	www.caregiver.org
Generations United	www.gu.org
International Longevity Center-USA	www.ilcusa.org
Kaiser Family Foundation	www.kff.org
MetLife Mature Market Institute	www.metlife.com
National Alliance for Caregiving	www.caregiving.org
National Association for Home Care and Hospice	www.nahc.org
National Association of Area Agencies on Aging	www.n4a.org
National Association of Long Term Care Hospitals	www.nalth.org
National Association of Professional Geriatric Care Managers	www.caremanager.org
National Council on Aging	www.ncoa.org
National Family Caregivers Association	www.thefamilycaregiver.org
National Senior Citizens Law Center	www.nsclc.org
Network of Care Virtual Community	www.networkofcare.org
New York Association of Homes and Services for the Aging	www.nyahsa.org
Robert Wood Johnson Foundation	www.rwjf.org
Society for Human Resource Management	www.shrm.org

United Hospital Fund	www.uhfnyc.org
United Jewish Communities	www.ujc.org
U.S. Administration on Aging	www.aoa.gov
U.S. Department of Health and Human Services	www.hhs.gov
Volunteers of America	www.voa.org
Working Caregiver Virtual Community	www.workingcaregiver.com

NOTES

1. FROM DAUGHTER TRACK TO DAUGHTER TRAP

1. Jane Gross, "The Daughter Track: Caring for the Parents," *New York Times,* November 24, 2005, http://www.nytimes.com/2005/11/24/world/ameri cas/24ihtdaughter.html.

2. Ibid.

3. Jane Gross, "Elder-Care Costs Deplete Savings of a Generation," *New York Times*, December 30, 2006, http://www.nytimes.com/2006/12/30/us/ 30support.html?_r=1&th=&emc=th&pagewanted.

4. Ibid.

5. "Thirteen Million Baby Boomers Care for Ailing Parents, 25% Live with Parents," Press Release, Business Wire, October 19, 2005.

6. "Long Term Care Financing Options," Genworth 2009 Cost of Care Study, 7. http://www.genworth.com/content/etc/medialib/genworth_v2/pdf/ltc_ cost_of_care.Par.8024.File.dat/cost_of_care.pdf.

7. James Surowiecki, "Lifers," *The New Yorker*, The Talk of the Town, January 16, 2006, http://www.newyorker.com/archive/2006/01/16/060116ta_talk_ surowiecki.

8. *"Baby Boomers Approach 60: From the Age of Aquarius to the Age of Responsibility,"* Pew Research Center, December 8, 2005.

9. Ibid.

10. *Baby Boomers Struggling to Care for Aging Parents*, Joint Study by *Family Circle* and Kaiser Family Foundation, September 25, 2000, www.kff.org/docs/ parents.

11. *Exploding the Myths: Caregiving in America.* Select Committee on Aging, U.S. House of Representatives, Subcommittee on Human Services Publication No. 99-611, Washington, D.C.: U.S. Government Printing Office, January 1988.

12. *Ahead of the Curve: Emerging Trends and Practices in Family Caregiver Support*, Report prepared for the National Center on Caregiving, Family Caregiver Alliance, and AARP, March 2006, Doc. 2006–09, p. 1.

13. "Your Retirement Health-Care Bill: $200,000," *MSN.com*, Money. http:// articles.moneycentral.msn.com/Insurance/InsureYourHealth/Your Retirement.

14. "Many Americans' Retirement Hopes Are Filled with Holes," *EBRI News*, April 4, 2006.

15. *Caregiving Across the Life Cycle*, National Family Caregivers Association, 1998, https://www.thefamilycaregiver.org/who_are_family_caregivers/care giving_survey.cfm.

16. C. C. Cannuscio, C. Jones, I. Kawachi, G. A. Colditz, L. Berkman, and E. Rimm, "Reverberation of Family Illness: A Longitudinal Assessment of Informal Caregiver and Mental Health Status in Nurses' Health Study," *American Journal of Public Health*, 92 (2002): 305–1311.

17. *101 Facts on the Status of Workingwomen*, Business and Professional Women's Foundation, July 2005.

18. Marco R. della Cava, "When Mom (or Dad) Moves In," *USA Today*, May 14, 2006, http://www.usatoday.com/news/nation/2006-05-14-parents-mov ing-in_x.htm.

2. THE MOMENT FOR A MOVEMENT

1. "The National Organization for Women's 1966 Statement of Purpose," http://www.now.org/history/purpos66.html?printable.

2. Vivianne Rodrigues, "U.S. Women Far from Equality, Lawmaker's Book Says," Reuters, June 25, 2008, http://www.reuters.com/articlePrint?articleID=USN2525969920080625.

3. Shankar Vedantam, "Women in Top Ranks Pull Up the Pay of Others," *Washington Post*, August 13, 2006, http://www.washintonpost.com/wp-dyn/content/article/2006/08/12/AR2006081200858_p.

4. P. N. Cohen and Matt L. Huffman, "Working for the Man? Female Managers and the Gender Wage Gap," American Sociological Association annual meetings, Montreal, 2006.

5. Rodrigues, "U.S. Women Far from Equality."

6. Vedantam, "Women in Top Ranks."

7. "The Wage Gap Favoring Men Doesn't Just Hurt Women's Pay, According to New Research," Press Release, American Psychological Association, August 24, 2003, http://www.printhis.clickability.com/pt/cpt?action=cpt&title=The+Wage+Gap+Favoring+Men.

8. *To Hell with All That: Loving and Loathing Our Inner Housewife*, New York: Little, Brown and Company, (2006), p. xx.

9. "The MetLife Caregiving Cost Study: Productivity Losses to U.S. Businesses," *MetLife Mature Market Institute*, July 2006, p. 5, http://www.metlife.com/FileAssets/MMI/MMIStudiesCaregiverCostStudy.pdf.

10. Frank B. Hobbs, "Population Profile of the United States: The Elderly Population," U.S. Census Bureau, http://www.census.gov/population/www/pop-profile/elderpop.html.

11. Lesbian Health Research Center FAQ, http://www.lesbianhealthinfo.org/about_us/faq.html.

12. "Exactly How Much Housework Does a Husband Create?" University of Michigan News Service, Press Release, April 3, 2008, http://www.ns.umich.edu/htdocs/releases/print.php?htdocs/releases/plainstoryphp?id=645.

13. http://www.michaeljfox.org/.

14. "An Age Old Problem: TV Newswomen Say Discrimination Persists: It's Just Harder to Prove," *Broadcasting & Cable*, October 31, 2005, http://www.broadcastingcable.com/article/CA6278784.html.

15. "Toward a National Caregiving Agenda: Empowering Family Caregivers in America," Proceedings of a Caregiver Empowerment Summit 2001, p. 10–11, http://www.caregiving.org/data/summit.pdf.

16. "Family Caregiving and Long-Term Care: A Crucial Issue for America's Families," Policy Brief, June 2004, http://www.caregiver.org/caregiver/jsp/content/pdfs/op_2004_presidential_brief.pdf.

17. Daniel Arnall, "Role Reversal: The High Cost of Elder Care," ABC News, June 23, 2007, http://www.abcnews.go.com/print?id=3307546.

18. Abby J. Cohen, "A Brief History of Federal Financing for Child Care in the United States," *The Future of Children* 6, no. 2 (1996): 26–37.

19. Ibid, 30.

20. Ibid, 31.

21. "Claiming the Child and Dependent Care Credit," Tax Tip 2008-46, Internal Revenue Service, http://www.irs.gov/newsroom/article/0,,id=106189,00.html.

22. *Quick Stats 2007*, July 18, 2008, http://www.dol.gov/wb/stats/main.htm.

23. Joe Nocera, "On Day Care, Google Makes a Rare Fumble," *New York Times*, Talking Business, July 5, 2008, http://www.nytimes.com/2008/07/05/business/05nocera.html?pagewanted=2&partner=rssnyt.

24. Parents and the High Price of Child Care: 2009 Update, National Association of Child Care Resource and Referral Agencies, 5 and 7 http://issuu.com/naccrra/docs/parents-and-the-high-price-of-child-care-2009

25. "Aging Services: The Facts," American Association of Homes and Services for the Aging, p. 2, http://www.aahsa.org/aging_services/default.asp.

26. Jane Gross, "Study Finds Higher Costs for Caregivers of Elderly," November 19, 2007, *New York Times*, http://www.nytimes.com/2007/11/19/us/19caregiver.html?_r=1&pagewanted=print&oref=slogin.

27. Ibid.

28. Ibid.

3. NOT-SO-GREAT EXPECTATIONS

1. G. R. Lee, I. W. Dwyer, and R. T. Coward, "Filial Responsibility Expectations and Patterns of Intergenerational Assistance," *Journal of Marriage and the Family* 56 (1994): 559–65.

2. "Motivations for Filial Responsibility," http://family.jrank.org/pages/635/ Filial-Responsibility-motivations-Filial-Responsibility.html.

3. J. English, "What Do Grown Children Owe Their Parents?" in *Having Children: Philosophical and Legal Reflections on Parenthood*, ed. O. O'Neill and W. Ruddick, (New York: Oxford University Press, 1979).

4. C. L. Johnson, "Cultural Diversity in the Late-Life Family," In *Aging and the Family: Theory and Research*, ed. R. Blieszner and V. Bedford (Westport, CT: Greenwood Press, 1996).

5. B. Ingersoll-Dayton and C. Saengtienchai, "Respect for the Elderly in Asia: Stability and Change," *International Journal of Aging and Human Development* 48 (1999):113–30.

6. M. Blenkner, "Social Work and Family Relationships in Later Life with Some Thoughts on Filial Maturity," In *Social Structure and the Family: Generational Relations*, ed. E. Shanas and G. F. Streib (Englewood Cliffs, NJ: Prentice Hall, 1965).

7. "Sixty-Five Plus in the United States," Statistical Brief, U.S. Census Bureau, July 7, 2001, p. 5, http://www.census.gov/population/socdemo/statbriefs/ agebrief/html.

8. Gayle Ehrenman, "Fly the Grayer Skies," *Mechanical Engineering*, Design Features, March 2005. http://www.memagazine.org/desmar05/grayskies/ grayskies.html.

9. "The MetLife Caregiving Cost Study: Productivity Losses to U.S. Businesses," *MetLife Mature Market Institute*, July 2006, p. 5. http://www.metlife .com/assets/cao/mmi/publications/MMI-Studies-Caregiver-Cost-Study .pdf.

10. Leah Dobkin, "How to Confront the Elder Care Challenge," *Workforce Management Online*, April 2007, www.workforce.com/section/09/feature/24/ 85/10/index_printer.html.

11. "Dr. Murphy Interview." "Caring for your Parents," PBS September 20, 2007. http://www.pbs.org/wgbh/caringforyourparents/interviews/interviews _1.html.

12. "The MetLife Caregiving Cost Study."

13. I. A. Connidis, *Family Ties and Aging* (Thousand Oaks, CA: Sage Publications, 2001).

14. J. Finch and J. Mason, "Obligations of Kinship in Contemporary Britain: Is There Normative Agreement?" *The British Journal of Sociology*, 42, no. 3 (1991): 345–67.

15. Mindy Fetterman, "Prepare Yourself Now to Help Care for Parents Later," *USA Today*, June 28, 2007, http://usatoday.printthis.clickability.com/pt/ cpt?action+cpt&title+Prepare+yourself+now+to.

16. "The MetLife Caregiving Cost Study," p. 4.

17. Fetterman.

18. "2008 Genworth Financial Cost of Care Study," April 29, 2008, http:// www.genworth.com/content/etc/medialib/genworth/us/en/Long_Term_ Care.Par.14291.File.dat/37522%20CoC%20Brochure.pdf.

19. Sandy Hotchkiss, *Why Is It Always About You? The Seven Deadly Sins of Narcissism* (New York: The Free Press, 2002).

20. Diagnostic Criteria for 301.81, *Diagnostic and Statistical Manual of Mental Disorders*, 4th ed., Arlington, VA: American Psychiatric Association 1994.

21. "Filial Responsibility Laws: The Next Iceberg for GLBT People?" http:// www.doaskdotell.com/controv/filial.htm.

4. SIBLING RIVALRIES REVISITED

1. Jane Mersky Leder, "Adult Sibling Rivalry: Sibling Rivalry Often Lingers Through Adulthood," *Psychology Today*, Jan/Feb 1993, http://www .psychologytoday.com/articles/index.php?term+pto-19930101-000023& print=1.

2. Ibid.

3. Susan Lang, "Study: Older Moms Have Favorite Children—But Children

Get It Wrong," *Cornell Chronicle,* December 4, 1997, http://www.news.cor
nell.edu/chronicle/97/12.4.97/Pillemer.html.

4. "Why Isn't Willy a Doctor? Study at Cornell Finds that Aging Moms Have
Conflicted Relationship with Lower-Achieving Adult Children," Press Release, Cornell University, November 14, 2002, http://www.news.cornell
.edu/releases/Nov02/ambivalent.moms.ssl.html.

5. Ibid.

6. "Adult Sibling Relationships," *Ohio State University Fact Sheet*, Family Life
Month Packet 1999, http://ohioonline.osu.edu/flm99/fs06.html.

7. Ibid.

8. Leder.

9. "Adult Sibling Relationships."

10. Karl Pillemer and J. Jill Suitor, "Making Choices: A Within-Family Study of
Caregiver Selection," *The Gerontologist* 46 (2006):439–48.

11. Leder.

12. Elizabeth Rosenthal, "Troubled Marriage? Sibling Relations May Be at Fault,"
New York Times, August 18, 1992, http://query.nytimes.com/gst/fullpage
.html?res=9E0CE6D91531F93BA2575BC0A964958.

13. National Association of Professional Geriatric Care Managers, www.care
manager.org.

14. "Find A Care Manager," National Association of Professional Geriatric Care
Managers, http://www.caremanager.org/displaycommon.cfm?an=1&sub
articlenbr=94.

15. Phone interview, Carolyn L. Rosenblatt, June 16, 2008.

16. Stephen R. Marsh, "The Truths Behind Mediation," 2000, http://adrr.com/
adr3/other.htm.

17. Phone interview, Brian Carpenter, June 6, 2008.

6. IT'S OKAY TO FEEL BAD

1. *Caregiving in the United States*, Executive Summary, Stress and Strain of Caregiving, National Alliance for Caregiving and AARP, 2005, p. 18, http://
www.caregiving.org/data/04execsumm.pdf.

2. *Caregiving in the United States*, Stress and Strain of Caregiving, National Alliance for Caregiving and AARP, 2004, http://www.caregiving.org/data/04finalreport.pdf.

3. "Definition of a Disability, Functional Limitations, Activities of Daily Living [ADLs], and Instrumental Activities of Daily Living [IADLs]," http://www.census.gov/hhes/www/disability/sipp/disab02/ds02f1.pdf.

4. *Caregiving in the United States*, Executive Summary, Emotional Health, National Alliance for Caregiving and AARP, 2005, p. 19, http://www.caregiving.org/data/04execsumm.pdf.

5. "Family Caregivers—What They Spend, What They Sacrifice," Evercare, 2007, p. 7, http://www.caregiving.org/data/Evercare_NAC_Caregiver CostStudyFINAL20111907.pdf.

6. Ibid.

7. Ibid.

8. "MetLife Juggling Act," National Center on Women and Aging and MetLife, 1999.

9. "The Female Factor 2008: Why Woman Face Greater Retirement Risk and What Can Be Done to Help Beyond Employee-Based Retirement Programs," Americans for Secure Retirement, Executive Summary, p. 1, http://www.paycheckforlife.org/uploads/ASR-white_paper_FINAL.pdf.

10. Ibid.

11. Ibid.

12. Jo Horne, "A Caregiver's Bill of Rights," www.caregiver.com/articles/caregiver/caregiver/caregiver_bill_of_rights.htm.

13. Personal interview.

14. "Valuing the Invaluable: 2006 Economic Value of Family Caregiving is $350 Billion," http://www.aarp.org/families/caregiving/caring_parents/valuing_the_invaluable.html?print=yes.

15. Personal interview.

16. Personal interview.

7. BOY POWER

1. Jerome Tognoli, "Male Friendship and Intimacy Across the Life Span," *Family Relations* 29, no. 3 (1980): 273–79.

2. "WISER's Top Five Retirement Challenges for Women," http://www.wiser women.org/portal/index.php?option=com_content&task=view&id=50.

3. "Can Women Bridge the Retirement Savings Gap?" *BusinessWeek*, Your Retirement, August 11, 2008, http://www.businessweek.com/print/investor/ content/aug2008/pi2008088_307392.htm.

4. Ibid.

5. Daniel Chandler, "Television and Gender Roles," Media Studies Department, Aberystwyth University, Australia, http://www.aber.ac.uk/media/ Modules/TF33120/gendertv.html. See also David Morley, *Family Television: Cultural Power and Domestic Leisure*, (London: Routledge, 1986).

6. Chandler.

7. Quoted in Chandler, "Television and Gender Roles."

8. THE DOCTOR IS IN

1. "A Statement of Principles: Toward Improved Care of Older Patients in Surgical and Medical Specialties," *Journal of the American Geriatrics Society* 48 (2000):699–701.

2. U.S. Department of Health and Human Services, Centers for Disease Control and Prevention, National Center for Health Statistics, "Health, United States, 2007: With Chartbook on Trends in the Health of Americans," November 2007, DHHS Publication No. 2007-1232, p. 175, http://www.cdc .gov/nchs/data/hus/hus07.pdf#027.

3. Jane Gross, "New Options (and Risks) in Home Care for Elderly," *New York Times*, March 1, 2007, http://www.nytimes.com/2007/03/01/us/01aides .html?pagewanted+print.

4. Centers for Disease Control and Prevention, Merck Institute of Aging and Health, "State of Aging and Health in America, 2004," p. 2, http://www .cdc.gov/aging/pdf/State_of_Aging_and_Health_in_America_2004.pdf.

5. Ibid.

6. Centers for Disease Control and Prevention, Merck Institute of Aging and Health, "State of Aging and Health in America, 2004," Executive Summary, http://www.cdc.gov/aging/pdf/State_of_Aging_and_Health_in_America_2004.pdf.

7. Ibid.

8. Gerard Anderson, "Chronic Conditions: Making the Case for Ongoing Care," November 2007, Johns Hopkins Bloomberg School of Public Health, p. 8.

9. "People with Multiple Chronic Conditions Account for 65 Cents of Every Health Care Dollar," Press Release, December 10, 2007, Partnership to Fight Chronic Disease, http://www.fightchronicdisease.com/news/pfcd/pr12102007.cfm.

10. Ibid.

11. Anderson, p. 22.

12. Ibid, p. 16.

13. Ibid, p. 23.

14. Ibid, p. 30.

15. "People with Multiple Chronic Conditions Account for 65 Cents of Every Health Care Dollar."

16. Anderson, p. 30.

17. "Frequently Asked Questions About Geriatricians and the Shortage of Geriatrics Health Care Providers," The American Geriatrics Society, http://www.americangeriatrics.org/news/geria_fa8sPF.shtml.

18. Ibid.

19. Ibid.

20. Ibid.

21. "About Depression," National Institute of Mental Health, http://nihseniorhealth.gov/depression/aboutdepression/04.html.

22. "Frequently Asked Questions About Geriatricians."

23. "Depression: Causes and Risk Factors," National Institute of Mental Health, http://nihseniorhealth.gov/depression/aboutdepression/04.html.

24. "Seniors and Depression," PsychCentral, National Institute of Mental Health, http:/psychcentral.com/lib/2007/seniors-and-depression/.

25. Ibid.

26. Jennifer Blair, "Taking the E-ROAD," *Yale Medicine*, Autumn 2007, http://yalemedicine.yale.edu/ym_au07/feature3_eroad.html.

27. "Frequently Asked Questions About Geriatricians."

28. J. P. Leigh, R. L. Kravitz, M. Schembri et al., "Physician Career Satisfaction Across Specialties," *Archives of Internal Medicine*, 162, no. 14 (2002): 1577–84.

29. "Frequently Asked Questions About Geriatricians."

30. Personal interview, Robert Butler, July 28, 2008.

31. "What Is Loan Forgiveness?" American Geriatrics Society, http://www.americangeriatrics.org/policy/loan_forgiveness.shtml.

32. Ibid.

33. Ibid.

34. "Retooling for an Aging America: Building the Health Care Workforce," Institute of Medicine, Committee on the Future Health Care Workforce for Older Americans, Report Brief, April 2008, http://www.iom.edu/?id=53513.

35. Personal interview, Robert Butler.

36. Jane Gross, "Geriatrics Lags in Age of High-Tech Medicine," *New York Times*, October 18, 2006, http://www.nytimes.com/2006/10/18/health/18aged.html?pagewanted=print.

37. Howard Kim, "As Population Grows Older, Geriatricians Grow Scarce," *Washington Post*, March 11, 2008, http://www.washingtonpost.com/wp-dyn/content/article/2008/03/10/AR2008031001655_.

38. Personal interview, Robert Butler.

39. "Medical Home: Why Is This Concept Important?" *Wikipedia*, http://en.wikipedia.org/wiki/Medical_home.

40. "Joint Principles of the Patient-Centered Medical Home," March 2007, p. 1 http://www.medicalhomeinfo.org/Joint%20Statement.pdf.

41. "CIGNA and Dartmouth-Hitchcock Launch 'Patient-Centered Medical Home Model' Program," Press Release, June 10, 2008, http://www.reuters.com/article/pressRelease/idUS158071+10-Jun-2008+BW20080610.

42. Milt Freudenheim, "Trying to Save by Increasing Doctor's Fees," *New York*

Times, Business Section, July 21, 2008, http://www.nytimes.com/2008/ 07/32/business/21medhome.html. See also "Trend: Medical Home Funding Sources Grow," FierceHealthcare, July 21, 2008, http://www.fiercehealth care.com/story/trend-medical-home-funding-sources-grow/2008-07-21.

43. Freudenheim.

44. Julie Appleby, "Old-Fashioned Docs Inspire New Medical Homes," *USA Today*, July 13, 2008, http://www.usatoday.com/news/health/2008-07-13-medical-homes_N.htm.

45. "Trend: Medical Home Funding Sources Grow."

46. Stephen J. Spann, "Report on Financing the New Model of Family Medicine," *Annals of Family Medicine* (2004): S1–S21, p. s1. http://www.annfammed. org/cgi/content/abstract/2/suppl_3/s1.

47. Jim Duffy, "A New Age for Old Age," *Johns Hopkins Public Health Magazine*, Spring 2007, p. 2, http://magazine:jhsph.edu/2007/Spring/features/aging_ health/?page=2.

9. IT TAKES A VILLAGE

1. Stephen Levitt and Stephen Dubner, *Freakonomics: A Rogue Economist Explores the Hidden Side of Everything* (New York: Penguin, 2005), pp. 77–79.

2. *Ageism in America*, International Longevity Center, http://www.ilcusa.org/ media/pdfs/Ageism%20in%20America%20-%20The%20ILC%20Report .pdf.

3. "Adecco USA Survey Finds Age #1 Form of Discrimination at the Office," Press Release, July 30, 2008, http://www.adeccousa.com/AboutUs/Pages/ NewsContent.aspx?submenuid=4.0&webid=a9b9dac5-6c08-4fa9-9e01-2724e59af745&pageid=dc5e4028-b9a0-4227-bbe7-1ee3f92b27ef.

4. Quote in Amy M. Horgan and Bronwyn S. Fees, "Children's Perceptions of Older Adults," Kansas State University, http://www.kon.org/urc/horgan .html.

5. Ibid.

6. "Community Movies: Act Your Age," http://www.communitymovies.com/ voices.htm.

7. "9 in 10 Adults Aged 60+ Prefer to Stay in Their Home and Community Rather than Move," October 27, 2006, AARP Press Release. http://www .aarp.org/research/press-center/presscurrentnews/9_in_10_adults_age_ 60_prefer_to_stay_in_their_home.html.

8. Personal interview.

9. "Senior Housing," *Private Equity Real Estate*, June 2006, p. 48.

10. Quoted in Lynn Greenleaf Sheila Malynowski, and the New Hampshire Housing Finance Authority, *Increasing Service Availability to Seniors in Housing: Final Report* (Bedford, NH: New Hampshire Housing Authority, 1993).

11. Marlene Piturro, "The Place They Have Always Called Home," *Future Age*, November/December 2006, pp. 6–8, 44.

12. "All About NORCS," http://www.norcs.com/page.aspx?id+119552.

13. http://www.aoa.gov/oaa2006/Main_Site/oaa/oaa_full.asp.

14. "Appropriations Overview," http://www.ncoa.org/PrintPage.cfm?section ID=336&detail=1860; http://www.nhpf.org/pdfs_basics/Basics_Older AmericansAct_04-21-08.pdf.

15. Ibid.

16. Haya El Nasser, "Granny Flats Finding a Home in Tight Market," *USA Today*, January 5, 2004, http://www.usatoday.printthis.clickability.com/pt/cpt? action=cpt&title=USATODAY.com.

17. Ibid.

18. Personal interview, Paul Dean.

19. Sarah Max, "Living with the In-Laws," *CNN/Money*, April 22, 2004, http:// cnnmoney.printthis.clickability.com/pt/cpt?action=cpt&title=Multi generational+housing.

20. Ibid.

21. "Home Sharing Program," New York Foundation for Senior Citizens, http:// www.nyfsc.org/services/home_sharing.html.

22. Personal interview, Craig Ragland.

23. "Green House Nursing Homes Expand as Communities Reinvent Elder Care," Transcript, *NewsHour*, PBS, January 23, 2008, http://www.pbs.org/ newshour/bb/health/jan-june08/nursing_01-23.html.

24. Lucette Lagnado, "Home Remedy: Rising Challenger Takes on Elder-Care System," *Wall Street Journal*, June 24, 2008, p. A1, http://www.webreprints .djreprints.com/1993710401839.html.

25. Caroline Hsu, "The Greening of Aging: William Thomas, Physician, Farmer," *U.S. News and World Report*, June 11, 2006, http://www.usnews.com/ usnews/biztech/articles/060619/19leader_print.html.

26. Ibid.

27. "Welcome to Eden," Eden Alternative, http://www.edenalt.org/home .html.

28. "Our 10 Principles," Eden Alternative, http://www.edenalt.org/about/our-10-principles.html.

29. Lagnado.

30. "Green Houses Growing in Numbers Across the States," Robert Wood Johnson Foundation, http://www.rwjf.org/pr/product.jsp?id=28231.

31. Lagnado.

10. IT TAKES A COMPANY

1. Thomas J. Clifton and Edward Shepard, "Work and Family Programs and Productivity," *International Journal of Manpower*, 25, no. 8 (2004): 714–28.

2. Kelly Edmiston, "The Role of Small and Large Businesses in Economic Development," *Economic Review*, Second Quarter, 2007, p. 79, http://www.kc .frb.org/publicat/ECONREV/PDF/2q07edmi.pdf.

3. "2003 Eldercare Survey," Society for Human Resource Management, December 2003, table 4, p. 7, statistic 806, http://www.agingandwork.bc.edu/ statprint_188.

4. Personal interview, Jacquelyn James.

5. "Everyone Wants an Engaged Workforce: How Can You Create It?" *Workspan*, January 2006, p. 39, http://www.wfd.com/PDFS/Engaged%20Workforce %20Amy%20Richman%20Workspan.pdf?%22.

6. Ibid., p. 38.

7. Ibid.

8. Personal interview, Elinor Ginzler.

9. http://www.metlife.com/FileAssets/MMI/MMIStudiesCaregiverCost
   Study.pdf.

10. "The MetLife Juggling Act Study," MetLife Mature Market Institute, No-
    vember 1999, p. 7, http://www.maturemarketinstitute.com.

11. "How Employers Can Support Working Caregivers," http://www.aarp.org/
    money/careers/employerresourcecenter/retention/how_employers_can_
    support_working_caregivers.html.

12. "Elder Care Programs Take Center Stage as Baby Boomers Age," *Workforce
    Management*, September 2008, http://www.workforce.com/section/02/
    feature/25/73/52/index_printer.html.

13. "How Employers Can Support Working Caregivers."

14. Personal interview, Sandra Timmermann.

15. "2003 Eldercare Survey," p. 6.

16. Molly Selvin, "An Aging Population Brings Employer Elder-Care Benefits,"
    Los Angeles Times, December 31, 2006, http://www.chron.com/disp/story
    .mpl/headline/biz/4435912.html.

17. "Retention Strategies: How Employers Can Support Working Caregivers,"
    http://www.aarp.org/money/careers/employerresourcecenter/retention/
    how_employers_can_support_working_caregivers.html.

18. "Balancing Work While Caring for Aging Parents," ABC News, June 27,
    2007, http://www.abcnews.go.com/print?id=3318633.

19. "Retention Strategies."

20. Leah Dobkin, "How to Confront the Elder Care Challenge," *Workforce Man-
    agement Online*, April 2007, http://www.workforce.com/section/09/fea
    ture/24/85/10/index_printer.html.

21. "Elder Caregiving: Question 3: What Do Employers Do to Help Their Em-
    ployees Fulfill Their Elder Care Responsibilities?" *The Center on Aging and
    Work, Fact Sheet 2*, October 2006, p. 1.

22. Lydell C. Bridgeford, "Backup Elder Care Helps Caregivers Balance Work
    and Family Responsibilities," *Employee Benefit News*, June 1, 2008, http://
    ebn.benefitnews.com/asset/article-print/586401/printPage.html.

23. Ibid.

24. "2003 Eldercare Survey," statistic 801.

25. "Backup Care Ranked as Fastest Growing Employee Benefit," Press Release, July 17, 2007, *Businesswire*, http://www.businesswire.com/portal/site/google/?ndmViewId=20070 news_.

26. "Backup Elder Care Is Latest Benefit Offered by Big Law Firms," *ABA Journal / Law News Now*, July 23, 2008, http://abajournal.com/news/backup_elder_care_is_latest_benefit_offered_by_big_law_firms.

27. Sukanya Mitra, "Managing Absenteeism and Presenteeism in the Workplace," AICPA, January 17, 2008, http://www.cpa2biz.com/browse/print_articles_landing.jsp.

28. W. Stewart, D. Matousek, and C. Verdon. *The American Productivity Audit and the Campaign for Work and Health*, The Center for Work and Health, AdvancePCS, 2003.

29. *AARP Bulletin Today*, May 19, 2006, http://www.aarp.org/family/caregiving/articles/cost_elder_care_html?print=1.

30. "The Elder Care Gap," *HR Magazine*, May 2000, http://findarticles.com/p/articles/mi_m3495/is_5_45/ai_62303387(May.

31. Ibid.

32. "Elder Care Programs Take Center Stage."

33. Ibid.

34. http://www.bc.edu/centers/cwf/meta-elements/pdf/Flex_Executive Summary_for_web.pdf.

11. IT TAKES A TECHNOLOGY

1. "TV Acres: Huge and Gigantic Robots," http://www.tvacres.com/robots_huge_tobor.htm.

2. "Captain Video and His Video Rangers," http://www.museum.tv/archives/etv/C/htmlC/captainvideo/captainvideo.htm.

3. "Captain Video and His Video Rangers," http://everything2.com/e2node/Captain%2520Video%2520and%2520His%2520Video%2520Rangers.

4. "ASIMO, Humanoid Robot," Honda, http://www.honda.com/asimo/?ef_
id+1097:3:s_73798abdbadb7939d3e16be787119bc_84; "Paro (robot)," Wiki
pedia, http://en.wikipedia.org/wiki/Paro_(robot).

5. "Huggable Robotic Bear Companion from MIT," http://www.technovelgy
.com/ct/Science-Fiction-News.asp?NewsNum=706.

6. "Research Group Projects and Descriptions," MIT Media Lab, http://www
.media.mit.edu/research/53.

7. "Huggable Robotic Bear Companion from MIT."

8. "Up Close with MIT's Huggable Robot," http://www.physorg.com/print
news.php?newsid+98613563.

9. "Paro (robot)."

10. "Paro's Goal (Purpose) and Effects," http://paro.jp/english/therapy.html.

11. "AIBO," Wikipedia, http://en.wikipeida.org/wiki/AIBO; "Robotic Pet Won't
Soil Your Carpet," San Francisco Chronicle, March 3, 2008, http://www
.sfgate.com/cgi-bin/article.cgi?f=/c/a/2008/03/03/BUQUVB295.DTL&
type=p.

12. "HAL Offers Mobility—By the Month," Chicago Tribune, October 8, 2008,
Section 1, p. 21.

13. "HAL Robot Suit Almost Summits with Quadriplegic Man in Tow," Engad-
get, August 8, 2006, http://www.engadget.com/2006/08/08/hal-robot-
suit-almost-summits-with-quadriplegic.

14. "What's HAL?" http://www.cyberdyne.jp/english/robotsuithal/index.html.

15. "2007: 6.5 Million Robots in Operation World-wide," Press Release,
Statistical Department, International Robotics Federation, October 15,
2008, p. 1.

16. "New Robots Can Provide Elder Care for Aging Baby Boomers," Science
Daily, April 21, 2008, http://www.sciencedaily.com/releases/2008/04/
080416212725.htm.

17. Ibid.

18. Victoria Groom, "What's the Best Role for a Robot?" International Conference on Informatics in Control, Automation and Robotics, 2008, pp. 323,

325, http://chime.stanford.edu/downloads/groom_robot_role_ICINCO _2008.pdf.

19. Alex S. Taylor and Laurel Swan, "Notes on Intelligence," http://research .microsoft.com/users/Cambridge/ast/files/Taylor_Intelligence_2008.pdf.

20. J. Forlizzi and C. DiSalvo, "Service Robots in the Domestic Environment: a Study of the Roomba Vacuum in the Home," ACM SIGCHI/SIGART Human-Robot Interaction, 2006, pp. 258–65.

21. Ja-Young Sung, Rebecca E. Grinter, Herik I. Christensen, and Lan Guo, "Housewives or Technophiles? Understanding Domestic Robot Owners," HRI'08, March 12–15, 2008, Amsterdam, Netherlands.

22. Groom.

23. "Robots Help Japan Care for Its Elderly," *Popular Mechanics*, June 2004, http://www.popularmechanics.com/technology/industry/128841.html? nav=hpPrint&do=.

24. James Brooke, "Machida Journal: Japan Seeks Robotic Help in Caring for the Aged," March 5, 2004, *The New York Times*, http://query.nytimes.com/ gst/fullpae.html?res=9C07E4DE113FF936A35750C0A9629C.

25. "Robot Pharmacist!—Part 2," Pharmainfo.net, http://www.pharmainfo .net/praseengp/robot-pharmacist-part-2.

26. Ibid.

27. Elaine D. Seeman and David A. Rosenthal, "Electronic Intensive Care: A Technical Solution to the Intensivist Shortage," *Proceedings of the Academy of Health Care Management*, 1, no. 1 (2004): 13–17, p. 14.

28. Ibid., p. 15.

29. "Coronary/Medical ICU—eICU," Parkview Hospital, http://www.parkview .com/body.cfm?id=358.

30. "How Stuff Works: Advantages of Robotic Surgery," http://science.how stuffworks.com/robotic-surgery1.htm.

31. "No Hands: R2-D2 to Perform Heart Surgery?" ABC News, April 26, 2008, http://abcnews.go.com/Video/playerIndex?id=4732675.

32. "Intuitive Surgical: Products," http://www.intuitivesurgical.com/products/ index.aspx.

33. "Doc at a Distance," http://www.spectrum.ieee.org/print/4667.

34. "Intel's Health Guide Puts Telehealth in the Spotlight," http://www.american telemed.org/files/public/IntelsHealthGuidePutsTelehealthinSpotlight.pdf; "Intel to Launch Home Telehealth System," *Portland Business Journal*, August 22, 2008, http://tie.telemed.org/homehealth/news.asp#item1709.

35. "Intel to Launch Home Telehealth System."

36. "Telemedicine Defined," American Telemedicine Association, http://www .americantelemed.org/i4a/pages/index.cfm?pageid=3333.

37. "Mainstream Healthcare Paying Attention to Home Telehealth's Benefits," *Health News*, July 15, 2008, http://www.americantelemed.org/i4a/pages/ index.cfm?pageid=3333.

38. Ibid.

39. "Telemedicine Defined."

40. "Online Doctor Consults Slowly Becoming More Popular," *Florida Sun-Sentinel*, July 21, 2008, http://www.americantelemed.org/i4a/pages/index .cfm?pageid=3333.

41. J. F. Coughlin, L. A. Ambrosio, B. Reimer, and M. R. Pratt, "Older Adult Perceptions of Smart Home Technologies: Implications for Research, Policy and Market Innovations in Healthcare," White Paper, presented at IEEE Proceedings of the Engineering in Medicine and Biology Annual Conference, Lyon, France, August 2007.

42. "Innovations in Health, Wellness and Aging-in-Place," *IEEE Engineering in Medicine and Biology Magazine*, July/August 2008, p. 48.

43. Andrew Carle, "More Than a Game; Brain Training Against Dementia," *Nursing Homes*, August 1, 2007, http://www.allbusiness.com/medicine-health/ diseases-disorders-neurological/5515335-1.html.

44. Ibid.

45. "FAQs," Continua Health Alliance, 2009. http://www.continuaalliance .org/faqs.html.

46. http://www.agingtech.org/about.aspx.

47. Kelly Greene, "Report Finds Heavier Cost for Caregivers," *Wall Street Journal*, Personal Finance, November 20, 2008, p. D4.

48. Coughlin, et al.

49. Ibid.

12. IT TAKES YOU

1. "New MacArthur Research Network to Examine Impact of Aging Society," Press Release, November 21, 2008, http://www.macfound.org/site/apps/ s/content.asp?ct=6355093&c=KXH8NQKrH&b=41.

2. Ibid.

3. " 'Green Houses' Provide a Small Group Setting Alternative to Nursing Homes—and a Positive Effect on Residents' Quality of Life," Robert Wood Johnson Foundation, http://www.rwjf.org/pr/product.jsp?id=17402.

4. "Grants at Work: HGNI Summit Seeks New Heights for Geriatric Nursing" and "Integrating Geriatrics into the Specialties of Internal Medicine," The John A. Hartford Foundation, http://www.jhartfound.org/grantsatwork .htm.

5. "What Kind of Genius Are You?" *Wired* magazine, http://www.wired.com/ wired/archive/14.07/genius_pr.html.

6. See www.innocentive.com, http://fold.it, http://www.nap.edu/catalog .php?record_id=11816 for examples.

7. Cornelia Dean, "If You Have a Problem, Ask Everyone," *New York Times*, Science section, July 22, 2008, http://www.nytimes.com/2008/07/22/ science/22inno.html?_r=1&th=&oref+slogin&emc=t.

8. "Crowdsourcing," Wikipedia, http://en.wikipedia.org/wiki/Crowdsourcing.

9. "National Pace Association: About Us," http://www.npaonline.org/web site/article.asp?id=5.

10. "Demographics—Older Persons," United Nations, http://www.un.org/ NewLinks/older/99/older.htm.

INDEX